PRIDE OF THE ROCKIES

Hungarian Mills, Denver, Colorado. Courtesy, Timothy O'Connor collecton.

PRIDE OF THE ROCKIES

The Life of Colorado's Premiere Irish Patron,
John Kernan Mullen

WILLIAM JOSEPH CONVERY, III

University Press of Colorado

Copyright © 2000 by the University Press of Colorado
International Standard Book Number 0-87081-591-1

Published by the University Press of Colorado
5589 Arapahoe Avenue, Suite 206C
Boulder, Colorado 80303

The University Press of Colorado is a cooperative publishing enterprise supported, in part, by
Adams State College, Colorado State University, Fort Lewis College, Mesa State College,
Metropolitan State College of Denver, University of Colorado, University of Northern
Colorado, University of Southern Colorado, and Western State College of Colorado.

The paper used in this publication meets the minimum requirements of the American
National Standard for Information Sciences—Permanence of Paper for Printed Library
Materials. ANSI Z39.48-1992

Library of Congress Cataloging-in-Publication Data

Convery, William Joseph.
    Pride of the Rockies : the life of Colorado's premiere Irish patron, John Kernan Mullen /
  William Joseph Convery, III.
        p. cm.
    Includes bibliographical references (p.) and index.
    ISBN 0-87081-591-1 (alk. paper)
      1. Mullen, John Kernan, 1847–1929. 2. Irish Americans—Colorado—Denver—
  Biography. 3. Pioneers—Colorado—Denver—Biography. 4. Industrialists—Colorado—
  Denver—Biography. 5. Philanthropists—Colorado—Denver—Biography. 6. Denver
  (Colo.)—Biography. 7. Denver (Colo.)—Social conditions—19th century. I. Title.
F784.D453 M853 2000
978.8'03'092—dc21   00-056803

Designed by Laura Furney
Typeset by Daniel Pratt

09 08 07 06 05 04 03 02 01 00   10 9 8 7 6 5 4 3 2 1

To my first teacher, Lyra Armeling Garson.
And to all the teachers in my life.

CONTENTS

CONTENTS

CONTENTS

ACKNOWLEDGMENTS

I OWE THE INSPIRATION FOR THIS BIOGRAPHY to my work as an intern for Peg Ekstrand and the Colorado Historical Society. While writing *Colorado Historical Moment* segments for the KCNC television program, *Colorado Getaways*, I came across the practically untouched Mullen manuscripts at the Colorado History Museum archive. Their manuscript collections made me realize that John Kernan Mullen was an important, interesting, and relatively underreported figure in Denver and Colorado history. I therefore must first thank Peg and *Colorado Getaways* producer Doug Whitehead for helping open this particular door to opportunity.

This book would not exist without generous research funding provided by the J. K. Mullen Foundation, the Weckbaugh Foundation, Inc., the Eleanore Mullen Weckbaugh Foundation, Peter Grant, and the Michael J. Collins Chapter of the Ancient Order of Hibernians. These groups and individuals continue to prove that J. K. Mullen's spirit of philanthropy is alive and well in Denver. Thanks are also due to Julius Johnson and Theresa Polakovic and to family members Peter Grant, John F. Malo, Elaine Tettemer Marshall, Beth Matthews, Timothy O'Connor, Sheila Sevier, Anne Weckbaugh, Heather Weckbaugh, Larry Weckbaugh, and Walter S. Weckbaugh for their graciousness and their willingness to share documents in their possession. Their interest and encouragement was essential to this project.

I am particularly grateful to Thomas J. Noel, Ph.D., of the University of Colorado, Denver. Dr. Noel provided important research materials as well as tireless fundraising advocacy and exhaustive editing. This manuscript also benefited from close readings and thoughtful commentary by Pamela Laird, Ph.D., Mark Foster, Ph.D., and James Whiteside, Ph.D., of UCD, and Stephen J. Leonard, Ph.D., of the Metropolitan State College of Denver.

Valuable archival assistance was provided by Sister Mary Hughes of the Archdiocese of Denver; Rev. Vincent J. Kelly of St. Joseph's Church in Oriskany Falls, New York; the archive staffs of the Western History Department of the Denver Public Library, the State Historical Society of Colorado, the Utica Public Library, and the Oneida County Historical Society; Stella Cieslak of the Limestone Ridge Historical Society; and the Minnesota Historical Society.

Rosemary Fetter of the Auraria Higher Education Center, Robert Pulcipher, Jim Kimmett, Denver City Councilman Dennis Gallagher, Rev. John Anderson of Denver's Immaculate Conception Cathedral, and Michael J. Convery all generously provided information and expertise that kept me on track. Additionally, Paula Aven, Marcie Morin, Thomas and Helen Mullen of Oriskany Falls, New York, Thorvald A. Nelson, esq., Caron Stone, Heather Weckbaugh, and Patrice Weddig reviewed all or part of this manuscript. Thanks most of all to my patient wife, Cara, who helped edit this manuscript, coped with my long ramblings, and gave up her vacation time to track through the wilds of Onieda County, New York. I deeply appreciate her tolerance. Finally, thanks to my parents, William and Eileen Convery, for their assurances that everything would be all right.

FOREWORD

SHAKING HANDS WITH J. K. MULLEN was unforgettable. After working in flour mills since the age of fourteen, his hands were imbedded with millstone shards.

The painful handshake epitomized the stony-faced millionaire who became an unsmiling philanthropist. He refused to pay for the usual publicity puffs and flattering biographical sketches in booster history books. A brusque man who often struck even his family and closest associates as cold, he could be admired only from afar.

Perhaps because of his stern personality, little has been written about one of the West's most important and influential Irish immigrants. Mullen built a grainy empire stretching from Texas to Oregon, from Missouri to California. His flour mills sustained thousands of Rocky Mountain and High Plains mill hands, elevator operators, and wheat farmers, including many of his countrymen, and put bread on the table for millions of consumers. Yet critics charged that Mullen made his millions by paying as little as possible.

Mullen's descendants—the Grant, Malo, O'Connor, and Weckbaugh families—helped author William J. Convery III trace the tycoon back to his County Galway birthplace, and to Oriskany Falls, New York, where the penniless immigrant boy learned milling. They also gave Bill access to previously closed family collections, enabling him to present fully both the public and private man.

Author Bill Convery, a fourth-generation Irish Coloradoan coming from a long line of teachers, politicians, and wheat farmers, has his own deep roots in Mullen country. His previous research on Irish-

American history has won prizes and funding from the Ancient Order of Hibernians.

Convery spent four years tracking down this elusive milling mogul who had previously defied biographers. The result is in your hands—a well-told, thoroughly researched tale. Readers may decide the character whom Convery depicts here was neither saint nor satan, although many called him one or the other.

These pages explain how one of Colorado's shrewdest tycoons emerged as one of the state's most heroic givers. His donations range from churches and schools and nursing homes to previously hidden benefactions such as bankrolling Baby Doe Tabor in her final years at the Matchless Mine. "Some of my good friends appear to think that I am a little daffy on the subject of giving away large amounts of money," Mullen wrote to a daughter. "But I have always felt that God Almighty had a purpose in giving me the opportunity to accumulate, and that he would hold me to a stern responsibility."

No one did more to uplift Colorado's Irish community and to persuade a provincial Roman Catholic clergy to drop its militant anti-Protestantism. Mullen insisted that his countrymen and his church make peace with WASP-ish America. While giving millions to the Catholic Church and to Irish immigrants, he also donated heavily to Protestant causes and to Denver mayor Robert W. Speer's City Beautiful Crusade to transform Denver from a dusty, drab town into "a Paris on the Platte."

This book will take you back to when Colorado was young and bright-eyed immigrants such as J. K. Mullen arrived with ruthless ability and ambition that would take them to the top. Few men took so much and then gave it back; giving as well as taking in Mullen's stony fashion.

—Tom Noel

PRIDE OF THE ROCKIES

1

ECHOES OF CHARITY

"He was Irish and American both—but he was more than both, for all humanity was his kin." The secret of his inner power to capture and to hold the love of those who knew him . . . was the instinct of his race—an instinct that has often cost them dearly—his sympathy was ever and always with the loser on the battlefield of life.

—SISTER JUSTINE, Little Sisters of the Poor, quoting John Boyle O'Reilly, in honor of J. K. Mullen, 1932.[1]

THE 150TH ANNIVERSARY OF JOHN KERNAN MULLEN'S BIRTH on June 11, 1997, passed as any normal day in Denver. Newspapers reported the usual complement of scandals and the normal quotient of crime without mentioning Mullen's anniversary—poor recompense for one of the city's leading benefactors. The Denver Catholic Archdiocese, which had once counted Mullen among the seraphim of its laity—he once graced the parish, after all, as a Knight of St. Gregory, a Knight of Malta, and the greatest supporter of the Denver's early Catholic community—let Mullen's sesquicentennial lapse without fanfare. As the twentieth century slipped away, awareness of J. K. Mullen, among Denver's and Colorado's best known citizens at the start of the century, seemed to be fading away.

There remain, to be sure, tangible reminders of J. K. Mullen's life and largesse. Visitors to Denver's Civic Center may not know who Mullen was, but they see his vine-covered name among the donors of Civic Center Plaza. Tourists snap pictures of the plaque that identifies him as the donor of the *Broncho Buster* statue, one of the city's most famous symbols of the wide-open frontier—a frontier Mullen helped tame and close. A few blocks from the Civic Center, the twin spires of the Roman Catholic Cathedral of the Immaculate Conception grace Capitol Hill. There, worshipers occasionally notice Mullen's name among the church's benefactors, likely without realizing that without him that grand church, so long the pride of Colorado's Catholics, would not exist.

Reminders of J. K. Mullen's benevolence appear to the attentive visitor all over town. At the lower end of downtown, near Cherry Creek, students toss frisbees in the shadow of St. Cajetan's Center—a former church but now a conference center on the Auraria Higher Education Center campus. This modest mission revival church sits on the site of Mullen's West Denver home. An interior plaque commemorates the contributions of J. K.'s wife, Kate, to Denver philanthropy. J. K. and his wife financed the church that once anchored Denver's Spanish-speaking community. Across from the Civic Center, researchers pore over manuscripts underneath Mullen's portrait in the Western History Department of the Denver Public Library—a reminder of his sponsorship of Denver's library system. In northwest Denver, elderly residents of Mullen's Home for the Aged pass their closing days in peace, dignity, and comfort in the building J. K. built for them. In southwest Denver, young men and women attend an elite Catholic preparatory school—a legacy of J. K.'s concern over the fate of orphan boys.

Evidence of Mullen's contribution to the architectural landscape stretches beyond Denver. The tallest structure in many farming towns throughout the Rocky Mountain West is the grain elevator constructed by Mullen's Colorado Milling and Elevator Company. J. K.'s name adorns a plaque commemorating the construction of St. Joseph's Catholic Church in his boyhood home of Oriskany Falls, New York. In Washington, D.C., the J. K. Mullen Memorial Library adorns the campus of the Catholic University. The Catherine Smith Mullen Nurse's Home and the Ella Mullen Weckbaugh Memorial Chapel at St. Joseph's Hospital, Camp St. Malo, located near Long's Peak, and Camp Santa Maria along the South Platte River all exist as a result of his fortune as well as his inculcation of philanthropy in his descendants. Through modern donations by the charitable foundation that bears his name, children enjoy the Tropical Discovery and Primate Panorama exhibits at the Denver Zoological Gardens. Other foundations created by his daughters and grandchildren continue as important sources of medical, social, and religious giving.

J. K. Mullen, the poor Irish immigrant boy who grew up to found a multimillion-dollar flour-milling empire, appears cast in the model of an instructive Horatio Alger story. Indeed, like his fellow temperance advocate William Makepeace Thayer, Mullen believed that Providence guided "each one [who] possessed character, a noble purpose, ability to do, industry, perseverance, and patience . . . Whatever other qualities they possessed, these led the van and controlled all."[2] Like many of his contemporary business associates, such as John D. Rockefeller and Andrew Carnegie, and such contemporary Colorado capitalists as John Evans, Winfield Scott Stratton, Charles Boettcher, and Albert Humphreys, J. K. Mullen considered his investments in the spiritual, cultural, and moral fabric of his community as part of his obligations as a successful businessman. As a self-recognized "self-made man," Mullen embodied a desire to channel his success for the benefit of others.

His efforts to acquire and maintain a personal fortune contributed to Colorado's financial, civic, and commercial climate. Mullen's investment in the Colorado cattle industry and his transformation of Colorado's competing flour mills into the mighty Colorado Milling and Elevator Company bolstered the agricultural facets of western economic development. His success was typical of intelligent, hard-working speculative capitalists who operated in the boom-bust climate of the late nineteenth and early twentieth centuries. Yet, J. K. avoided the reckless plunging that brought ruin on some of his contemporaries.

Diminutive in stature—he stood just five feet eight—and childlike in his facial features, J. K. surprised those who assessed him with a strong-mindedness that belied his outward appearance. His bright, soft, babyish eyes beamed benevolence that disarmed his admirers and foes alike. Yet a friend recalled that the little Irishman was "a giant in physical strength and in power of endurance, [who] could put in longer hours of hard work, on less sleep, than was possible with most men."[3] His height disadvantage was offset by a broad, muscular girth developed through long hours of swinging picks, shovels, and heavy flour sacks. An early photograph shows that he possessed a slender, angular profile, softened by a bristly goatee. His head rests on a muscular neck, which strains through the tight collar of his shirt. His large hands and feet appear out of balance with his husky bantamweight frame. In later years, his face softened up with the fleshiness of prosperity.

John Kernan Mullen, c. 1910. Soft eyes and the babylike roundness of his facial features belied an indomitable will. Courtesy, Western History Dept., Denver Public Library.

The businessman exuded a calm reserve and dignified formality that repeatedly earned him the description "gentlemanly." He dressed in immaculate clothing and kept impeccably groomed hair (reportedly maintained by daily visits to a barber). In conflict he preserved an air of gentle good humor as long as his patience lasted. True anger dispelled his softness and darkened his features into a forceful scowl. Flexing his rough, work-scarred hands, he emitted an iron-cold remoteness that chilled even those dearest to him. A private man, unknowable to strangers, J. K. suppressed his deepest feelings behind a mask of benevolence and hid away his passions in all but the most intensely emotional moments. The mask proved to be a frustrating barrier for those friends and relatives who wished to know the entrepreneur's inner self.[4]

Remembered for good works, which earned unqualified praise, Mullen also aggravated friends, family, clergymen, and colleagues by his drive to dominate all aspects of his business, family, and religious life. His single-handed domination of the Colorado milling industry fostered bitter mistrust in the regional farming community and dissension among his board of directors. His firm opinions on religious issues led to ecumenical arguments with Denver's pioneer bishops. His attempts to control the financial behavior of his unruly younger brother led to a lawsuit and a bitter deathbed rift between the families. Yet if the price to pay for his ambition was high, J. K. never expressed regret.

Ironically, Mullen displayed a willingness to acculturate to Protestant American values, despite his uncompromising self-identification as a Catholic. The philanthropist witnessed anti-Catholic intolerance from a very early age. Feeling vulnerable to the sheer numeric weight of Protestant culture in American society, the businessman chose to react to nativism—including the antiforeigner, anti-Catholic American Protective Association movement of the 1890s and dominance of the Ku Klux Klan in the 1920s—by turning the other cheek. He drove himself hard to prove to his religious antagonists how far a Catholic could succeed in a Protestant society. His behavior contrasts with that of working-class Irish miners in the Irish-dominated copper-mining town of Butte, Montana. There, writes historian David Emmons, the Irish-dominated work environment allowed for a strong expression of ethnic and labor solidarity.[5] Unable to control the cultural climate in New York, Kansas, or Colorado, Mullen downplayed his ethnic identity and strove instead to fulfill the success and tolerance ideals of the dominant Protestant middle-class culture. He reconciled his self-identification as a defender of Catholic values and institutions with an acceptance of Protestant associates and influences. To the exasperation of his more traditionally minded bishops, J. K. pioneered a new path chosen by many twentieth-century American Catholics by blending traditional cultural views on religion with new ecumenical perspectives.

In the tradition of contemporary businessman-philanthropists, Mullen's motivation to give came as a cultural attachment to his success. J. K. identified himself as an economic pioneer whose construction of the Colorado Milling and Elevator Company enriched the state's economic growth. Likewise, his philanthropy buttressed Colorado's religious, educational, and social life. Unaccustomed to celebrity, the philanthropist preferred to give in anonymity. Yet, when he wished to make a moral point, he very often demanded the attention that his position in society enjoined.

Mullen committed a significant share of his fortune to the development of Colorado's philanthropic community, but his desire to give was tied closely to his family life. The businessman struggled to reconcile material success with domestic values. Success achieved through long periods in the office or on the road came at the expense of his family life. Yet on the whole, J. K. created a stable family structure through which to pass on his values and the responsibility of his philanthropic beliefs. Often, business matters served to alienate J. K. from his brothers, his daughters, and his sons-in-law. Philanthropy, shared and shaped by the entire household, was the strongest of bonds, which tied the family together over time.

NOTES

1. Sister Justine, L.S.o.P., "Dedication of Mullen Home for the Aged Recreation Center," speech transcript, 1932, Little Sisters of the Poor/Mullen Home for the Aged papers, Archdiocese of Denver.

2. William Makepeace Thayer, quoted in Richard M. Huber, *The American Idea of Success* (New York: McGraw-Hill, 1971), 54.

3. Charles W. Hurd, "J. K. Mullen, Milling Magnate of Colorado," *The Colorado Magazine* XXIX:2 (April 1952): 110.

4. Ibid., 111; Thomas J. Noel, *Colorado Catholicism and the Archdiocese of Denver, 1857–1989* (Niwot: University Press of Colorado, 1989), 316.

5. David Emmons, *The Butte Irish: Class and Ethnicity in an American Mining Town, 1875–1925* (Urbana: University of Illinois Press, 1989), 198.

2

FROM IRELAND TO AMERICA

Galway, Ireland, to Oriskany Falls, New York, 1847–1867

IN THE FAMINE YEAR OF 1847, when John Mullen was born—he supposedly did not acquire his middle name, "Kernan," until a later date—105,536 Irish men, women, and children entered the United States. When John's father, Dennis, packed up his family for the trip to America in 1856, they joined another 54,350 refugees. During John Mullen's first nine years of life, nearly 1.2 million emigrants abandoned Ireland for the hope of a better chance in America.[1] Although Charles W. Hurd, the author of an admiring biographical sketch, contends that John Mullen "cherished fond boyhood memories of his native country," poverty and the chance for a better life in America carried John Mullen from his home at a very early age.[2] At fifty-one, Dennis Mullen (1806–1886), faced the difficult task of starting over in a new land. Dennis started his family late, even by Irish standards. When his wife, Ellen Mulray (1816–1888), delivered their first child, Bridget, in 1841, Dennis was already thirty-five. Other children followed, including Maria (1842), Patrick (1844), John (1847), Dennis (1850), Kate (1853), and Ella (1855).[3] With so many mouths to feed, emigration probably meant the difference between life and death for the rest of Dennis's family.

Prior to the famine, Dennis provided for his family in Ballinasloe, Ireland. The Shannon River market town was situated on the road between Galway and Dublin. Located in the heart of Ireland's oat-growing country, the town supported three oatmeal mills, two breweries, and a flour mill during the 1820s and 1830s. In more prosperous times, Dennis and his brother, Thomas, crafted barrels for the mills.

By 1856, prosperity was a distant memory—the oats that could have fed western Ireland were instead exported to the enrichment of absentee landlords. After ten years of famine, western Ireland's system of subsistence farming was in ruins. Even city-dwellers such as the Mullens found the prospect of emigration more appealing than unemployment, eviction, and starvation. The family joined the exodus that reduced the western Irish population by one-third.[4]

Dennis's search for work would lead through Boston to central New York. Their destination, Oriskany Falls, was a small village situated on a modest cascade of a tiny tributary to the Mohawk River in the farthest southeastern corner of Oneida County. The town of Oriskany Falls served as a milling station for the wheatlands of central New York. Cooper Street, the thoroughfare where barrel makers set up shop, emerged literally from the doors of the major Oriskany Falls gristmill. When Dennis and his brother arrived in the town, they each bought small adjacent houses in the shadow of the mill.[5]

Although soil exhaustion and the development of railroad networks and the Erie Canal had pushed the grain frontier to the Midwest, central New York was still a significant if declining center of wheat and flour production in the mid-1850s. Immigrant boys like John and his brothers Patrick and Denny were either expected to follow in their father's footsteps as coopers or obtain work at one of the nearby mills. Dennis enrolled his children in public school, but John quit as soon as he was old enough to take an apprenticeship at Miller's Flour Mill at the head of Cooper Street.[6] Education remained important to the immigrant, but for the moment, instruction in a skill outweighed the value of book learning, particularly among struggling Irish families who "needed the labors of all to survive."[7] Too young to take up arms in the Civil War, John took advantage of the opportunity created by the wartime manpower drain. At an age when late-twentieth-century boys are typically beginning their sophomore year of high school, John Mullen became one of the primary wage earners in his family. His education from that point on would be informal, practical, and self-regulated.

Indeed, as flour-mill historian Robert Murray Frame points out, "for a miller-millwright . . . little prior schooling beyond literacy was either assumed or considered necessary."[8] Miller's Mill utilized the traditional techniques that flour manufacturers had relied upon since

The falls of Oriskany Creek, New York, c. 1890. Miller's Mill, where fourteen-year-old J. K. Mullen first found employment, stands at right. At center is a frame church constructed by J. K.'s brother Patrick in 1872. Courtesy, Limestone Ridge Historical Society.

the 1790s. The two-story structure drew power from the falls on Oriskany Creek to drive its grinding stones—massive granite disks known as French burrs. As an apprentice, John cleaned the wheat kernels by hand and poured them from the second story into the granite wheels on the first floor. The higher burr spun like a top on a spindle, pressing the wheat berries against its fixed twin on the bottom. Sharp grooved channels pulled the bran from the germ and mashed the kernels into a coarse powder. Operators next sifted—or "bolted"—the slurry through a silk or wire mesh to separate the unground middlings and bran from the finely powdered flour. Apprentices learned the secrets of flour milling from their masters in a time-honored fashion that predated the industrial revolution.[9]

In time, Mullen would embrace innovation that would overturn this preindustrial system. For now, his training was grounded in eighteenth-century tradition. Before technical innovations demanded increasing specialization, millers were expected to perform a wide range of operations. Master millers guided their apprentices through tricky lessons in physics, engineering, applied mathematics, marketing, and business practices. With the help of assistants, millers built and repaired each part of the mill by hand—all while coordinating a whirling dance of belts, cogs, pulleys, cams, shafts, levers, and engines.[10]

"Millwrights, as a rule," explained milling engineer R. James Abernathey, "were fairly good mechanics."[11] To assist their training, most American millers relied on Oliver Evans's *Young Mill-Wright and Miller's Guide.* This guide, which had remained virtually unchanged since its first publication in 1795, contained the mechanical principles and business techniques that comprised "a complete education for a miller-millwright."[12] Yet during Mullen's apprenticeship, times—and technologies—were changing. In 1860, Evans's handbook underwent its fifteenth and last reprinting. Within the next two decades, new innovations, increased specialization, and new management techniques both increased the efficiency of mills and rendered the *Young Mill-Wright and Miller's Guide* obsolete.[13]

As an apprentice, John Mullen struggled to channel the forces of friction that simultaneously produced the whitest flour and inevitably dulled the edges of the brittle granite millstones. Mullen earned much of his weekly two-dollar salary by "dressing" the worn-out burrs—sharpening their grooves with a pickaxe. This tedious job physically

Burr dressers, who sharpened the teeth of granite millstones with an iron pick, endured demanding labor that left physical scars on apprentices and journeymen alike. These Minnesota dressers display their toughness in an 1858 photo. Courtesy, Minnesota Historical Society.

identified him with the working class. Chips of granite, dislodged by his pick, imbedded in the backs of the boy's hands. They left permanent calluses and dark scars resembling powder burns that one witness claimed made him looked like "he had been shot at short distance." Until the end of his life John proudly displayed his scarred hands to visiting schoolchildren as the badge of distinction for a self-made man.[14]

THE ACCULTURATION DILEMMA

The Irish who fled the Great Famine often faced the challenge of preserving their cultural identity in America. One of the common methods of coping with this problem was to cling fiercely to their religious/spiritual devotion. This "devotional revolution," as historians Emmett Larkin and Andrew M. Greeley call the phenomenon, left the American Irish with "a stubborn, dogged, counter-Reformation form of Irish Catholicism, about the only explicit cultural form left them by their tragic history."[15] The immigrants practiced their religion in a climate of religious intolerance, which forced the most visible Irish Catholics to regulate their behavior, accommodate to the cultural backdrop, or face persecution from members of the Protestant majority.

Under the guidance of his parents and circuit-riding Catholic priests, John Mullen received the spiritual indoctrination by which he ordered his life. The young miller shared the traditional Irish respect for the clergy as well as the weekly ritual of Mass. With only forty Catholic families in Oriskany Falls, Catholic services were held irregularly in the village, often in the homes of the parishioners. John frequently traveled to neighboring towns to attend Mass.[16] He learned to habitually go out of his way to find Catholic services. On his way west, and over the course of his lifetime, he strove to attend Sunday Mass wherever his travels took him, dutifully reporting his attendance, or lack thereof, in his letters and reminiscences.

Church appealed to the young man because it blended spiritual and moral fulfillment with social intercourse. By contrast, another common meeting place for Irish immigrants, the saloon, provided only the social environment without the uplifting qualities of the former two. For many working-class Irishmen, immigrant saloons were havens of recreation, nationalism, and employment where alcohol formed social glue.[17] J. K. broke the stereotype set by many of his tippling fellow countrymen when he developed an aversion to alcohol at an early age. Perhaps as a sign of his growing responsibility to his family, he signed a pledge of sobriety at the same time that he began working at the mill. Thereafter, he pursued temperance as conscientiously as regular church attendance.[18]

The importance of sobriety and a clean standard of conduct became apparent whenever Mullen traveled to Utica, where anti-Irish sentiments often ran high. Each Fourth of July, the Mullen family took advantage of reduced train fares to attend the annual fireworks display in the regional capital. Displays of public drunkenness among Irish and native-born Americans alike often marred their holiday excursions.[19]

On other occasions, the Mullens probably witnessed or, if they could, avoided darker demonstrations of patriotism. Beginning with the construction of the Erie Canal in the 1820s and lasting into the 1860s, native-born laborers staged mocking parades to protest the presence of the Irish. Demonstrators carried effigies of stereotypic Irishmen decked out in "rosaries of potatoes." "Paddy baiting" rowdies beat Irish workers or provoked them into fights on public holidays such as the Fourth. When Irishmen fought back, local papers carried sensational accounts of the disturbances of "drunken paddies."[20] Other than keeping out of the mob's path, there was little that working-class families such as the Mullens could do to prevent such confrontations. It fell to local Irish political and business leaders to counteract this unfavorable treatment.

In the forefront of Utica's conservative Irish leaders was John Mullen's hero, Francis Kernan (1816–1892). As the head of the richest Irish Catholic family in Utica, the successful attorney presented himself as a role model for aspiring young Irish Catholics. Kernan, a prominent Democratic politician, championed the Tammany political machine in its battle against the Republican boss Roscoe Conkling for control of Oneida County. Kernan served as state assemblyman from Utica, U.S. congressman, contender for the office of New York State governor, and U.S. senator. Although a member of the corrupt Democratic organization centered at New York's Tammany Hall, Kernan strove to keep his personal reputation beyond reproach. All too often, Protestant representatives in the New York State assembly shared New York State assemblyman Theodore Roosevelt's opinion that the Irish Democrats were "a stupid, sodden, vicious lot, most of them being equally deficient in brains and virtue."[21] Kernan sought to prevent such characterizations from ruining his own political career. He demonstrated abstinence as president of the Utica Temperance Society, meticulously attended church, and distanced himself from the odium of Tammany affiliation by identifying himself as the party's reform candidate.[22]

Kernan's example had its effect on John Mullen. The extent to which the milling apprentice wished to identify with the politician is suggested in an unverifiable story related by Mullen's daughter Ella.

As a boy, Mullen was supposedly teased good-naturedly by Kernan about his lack of a middle name. Without the respectable weight of three names, Kernan chided, "You'll never amount to anything, Johnny Mullen." To counter this, Mullen adopted the name of the man he most admired—Kernan.[23]

At first glance, the smooth politician seems an unlikely moral beacon. However, the ward boss's well-groomed image as a moral, upstanding, Irish Catholic gentleman impressed other members of J. K.'s family. Mullen's brother Patrick praised Kernan in the highest terms he could articulate. "He is an honest leader," Patrick insisted, "which is accounted for by the fact that he is a good practical Irish Catholic."[24]

Kernan's example held one more lesson for a mature J. K. Mullen. As a young man in Denver, Mullen closely followed the politician's unsuccessful campaign for New York governor in 1872.[25] Although praised as a "cultivated gentleman" by the *New York Times*, Kernan was nevertheless condemned as a tool of the Tammany bosses. The *Times* charged that "a vote for Kernan is a vote for the restoration to power of Tammany Hall." Moreover, when Kernan boasted of being "'a severe'— that is bigoted—Roman Catholic," the *Times* editorialized, "Ninety-nine out of every hundred Irish-born Roman Catholics vote whatever is commended to them as the Democratic ticket." Backed by the anti-Catholic rhetoric of the *Times*, as well as the recent Tweed Ring scandal, Republican candidate John A. Dix won the election by casting himself as the true reform candidate.[26]

Kernan's defeat, underscored by the fact that Protestant Democrats won the next three gubernatorial elections with massive Tammany support, emphasized the perils of die-hard Catholicism in a society dominated by Protestants.[27] Mullen drew from the lesson the idea that personal integrity alone could not guarantee success. Instead, accommodation appeared to succeed in a potentially intolerant culture.

NOTES

1. U.S. Dept. of Commerce, Bureau of the Census, "Immigrants by Country: 1820–1970," *Historical Statistics of the United States: Colonial Times to 1970*, vol. 1 (Washington, D.C.: GPO, 1976), 106.
2. J. K. Mullen, Letter to Ella M. Weckbaugh, August 25, 1925, Weckbaugh family collection; Charles W. Hurd, "J. K. Mullen, Milling Magnate of Colorado," *The Colorado Magazine* XXIX:2 (April 1952): 117.

3. U.S. Dept. of Commerce, Bureau of the Census, *Manuscript Census, Population Schedules: 1865,* Town of Augusta, Oneida County, New York, microfilm copy, Utica Public Library, Utica, New York; East Galway Family Historical Society Company Ltd., Letter to John F. Malo, November 30, 1999.

4. Samuel Lewis, *A Topographical Dictionary of Ireland,* vol. 1, 1837 (Reprint, Port Washington, N.Y.: Kennikat Press, 1971), 110; Ruth Dudley Edwards, *An Atlas of Irish History* (London: Meuthen & Co., 1973),168–169, 218–219.

5. U.S. Dept. of Commerce, Bureau of the Census, *Manuscript Census, Population Schedules: 1865,* Town of Augusta, New York.

6. A. Stella Cieslak, ed., *The Colonel's Hat: A History of the Township of Augusta* (Oriskany Falls, N.Y.: Limestone Ridge Historical Society, 1979), 82; J. K. Mullen, Letter to Ella M. Weckbaugh, May Dower, Catherine O'Connor, and Edith Malo, Denver, Colorado, 1928, Weckbaugh family collection; Hurd, 105.

7. Hasia R. Diner, *Erin's Daughters in America: Irish Immigrant Women in the Nineteenth Century* (Baltimore: Johns Hopkins University Press, 1983), 13.

8. Robert Murray Frame, "The Progressive Millers: A Cultural and Intellectual Portrait of the Flour Milling Industry, 1870–1930" (Ph.D. diss., University of Minnesota, 1980), 16.

9. Ibid.

10. R. James Abernathey, *Practical Hints for Mill Building* (Moline, Ill.: R. James Abernathey, 1880, microfilm), 2.

11. Ibid.

12. Frame, 16.

13. Ibid., 15.

14. Hurd, 106; Anne Weckbaugh, personal interview, February 6, 1998.

15. Andrew M. Greeley, *That Most Distressful Nation: The Taming of the American Irish* (Chicago: Quadrangle Books, 1972), 84.

16. Cieslak, 23–24.

17. Thomas J. Noel, *The City and the Saloon, Denver, 1858–1916* (Lincoln: University of Nebraska Press, 1982), 84.

18. Patrick H. Mullin, Letter to J. K. Mullen, March 16, 1873, Weckbaugh family collection; Hurd, 114.

19. Patrick H. Mullin, Letter to J. K. Mullen, July 7, 1872, J. K. Mullen papers, State Historical Society of Colorado (hereafter cited as Mullen papers, CHS).

20. Cheryl A. Pula and Philip A. Bean, "Utica's Irish Heritage," in *Ethnic Utica,* James S. Pula, ed. (Utica, N.Y.: Utica College of Syracuse University, 1994), 74.

21. Cited in Edmund Morris, *The Rise of Theodore Roosevelt* (New York: Ballantine Books, 1979), 162.

22. "Francis Kernan," Biographical file, Oneida County Historical Society, Utica, New York.

23. Walter S. Weckbaugh, personal interview, Denver, Colorado, July 21, 1997.

24. Patrick Mullin, Letter to J. K. Mullen, August 3, 1872, Weckbaugh family collection.

25. Patrick Mullin, Letters to J. K. Mullen, August 3 and September 23, 1872; March 16, 1873, Weckbaugh family collection.

26. *New York Times*, October 27, 28, 1872.
27. David M. Ellis, James A. Frost, Harold C. Syrett, and Harry J. Carman, *A Short History of New York State* (Ithaca: New York University Press, 1957), 359, 361.

3

THE GRASSHOPPER YEARS

Oriskany Falls, New York, to Troy, Kansas, 1867–1871

HOWEVER MAINSTREAM SOCIETY MAY HAVE VIEWED IRISH CATHOLICS in
general during the 1860s, J. K.'s talents opened up avenues of ad-
vancement in the smaller world of Oriskany Falls. The apprentice
quickly absorbed the principles of milling. He was literate and skilled
in applied mathematics—so much so that his master, Dick Skinner, a
man of more exacting mathematical than grammatical standards, supposedly boasted, "[Mullen] ain't never made a mistake with figgurs."[1]
J. K.'s abilities, perhaps combined with the wartime manpower drain,
earned him rapid promotion. When J. K. later noted he had advanced
from apprentice to manager "before I reached my twentieth birthday,"
he recognized the mark of his own talent.[2]

A success he may have been, but by the spring of 1867, the young
journeyman—who at nineteen had begun to grow a beard that hardened the lines of his childlike face—was also growing restless. Milling
center or not, Oriskany Falls was a backwater compared to the vigorous new grain frontier developing along the Middle Border. Veterans,
whose absence had allowed J. K. to take employment, returned to
their former professions at the end of the Civil War. Accordingly, J. K.
formed plans with a boyhood friend, Dell Barker, to move west. The
road west, he later explained, led to opportunity: "We young fellows
started off to the West, hoping to find employment and better our
condition."[3] In so defining his aspirations, J. K. expressed the belief,
shared with those who subscribed to the doctrine of the self-made
man, in a fluid American class system based on geographic mobility.
"In the American experience," writes historian Richard M. Huber,

At nineteen, John Mullen—complete with his chosen middle name, "Kernan"—quickly advanced to manager of Miller's Flour Mill in Oriskany Falls. Although only possessing what would now be equivalent to a formal ninth-grade education, J. K.'s skill in mathematics led his boss at Oriskany Falls to proclaim, "He ain't never made a mistake with figgurs." Coming from a man of exacting mathematical, if not grammatical, standards, this was high praise. Perhaps as a momento for his family, nineteen-year-old Mullen poses for a photograph prior to his 1867 odyssey to Kansas. Courtesy, Colorado Historical Society.

"readiness to migrate across space . . . was restless motion with a purpose—moving out towards opportunity and up towards achievement."[4]
Mobility, in short, suited J. K.'s expanding horizons.

EASTERN KANSAS

Later in life, J. K. Mullen recalled that the two travelers roared out of
Oriskany Falls on a Conestoga stagecoach—the very symbol of western
adventure. In the more cosmopolitan Utica, and out of sight of their
family and friends, Mullen and Barker quickly traded their dusty,
bumpy stage for railroad passage. Further westward travel would be
done via the New York Central or other railway lines.[5] Their route led
through Buffalo to Niagara Falls. From Niagara, the two friends traveled due west through the Great Lakes region of Canada, then south
through Detroit and Chicago, before heading back into farming country. The friends split up at Quincy, Illinois. Dell's journey ended with
a job in Hannibal, Missouri. Mullen continued west to investigate
employment opportunities in Atchison, Kansas.[6]

Disappointment greeted J. K. in the West, as it had many others. In
1867, the large-scale milling frontier had stalled across the Missouri River
in eastern Kansas. Atchison represented both the end of the railroad line
and the edge of profitable commercial wheat farming and milling.
Sodbusters, inching westward on a ragged front, hesitated at the "water
line" between the ninety-fifth and hundredth meridians, which de-
marcated the midwestern prairies from the Great Plains. Softer eastern
varieties of wheat struggled in the arid trans-Missouri region. Russian
and German farmers had only recently introduced hard new varieties
of European spring wheat and the drought-resistant Crimean Red
strain into the Dakotas, Kansas, and Nebraska.[7] One consequence of
the introduction of these new varieties was a lag in milling technologies. The water-driven methods of grinding that J. K. Mullen had
learned did not remove impurities from the more robust immigrant
wheat as efficiently as it did the softer native varieties. New advances
in milling technology that could handle the vigorous new grains were still
four years away. Until engineers could solve the problem, mill capacities
were sharply reduced by the same hardiness that made dry-land wheat
more suitable for the western climate than softer native varieties.[8]

Atchison, J. K. observed, "was very dull . . . the entire crop had
been consumed by pesky grasshoppers."[9] The influx of pests, combined

with drought, ruined the Kansas wheat crop in 1867. As a result, the mills stood idle. Mullen hired on with the Blair and Ault mill, sacking corn for government contractors at a salary of five dollars per week. He moonlighted by dressing burrs at the dormant mills. Still unable to meet his boarding expenses, J. K. moved on to Doniphan, Kansas, where he helped operate a Missouri River ferry for two Oriskany Falls acquaintances. The following spring, the cash-strapped laborer "hitch-hiked" (by alternately walking and sharing a horse with a companion) to the Doniphan County seat of Troy to sign up with the Banner Flour Mills.[10]

There, he became acquainted with Troy's leading citizen—a man, who like Mark Twain's many-titled citizen of South Pass City, was "a perfect Allen's revolver of dignities." Frank Tracey was a town promoter, merchant, newspaperman, agricultural booster, Doniphan County treasurer, Kansas adjutant general, and the owner of Banner Mills. Best of all, the frontier entrepreneur offered hard but lucrative work.

J. K. recalled that, unlike the previous summer, 1868 promised to be "a good wheat year."[11] He pulled double shifts as a mill laborer and field hand, spending his twenty-first birthday in a sweltering Kansas field, forking heavy loads of wheat into a cradle. Tracey soon recognized the wasted assets of his highly experienced field hand. He promoted J. K. out of the fields and into the position of mill manager. In return, for a handsome monthly salary of $135, Mullen purchased wheat and oversaw the day-to-day operations at the mill in Tracey's absence. Mullen judged Tracey "the kindliest man I ever knew."[12] Along with the raise and the management assignment came a large amount of autonomy. Tracey's many responsibilities left little time to attend to mill business. As a result, J. K. enjoyed nearly complete control of the Banner Mills for the next two years.

SOFTENING A "STRICT CATHOLIC"

Although J. K. had managed a mill in Oriskany Falls, western mill operations required an altogether different mind-set. In New York, millers counted on their clients to produce steady harvests. Kansas millers shared with their customers the risks of their state's uncertain climate. Western wags claimed that Kansas produced only three consistent crops—"drought, grasshoppers, and politics."[13] The strain of uncertain harvests often told on farmers, who, in turn, resented the miller's control of wheat prices. The sodbuster's distrust of the millers required delicate treatment on J. K.'s part. In Kansas, Mullen had his first encounter with what he in time came to call "suspicious" western farmers.[14]

At the same time, the young Catholic absorbed new ideas from Troy's largely Protestant community. He was one of only two or three Catholics, in his own estimation, who lived in the county seat of three thousand. The Protestant atmosphere influenced the Catholic minority. J. K. had brought a fairly provincial set of beliefs and practices to his new home. He later admitted that the lax example of local Catholics caused him to relax some of his own observances. "I was so strict that . . . I was afraid I would break my fast on Fast Days, and so I didn't eat any meat on either Friday or any day during Lent." However, he capitulated when he noticed that a Catholic neighbor commonly ate meat on Fridays.[15]

Mullen's friends and spiritual companions among the Protestant community also contributed to his softening toward Protestant values. He developed a friendly theological rivalry with his boardinghouse roommate:

> Cad Chapman . . . was the son of a Presbyterian minister from Newark, New Jersey . . . who was studying for the ministry. He had his St. James' version of the Scriptures. I went down to St. Joseph [Missouri] and paid $28.00 for a Catholic bible, and together in the evenings and on Sundays we would go over the Scriptures from one end to the other. I guess likely I became somewhat more liberal.[16]

Troy exposed the layman to wider social experiences. Troy, like "Denver and many other small [western] towns," historian Stephen J. Leonard observed, "were places in which the immigrant underwent more rapid acculturation than he did in the large cities of the Northeast and Midwest."[17] As a frontier Roman Catholic, J. K. proved adaptable to the surrounding Protestant culture.

As one of only a handful of Catholics in Troy, Mullen's livelihood depended on mutual trust between him and his Protestant clients, friends, and co-workers. In 1923 he summarized his dependence on businessmen who looked beyond his religious creed:

> From the time I started in business by myself nearly fifty years ago—the very best friends that I had, and the very men that rendered me the greatest assistance and help, and who stood ready to comply with practically every call I made to them for assistance, were men who were not affiliated in any

way with the Catholic Church. I had to depend upon these men for assistance continually—and have to do so yet . . . I know that they are just as honest and just as anxious to do what is right and to save their souls as are men of my own denomination.[18]

Although the social atmosphere of Troy helped Mullen relax his parochialism, the miller was less willing to compromise on intemperance. "There was all kinds of drinking going on there," he worried.[19] He hoped to combat this abuse through organized, evangelical abstinence. Because the only abstinence organization in Troy was the Protestant Good Templars Society, Mullen asked and received permission to join from his diocesan priest in Atchison. Within three months, the Good Templars elected their sole Catholic member as financial secretary. Mullen encouraged tipplers to take the pledge by persuasion and example. He left Troy with the rank of Worthy Grand Chief in good standing.[20]

Because he worked hard to set forth an example of moral brotherhood, J. K. got along well with most of his middle-class neighbors in Troy. The key exception was Frank Tracey's brother-in-law and partner at the Banner Mills—a man known only as "Parker." Whatever his warm feelings for Tracey, J. K. admitted that he "didn't take kindly" to Parker. Sometime in late 1870 or early 1871, a feud erupted between Mullen and Parker over control of operations. Possibly, J. K. felt his authority at the mill compromised. Rather than make peace with Parker, he resigned. Tracey offered his manager a half-interest in his nearly completed hardware store. Mullen declined.[21]

Still other opportunities beckoned to the journeyman farther west. When J. K. arrived in the Jayhawk State in 1867, he was, for all practical purposes, at the end of the agricultural line. The lands beyond Kansas resisted easy exploitation, and without the railroad, few mills could expect more than modest returns on risky investments. By 1871, opportunity reached out in the form of the Kansas Pacific line to new markets in the Rocky Mountain mining camps. In the fall of 1871, J. K. Mullen politely turned his back on Troy and set out for Lawrence, where the railhead reached to Denver.[22]

NOTES

1. "J. K. Mullen Dies at 82," *The Southwestern Miller*, August 23, 1929: 33.
2. J. K. Mullen, Letter to Ella M. Weckbaugh, May Dower, Catherine O'Connor, and Edith Malo, Denver, Colorado, 1928, Weckbaugh family collection (hereafter cited as Letter to his daughters).

3. Ibid.
4. Richard M. Huber, *The American Idea of Success* (New York: McGraw-Hill, 1971), 112.
5. J. K. Mullen, Letter to his daughters, 1928.
6. Ibid.
7. Sean Dennis Cashman, *America in the Gilded Age*, 3d ed. (New York: New York University Press, 1992), 288. In 1871, Edmund N. La Croix solved the milling problem by inventing the gradual reduction process for Washburn Mills in Minneapolis, Minnesota. This new process crushed wheat kernels over ribbed rollers of gradually diminishing sizes.
8. Robert Murray Frame, "The Progressive Millers: A Cultural and Intellectual Portrait of the Flour Milling Industry, 1870–1930" (Ph.D. diss., University of Minnesota, 1980), 37.
9. J. K. Mullen, Letter to his daughters, 1928.
10. In a June 1, 1926, letter to his nephew John J. Mullen, J. K. Mullen described the "ride and tie" method of traveling that introduced the word *hitch-hiking* to the American lexicon: "Someone was going on horseback up to Troy . . . and he very kindly agreed to ride the horse . . . a half mile and hitch it to a post and go on, and then I would come on and get on the horse and ride the horse and pass him on the way and tie the horse, and then I would walk on." Mullen papers, Colorado Historical Society (CHS).
11. J. K. Mullen, Letter to his daughters, 1928.
12. Ibid.
13. *Colorado Farmer and Livestock Journal*, September 3, 1874: 569.
14. J. K. Mullen, Letter to W. S. Bunt, mgr., Claflin Flour Mills, February 12, 1924, Weckbaugh family collection, Denver, Colorado.
15. J. K. Mullen, Letter to John J. Mullen, June 1, 1926, Mullen papers, CHS.
16. Ibid.
17. Stephen J. Leonard, "Denver's Foreign Born Immigrants, 1859–1900," (Ph.D. diss., Claremont Graduate School, 1971), 115.
18. J. K. Mullen, Letter to Rt. Rev. Bishop J. Henry Tihen, March 3, 1923, J. Henry Tihen Papers, Archdiocese of Denver, Denver, Colorado (hereafter cited as Tihen papers).
19. J. K. Mullen, Letter to John J. Mullen, June 1, 1926, Mullen papers, CHS.
20. J. K. Mullen, Letter to John J. Mullen, June 1, 1926, Mullen papers, CHS.
21. J. K. Mullen, Letter to his daughters, 1928.
22. Mullen resided in Troy until at least July 25, when he loaned $150 to the Snow brothers, or possibly August 25,1871, when the debt came due. Robert M. Snow, Promissory note to J. K. Mullen, July 17, 25, 1871, Sheila Sevier private manuscript collection, Denver, Colorado.

4

DENVER, COLORADO TERRITORY, 1871–1874

WHEAT FARMERS AND FLOUR MAKERS first tried their luck with milling in Colorado long before J. K. Mullen's arrival. Spanish and Hispanic farmers introduced wheat into the San Luis and Purgatoire River valleys of southern Colorado by the 1850s. The pioneer *granjeros* cultivated long, narrow fields strung along rivers or irrigation ditches.[1] Small batches of soft *trigo Sonoreno* (Sonoran wheat) ground easily under the hooves of sheep or on stone pallets called *metates*, adopted from southwestern Indians.[2] Farmers sent larger harvests to water-powered mills in Taos or the San Luis Valley. Hispanic farmers built the earliest recorded grist mill near the southern Colorado town of Guadalupe between 1856 and 1857. This early mill used grinding stones made of six-inch-thick slabs of sturdy native lava rock. Pre–Gold Rush grist mills existed along Greenhorn Creek, the Huerfano River, and other southern Colorado watercourses.[3]

Hispanic wheat fields and mills supplied Colorado's relatively small communities in the pre–Gold Rush era. The Pikes Peak gold rush of 1859 created a hunger that outmatched the Hispanic mills. Early-arriving argonauts found "no provisions in the country—the Mexican supplies not yet having arrived—[and] no gold lying on the ground." Disgruntled "go-backers" quickly outnumbered those who stayed. Nevertheless, perhaps ten thousand miners remained in Colorado in early August 1859.[4]

The ten thousand required bread, even at the ruinously high prices demanded by slow, sometimes unreliable overland freight contractors. Hundred-pound bags of flour purchased for between $2.50 and $3.75

in Leavenworth, Kansas, resold for $12 to $15 in the gold camps. During the Indian troubles following the massacre at Sand Creek in 1864, flour prices rose to as much as $22 per hundred-pound bag.[5]

Colorado's boosters realized that in order to support the growth of the territory, farmers had to be lured into the region. The only way to accomplish this was to overturn Stephen Long's assertion that the Great Plains were, in fact, the "Great American Desert." Literally grasping at straws, Denver city boosters parlayed an errant wheat stalk discovered growing in the backyard corn patch of one "Mr. Parkison" into proof of a potential agricultural empire in October 1859. The wheat, spouting two heads from a single stem, was apparently an accidental traveler in a westbound bag of corn. Its symbolic importance was beyond any price. The 148 seeds yielded by the wheat were respectfully counted, planted, and nurtured. After inspecting the heads, *Rocky Mountain News* editor William Byers pinned the hopes of the Rocky Mountain Garden of Eden on this cereal Adam and Eve: "We have not a doubt that millions of acres of our plains and mountain valleys will produce wheat that for quantity and quality, the world cannot excel."[6]

Farmers responded to his challenge by risking Colorado's dry climate to plant wheat. The early results seemed to validate the risk. Wheat's value, durability, and long storage life all make the crop an attractive commodity for speculators. If Colorado's irrigation problems could be mastered, then wheat would flourish in the rich alluvial soil of the Great Plains to the enrichment of its growers.

With a market established, entrepreneurs began working out the problems of milling Colorado grain. Small water-driven mills appeared along Colorado's creeks like pendants on a charm bracelet. Mills harnessed the power of Beaver Creek in Fremont County (Louis Conley, c. 1860), and the Arkansas River near both Cañon City (H. E. Easterday and Ceran St. Vrain, 1860) and Pueblo (B. F. Rockafellow, c. 1862). Two mills stood alongside South Boulder Creek (Doughty & Son, 1862, and P. M. Housel, 1865). Others dipped into Bear Creek (David Barnes, c. 1864) and Fountain Creek (Colton & Co., 1864). Jefferson County boasted two (David Barnes and O. F. Barbour, 1865). Pioneer road builder Otto Mears constructed a mill in Saguache (1867). Richard Little and John G. Lilley's celebrated Rough and Ready Mill pulled power from the South Platte River in Littleton (1867). Anglo mills also competed with Hispanic mills on the Huerfano River (William Kroenig, c. 1859), and in the town of San Luis (J. B. Doyle, c. 1861).[7]

With the exception of the commercially successful Rough and Ready Mill, the proliferation of tiny mills represented, in historian David Brundage's words, "a classic form of home industry" in Colorado until railroad development created outside access to markets.[8] Colorado mills ground small batches of flour primarily for home consumption. Pioneer mills often folded quickly, or, like the Rockafellow Mill in Pueblo, were destroyed by fire.[9] Yet as early as the Civil War, Denver aspired to become the regional capital of the milling industry.

The first to dream of Denver's role as the Minneapolis of the West was John W. Smith, a forty-five-year-old Pennsylvanian of Welsh-Irish descent. Smith, who arrived in Denver on June 3, 1860, quickly realized the commercial possibilities of the emerging camp. Smith imported a variety of machines designed to finish raw materials, including a portable, steam-operated burr mill—the first of its kind recorded in Colorado. Denver's pioneer miller also discovered that fragile new technology

The mill race at Littleton's Rough and Ready Flour Mills. Pioneer Denver millers relied on power from ditches that dried up during hot summers and froze during the winter. Either way, Colorado's extreme climate forced the mills to cease operations—unless enterprising managers ordered young employees like J. K. to wade the ditch and break the ice. Courtesy, Western History Dept., Denver Public Library.

was sometimes worse than none at all. Overwhelming supplies of wheat and corn overloaded his five-horsepower mill, forcing him to revert to water power. In 1864, Smith built a larger turbine-driven flour mill, called the Excelsior, and dug a mill race that he named after himself.[10] The mill race was part of an elaborate water system that Smith built between 1864 and 1867. In the process, he expanded Denver's water delivery capacity and supplied water for a substantial portion of the city. At one time, Smith's ditch extended from the Platte River near Littleton to the West Denver neighborhood and ultimately to City Park. His excavations attracted other millers. Rival mills sprang up along the ditch in west Denver.[11] J. K. Mullen would one day benefit from John Smith's enterprises.

In 1871, those days still lay in the future. J. K.'s migration to Denver coincided with the territorial capital's emergence as the Queen City of the Rocky Mountains and Plains. The city that J. K. Mullen stepped into when he disembarked from his Kansas Pacific car had metamorphosed from a struggling village on the edge of the plains into one of the fastest-growing urban centers in the United States. The energetic boomtown thrived as the regional rail hub, storage depot, mining emporium, and political stronghold. J. K. was immediately struck by the energy of the brash young city around him. "When . . . I came here," he remembered, "there were no old people, we were all young."[12] Rough frontier types mingled with refined sports and gentlemen, while miners, Indians, and roughs prowled Denver's streets and saloons. Tuberculars and asthmatics of the "one-lunged army" congested the Queen City's boardinghouses and hotels. Exposed gaslight pipelines and streetcar tracks, still being laid in Denver's streets, seemed to gleam with the promise of Denver's shining future.[13]

The bustling city had agricultural potential as well. Farmers looked to Denver as a central marketplace for their produce. The fledgling city offered chances unlike any that the journeyman miller had previously encountered. With the advent of large-scale wheat farming imminent, milling, wheat's industrial handmaiden, stood to prosper.[14]

The talented young miller could at least expect a fair chance of employment despite his nationality. The Irish comprised less than 4 percent of the Queen City's population. Over half of J. K.'s countrymen crowded into the ranks of the unskilled and semiskilled labor force. Yet, the Irish enjoyed a higher level of toleration in Denver than

Denver's Larimer Street in 1871 was an emporium of goods and services for the nearby mines. The railroad that brought J. K. also heralded a boom in agriculture that the talented young miller rode to success. Courtesy, Western History Dept., Denver Public Library.

in many American cities. Because of their visible anti-British/pro-American sympathies, because of their political clout, and because Denver suffered from an acute labor shortage, the Irish could expect better opportunities than in the East. With extra advantage of his management experience, Mullen would not be barred by signs that read, "No Irish Need Apply."[15]

"I AM ONLY ASKING FOR A CHANCE TO WORK"

Mullen carried enviable credentials as a journeyman miller and manager, as well as terrific timing, into the territory. Colorado's agricultural epoch lay just ahead. Yet the young miller's expectations were at first disappointed. Flour mills and grain elevators that sprang up like yucca to anticipate the forthcoming bonanza in fact outpaced the rate of wheat production. Overcapitalized and overstaffed mills in Denver, Pueblo, and Manitou Springs all turned the applicant away. If the young man's confidence was shaken, he remained persistent. Taking a job digging irrigation ditches south of Denver, J. K. arranged more interviews during his off hours—often meeting with mill owners on Saturday nights when other young Irish workers typically retired to their neighborhood saloons. One such Saturday-night meeting with O. W. Shackleton, partner along with Charles R. Davis of the Merchant's Mills in West Denver, finally resulted in success.[16]

According to Mullen's reminiscences, shared in a 1928 letter to his daughters, the interview began tenuously. Shackleton expressed interest in Mullen's skills but was reluctant to hire an unproven applicant. His probing interview revealed the young man's ignorance of certain western milling techniques. When J. K. assured him that he was willing to learn any new process required, the proprietor relented, "Yes, I guess we can give you work, but we couldn't pay you much wages."

Mullen replied, "I never asked anyone what wages they would pay me. I am willing to work for whatever you see fit to pay me." Shackleton countered, "Well, we will pay your board down at the Williams's House on West Larimer Street."

"Very well," Mullen agreed, "When do you want me to begin work?"[17]

As a working salary, room and board was a setback from the $135-per month J. K. had given up in Kansas. Accepting the offer indicates a combination of economic pragmatism and confidence in his own abilities. Because he had worked his way up into management positions twice before, it is safe to assume that he expected to succeed again. Over time, the story increased in symbolic value as an example of Mullen's determination to prove himself through hard work, persistence, and character. Like his scarred hands and his labor in the wheat fields of Kansas, Mullen's first Denver job became part of the mythology of character that justified his later success. His willingness to work for room and board—or as Charles Hurd dramatically requoted him, "I am not asking for pay; I am only asking for a chance to work"—reinforced his identity as a self-made man.[18]

Self-confident or not, Mullen quickly compromised his religious principles for the sake of steady employment. Shackleton informed the miller that he would begin the next morning—a Sunday. Mullen objected, "I have never worked a Sunday in my life." His new boss replied that the young laborer "needn't come if [he] didn't want to." J. K. recalled that "I went to church at 5:00 . . . Sunday morning, and was over at work at 7:00."[19] Much later, as director of the Colorado Milling and Elevator Company, he made a special point of closing his mills on Sunday. "We consider Sunday a holy day," he declared, "the obligations of which should be observed by all good citizens."[20]

As a junior miller at the Merchant's Mills, J. K. received the toughest assignments. He dug mill races through the summer. During the winter, the young man spent his Sunday evenings wading through numbingly cold ditches, breaking up ice in the millraces.[21]

The Shackleton and Davis West Denver Flour Mill, c. 1871, stood at the corner of Eighth and Lawrence Streets. J. K. Mullen took the toughest assignments, including digging an extension of the Smith Ditch (foreground) through present-day Overland Park. By night, J. K. waded the ditch, freeing ice jams to maintain a steady flow to the mill race. Courtesy, Western History Dept., Denver Public Library.

As in New York and Kansas, Mullen soon demonstrated his value to his new employers. It was not long before he began to draw a regular salary and advance in rank. The owners of the Merchant's Mills promoted him to manager within two years. Anxious about his finances, J. K. took the advice of bank advertisements pasted on fences and telegraph poles between his boarding house and the mill, which encouraged him to save responsibly. Mullen deposited his paychecks and paid his living expenses out of the 1 percent interest. He saved up a modest sum of $1,200 while sending money back to friends and family in Oriskany Falls. His encouragement to his brothers to join him in Colorado fell on receptive ears. The New York economy was so depressed that his older brother, Patrick, complained that he was considering closing the family cooper's shop because there would be "no work next winter."[22]

The 1873 financial panic that caused this slump caught up with J. K. soon after. When his bank failed, J. K. urgently pressed his brother to collect on various loans he had made in Oriskany Falls to recoup his lost savings. Patrick replied pessimistically, "Business is dull here . . . I wish I could help you but I can't." Worse, Patrick added, "I probably never will be able to repay you what I owe you."[23] The crisis masked a silver lining. J. K. invested his subsequent paychecks in the Union Savings and Loan Association. This investment, he recalled, "turned out very profitably." Over the next eight years, he bought enough shares to become a director. By 1881, he was president. The Union Savings and Loan fund served Mullen as a foundation of both capital and credit.[24]

With financial stability, Mullen began planting roots. The stout Catholic volunteered to teach boy's Sunday school classes at Denver's St. Mary's Catholic Church. This act of faith was rewarded by new social contacts. At St. Mary's, he became infatuated with the girl's instructor, an Irishwoman from Central City named Catherine Smith. Suddenly, J. K.'s life took a new direction. The hardened bachelor found himself yearning for a family of his own.[25]

NOTES

1. Carl Abbott, Stephen J. Leonard, and David McComb, *Colorado: A History of the Centennial State*, 3d ed. (Niwot: University Press of Colorado, 1994), 41; Alvin T. Steinel, *History of Agriculture in Colorado* (Ft. Collins: Colorado State Agricultural College, 1926), 446.

2. Abbott, Leonard, and McComb, 41.

3. Steinal, 31.

4. Abbott, Leonard, and McComb, 56.

5. Duane A. Smith, *Rocky Mountain Mining Camps: The Urban Frontier*, 2d ed. (Niwot: University Press of Colorado, 1992), 196–199; One-hundred-pound bags (or hundrcdweight, or cwt.) were and are the standard wholesale unit for flour.

6. *Rocky Mountain News* (*RMN*), October 27, 1859: 2; Steinal, 447.

7. Steinal, 31–36; Stephen J. Leonard and Thomas J. Noel, *Denver: Mining Camp to Metropolis* (Niwot: University Press of Colorado, 1990), 278; Thomas J. Noel, Paul F. Mahoney, and Richard E. Stevens, *Historical Atlas of Colorado* (Norman: University of Oklahoma Press, 1994), 22.

8. David Brundage, *The Producing Classes and the Saloon: Denver in the 1880s* (New York: Tamiment Institute, 1985), 46.

9. John Everitt, "The Early Development of the Flour Milling Industry on the Prairies," *Journal of Historical Geography* 19:3 (1993): 279; *Colorado Business Directories*, 1877–1882.

10. Louisa Ward Arps, *Denver in Slices* (Denver: Sage Books, 1959), 72. The Smith Ditch, also called the City Ditch after the city bought it, is a designated Denver Landmark as it flows in an open ditch through Washington Park. It has been covered over most of its route in Denver.

11. Ibid., 67–68.

12. J. K. Mullen, Letter to Sister Germaine, Mother Provincial, Little Sisters of the Poor, June 12, 1916, Mullen papers, Western History Dept., Denver Public Library (hereafter referred to as WHDDPL).

13. Isabella L. Bird, *A Lady's Life in the Rocky Mountains*, 1st ed., 1878 (Reprint, Norman: University of Oklahoma Press, 1988), 138; Leonard and Noel, 54.

14. Abbott, Leonard, and McComb, 392; Leonard and Noel, 39.

15. Stephen J. Leonard, "Denver's Foreign Born Immigrants, 1859–1900" (Ph.D. diss., Claremont Graduate School, 1971), 118, 92, 101, 105.

16. J. K. Mullen, Letter to Ella M. Weckbaugh, May Dower, Katherine O'Connor, and Edith Malo, Denver, Colorado, 1928, Weckbaugh family collection (hereafter cited as Letter to his daughters).

17. Ibid.

18. Hurd recounts a more heroic version of the interview: "[Charles R.] Davis told him that he had no work for him. But the young man did not give up; he was sure that he could make good if given a chance, so he said, 'Well, can't you find something for me to do?' At that, Mr. Davis replied, 'Yes, but I can't afford to pay you for the work that I might hunt up for you to do.' Again the young man came back, 'I am not asking for pay; I am only asking for a chance to work.' [Davis replied,] 'Well if you want to work that bad, you may begin tomorrow morning. If we get along all-right I will pay you board and room.'" Charles W. Hurd, "J. K. Mullen, Milling Magnate of Colorado," *The Colorado Magazine* XXIX:2 (April 1952): 106.

19. J. K. Mullen, Letter to his daughters, 1928.

20. J. K. Mullen, Letter to W. S. Bunt, mgr., Claflin Flour Mills, February 12, 1924, Weckbaugh family collection.
21. Walter S. Weckbaugh, personal interview, July 21, 1997.
22. J. K. Mullen, Letter to his daughters, 1928; P. H. Mullin, Letter to J. K. Mullen, August 3, 1873, Weckbaugh family collection.
23. P. H. Mullin, Letter to J. K. Mullen, October 6, 1874, Mullen papers, CHS.
24. *RMN*, July 21, 1881: 5; J. K. Mullen, Letter to his daughters, 1928.
25. Thomas J. Noel, *Colorado Catholicism and the Archdiocese of Denver, 1857–1989* (Niwot: University Press of Colorado, 1989), 20.

5

"MY DARLING KATE"

Domestic Life, 1874–1900

LITTLE EVIDENCE EXISTS to illuminate J. K. Mullen's romantic interests before he encountered Kate. Considering his attempts to curtail his moral weaknesses, it is possible that this courtship was his first romantic venture. The relationship that blossomed between the two upright Sunday school teachers had a profound impact on Catholic philanthropy in Denver. In later years, J. K. Mullen claimed the right to call himself and his wife pioneers. By the accounting of the Sons of Colorado Territorial Pioneers, which the philanthropist and his wife joined in the 1910s, the appellation was technically correct for anyone who immigrated to Colorado before it became a state in 1876. Yet the title of "pioneer" more appropriately belonged to Catherine Smith Mullen, who, as J. K.'s wife, would at times dictate the direction of his philanthropy.

Whatever his romantic feelings, calculation appears to have mattered as much as impulse in J. K.'s selection of a suitable mate. Successful self-made men, according to Victorian doctrine, avoided moral dissolution by carefully choosing wives who complemented their achievements. Self-help writers advised:

> The young business man who desired a good name . . . to marry, because a good wife would be the means of saving him from loose women, gambling, drink, and other vices which damaged reputation . . . The good wife enriched her husband by bringing profitable qualities of character . . . into the home. She was economical, hard-working, orderly, neat, steady, and firm in disposition.[1]

So, too, Irish culture emphasized the "strength and centrality" of women within the Irish family.[2] The woman that J. K. Mullen married provided these qualities and more.

Catherine Theressa Smith was born in October 1851. She was the youngest of eight children born to the Smith family of County Cavan.[3] Katie, or Kate, as she was called by those close to her, was described as a "blue-eyed, pretty, bright-souled" girl.[4] Photographs reveal features more sturdy than pretty. Her round, almost stocky face and broad nose were offset by an apple-cheeked charm. Observers admired her clear, sparkling eyes, and her gently arched eyebrows. The lines of her mouth betrayed a thin-lipped pertness, softened by laugh lines in later years.[5] Shy and withdrawn, yet outspoken within her home, Kate revealed herself fully only to her closest friends and family.

Kate's birth coincided with the peak of the Great Migration. When Kate's father died suddenly in 1853, her mother, Mary Smith, packed up her children and joined the stream of immigrants flowing to North America. Three-year-old Katie entered the United States with her family via New Orleans. The Smith family migrated up the Mississippi and Ohio Rivers before settling in Burlington, Iowa. Kate's older brothers, John, Thomas, and Charles, opened a prosperous freighting company in St. Joseph, Missouri. Beginning with the 1859 Pikes Peak gold rush, the Smith brothers thrice yearly shuttled food and supplies from St. Joseph to the emerging Rocky Mountain gold camps.[6] In 1862, Kate's brothers earned the gratitude of Denver's fledgling Catholic community by hauling the first Catholic cathedral bell nearly 900 miles from St. Louis to St. Mary's Catholic Church.[7]

As the older boys prospered, their mother moved her remaining family to Atchison, Kansas, along the trail from St. Joseph to Denver. Inspired by her brothers' stories about the mining camps as well as the letters of her married sister, whose husband owned a share of the Kirk mine above Central City, the thirteen-year-old girl resolved to cross the prairies to visit the gold camps.

In 1864, Kate trekked the prairies three times in her brothers' wagons. Reaching Colorado, she returned to Kansas to fetch her mother.[8] The return trip to Gregory Gulch offered a taste of prairie hardships. Nighttime temperatures plummeted below zero. Kate's brothers had chosen a risky time to embark with their heavily loaded caravan. The Southern Cheyennes, retaliating for the atrocities committed by the Colorado militia at Sand Creek the previous November, had virtually cut off traffic and communication to and from Denver.[9] Like the journeys of many other pioneers, Kate's trek became the focus of family folklore. Kate's wagon train allegedly endured no less than three Indian raids on their journey to the mining camps.[10]

If the Smith ladies were disturbed by the violence of the prairies, they found in Gregory Gulch a maturing mining community. Nevadaville, where the ladies first settled with Kate's sister, proved to be too far removed from the social and religious activity centered in Central City. Kate disliked negotiating high snowdrifts in order to attend church services in the larger camp. Such inconveniences compelled Kate to move to Blackhawk before finally settling in Central City.[11]

If not for gold mining, no reasonable town planner would have imagined building in the location chosen by Central City. Attracted by the gold deposits that supposedly made the gulch "the richest square mile on earth," fortune hunters slapped haphazard frame and brick buildings up the sides of Gregory Gulch. Still, the slapdash camp boasted of its respectability. Boosters bragged about Central City's newspapers, churches, schools, "and all the best materials of government and society that the East can boast of."[12] Respectable, upright women such as Kate and her mother were welcome additions to the socially aspiring community. As historian Sandra L. Myers pointed out, "education and religion were considered the twin harbingers of civilization."[13] Women provided for both institutions in Gregory Gulch. Lacking an established Catholic parish, Central City was a mission town where the Catholic faithful first held services in a frame house donated by the town sheriff and his wife.[14] Kate and her mother joined Central City's Catholics in seemingly endless fund-raising activities required to support and extend the presence of the church.

Kate became a regular volunteer at Central City's annual Catholic fair. This combination handicraft exhibition and social gala sustained cash-strapped congregations throughout the mining frontier. Parishioners made and sold handicrafts, baked goods, and preserves, provided singing and entertainment, sponsored fortune-telling "sybils" and "voting contests," and offered raffle tickets for a glittering array of religious mementos.[15] The festivities often ended with a full-blown, if carefully monitored, ball. The Catholic fairs depended on young ladies

Catherine Theressa Smith, shown here c. 1890, worked steadily to acquire her own fortune before meeting John Kernan Mullen. Her work as a teacher in Central City and Denver allowed her to acquire real estate downtown. The real estate, along with capital raised by her brother's successful freighting company, grubstaked her husband's early business ventures. Courtesy, Western History Dept., Denver Public Library.

such as Kate to manage finances, sponsor craft tables, solicit contributions, and arrange for decorations. As late as 1880, a reporter noticed that the Central City table at Turner Hall "is under the direction of Mrs. John Mullen."[16] The struggling parish benefited from her volunteerism, which in turn instilled a sense of duty in the young woman.

In the mining camps, Kate formulated priorities that made her an indispensable force in her husband's later philanthropic activities. Her almost daily work with the poor, the sick, the orphaned, and the homeless placed her in sympathy with their needs. Her awareness of the constant pressures of fund-raising helped her channel her husband's wealth toward charitable ends. Although Mullen earned deserved credit for his later largesse, he freely admitted the debt he owed to his wife as a consultant, guide, and inspiration.[17]

If her moral strength alone failed to attract a potential suitor like John K. Mullen, Kate nurtured other attractive assets. She was a woman of property. Soon after arriving in Denver to teach girls' Sunday school classes, the bright-eyed schoolmarm acquired two lots and a house at Fifteenth and Glenarm Streets, a dozen shares of loan association stock, and various notes of debt. She enjoyed access to investment capital through her brothers' successful freighting business and her brother-in-law's mining ventures—capital that would indeed become important to the family's early milling enterprises.[18] Wealth like this was not an uncommon trait among Irish women. As social historian Hasia R. Diner pointed out, single Irish women often enjoyed a degree of economic independence in America. Desired as semiprofessional, white-collar laborers, single Irish women often earned better employment opportunities than their unskilled or semiskilled male counterparts.[19] That alone made Kate an attractive match. Her charm, her virtuous demeanor, her shared interest in church and charity, and her capital and business connections overwhelmed the young miller.

On October 12, 1874, J. K. and Kate wed at St. Mary's Catholic Church.[20] The wedding signified the level of prosperity that the partners had attained. In Ireland, couples married late, after "they were well established as grown-up members of their community."[21] At twenty-seven and twenty-three respectively, John and Kate were young by Irish standards. Their combined financial stability allowed them to buy a new, two-story house at 339 Ninth Street and accept a stream of guests, relatives, and children.[22]

A Mullen family portrait. Standing, from left to right, are J. K.'s sister-in-law Anne Hughes Mullen, brother Dennis W. Mullen, brother Patrick H. Mullen, and sister-in-law Hannah Mullen. Seated are J. K. and Kate's daughters, Katherine, May, Ella, and Edith Mullen. Alternately sources of pride and disappointment for the patriarchal J. K., his family relied on his support while chafing under his supervision. Courtesy, Weckbaugh family collection.

"MY HOME IS MY CLUB"

Domestic life included the responsibility for an extended clan of Irish immigrants. J. K. enjoyed the prospect of children, reminding his wife in 1876, "You know, Kate, that I was bound to have something in the cradle . . . ever since we were married, ain't that so?"[23] The couple filled their cradle quickly and regularly. On July 23, 1875, just nine months and eleven days after their wedding, Kate delivered the first of their five daughters, Ella Theressa, at home.[24] Ella was followed by Mary, or "May," Rose on May 30, 1877; Katherine on November 4, 1879; and Frances Edith on September 16, 1881. John and Kate's youngest daughter, Anne, was born on January 4, 1884. Precious and elfin, "Nannie" died of diphtheria just four years later.[25]

The steady succession of daughters, unbroken by a male heir, produced mixed emotions in their father. The proud papa delighted in his children and talked of little else when each was born. He enjoyed coddling them, protecting them from the harsh world, and instructing them in Catholic values. But the demands of his business forced him to compromise the intimacy of family life—a sacrifice that pained him greatly. On a fund-raising trip in 1900, J. K. wrote his family, "I felt more like staying than leaving you all but I did not want to show it."[26] He tried to make up for the loss by writing sentimental letters to his family from the road. One example, written to Kate and Ella, shows the tenderness that was intended to soften his frequent absences:

> My love to Papa's Little Girl. Learn [*sic*] her to say God Bless Papa in the mornings & Kiss her good night for Papa when she goes to bed in the evening & now Papa will say God Bless and preserve his Little Girl & Guard and Protect his faithful Wife who is watching over her—Who is the Life of us both.[27]

Yet the former mill hand's rough, working-class seasoning clashed against the ideal of indulging his daughters to the potential of his newfound wealth. Merely holding his babies proved to be difficult. His callused hands, the proud symbols of his working-class background, scratched their tender skin in a way that caused them to cry out. The noise upset and confused the awkward father. His pride suffered when his babies reached out for their mother instead.[28]

Ella, May, Katherine, and Edith. Precocious and feminine, J. K.'s beloved daughters grew up into "four wild hairs" of his own flesh and blood, instilled with their father's willfulness. They loudly proffered their opinions on all manner of subjects. They trespassed into the neighboring Tivoli brewery on dares. Worst of all, each new daughter underscored the absence of a male heir. As a result, J. K. instilled respect into his daughters that bordered on terror. Generous and sentimental with his children when relaxed, he could be a strict disciplinarian who generated "an absolute fear of God" when his patience reached its end. Although he encouraged them to call him "Papa," they often referred to him as "Mr. Mullen" when speaking of him in the third person. He sometimes expressed his disappointment in his daughters, reminding them of their shortcomings as women and openly wishing for a son. His disapproval hurt. No matter how obedient, reverent, or accomplished they were, they were unable to achieve this desire. As a result, each competed to gain an advantage of approval over the others.[29]

The girls grew up in a household crowded with grandparents, uncles, aunts, cousins, and other members of their extended family. The extended family was a by-product of immigration. In America, Irish families "provided support in the cycle of crises of poverty and illness, desertion and widowhood" that had disintegrated family bonds in famine-stricken Ireland.[30] J. K. had assumed partial responsibility for his family when he took his first job at fourteen. Wherever he went, he never forgot this obligation.

In West Denver, John and Kate hosted J. K.'s parents, Dennis and Ellen, his sister Kate, his brother Patrick and his family, as well as another brother, Dennis, and his family.[31] Catherine's mother, Mary Smith, lived with the couple from their marriage until her death twenty years later. J. K. blessed the memory of this "good soul" who lived under his roof. J. K.'s younger brother, Dennis W. Mullen (1850–1916), proved to be a more disruptive houseguest. "Denny" came west in 1873 to improve his health and to keep his then-bachelor brother company. J. K. encouraged his brother to escape the "very dull" economic conditions of New York and admonished him to "quit lying around doing nothing."[32] In Denver, Denny shared a boarding room with his older brother. J. K. secured him a job as a flour packer at the Merchant's Mills. Where J. K. went, his baby brother tagged along. When Mullen married and moved to Ninth Street, then to the house alongside the Star Mills, then back to Ninth Street, Denny followed.

A black sheep among his family, Dennis's behavior often exasperated his straight-laced older brother. J. K. frequently complained about Denny's excesses. Denny ran with fast company and plunged deep into the fledgling Denver Democratic machine. His gentlemanly demeanor and fast lifestyle earned him the political nickname "Honest Dennis." He squandered his wages on fine carriage teams. He speculated recklessly in mining and real estate schemes. When his investments faltered, he turned to his brother to help bail him out. He drank too much. His frequent illnesses required constant attention. Soon after his arrival in 1874, Dennis contracted typhoid fever. His older brother and pregnant sister-in-law strained to care for him. "When he lived with us there was but one bed in the house," Mullen recalled. "My wife and I slept on the floor and gave Dennis the bed. We nursed him for seven weeks when he was ill, because he was not strong and rugged."[33]

The family "homestead" on Ninth and Lawrence Streets in West Denver was home to the extended Mullen clan for twenty years. Built by flour miller O. L. Shackleton in 1869, this two-story Italianate house was purchased by J. K. in 1878 and secretly placed in Kate's name in 1889. Kate donated the house and lot to the St. Cajetan's parish in 1924. The first services of St. Cajetan's were held in the family parlor. Courtesy, Western History Dept., Denver Public Library.

Following the collapse of the New York flour industry and the depression of 1873, Mullen was obliged to support his parents and other siblings. For a time, Mullen sent $50 checks to his father in New York. Finally, with "no work next winter" expected in Oriskany Falls, John's family closed their cooper's shop and fled New York for the West. J. K. found each of them a job, often in his own firm.[34]

J. K. and Kate opened their doors to the following generation, as well. The newlyweds Ella and Eugene Weckbach initially lived with John and Kate. In 1912, the couple welcomed their widowed daughter, May, and her son, Frank Louis "Teddy" Tettemer. Kate, J. K. maintained, gave her blessing to May's second marriage only after May promised to reside with her husband in her parents' home. Many Irish families offered their hospitality naturally and the bustling household bothered Mullen not in the least. "I am sure you will all understand," he wrote of his many guests near the end of his life, "that they were very, very welcome."[35]

Home and family life became for the entrepreneur an imperfect sanctuary from the workaday world. Like the farmers with whom he

43

traded, Mullen worked hard. He spent several weeks out of every year among his rural customers, selling flour, buying equipment, inspecting mills, or borrowing money. "It was not uncommon," C. W. Hurd remembered, "for him to get off the train at two or three o'clock in the morning in a distant town and . . . drive into the country, visiting prospective wheat shippers."[36] Even at home, J. K. pushed himself through a rigorous work regimen. His stamina and concentration meant greater capacity for production at the firm even if it also meant a disrupted family life.

J. K.'s day began routinely before dawn. He ate a simple breakfast and departed quickly for work. His evening schedule was less predictable. Significantly, it was Kate who noticed how J. K.'s working habits disrupted domestic life:

> Mrs. Mullen said that for many years, seven o'clock in the morning never saw him at home, and she never knew when he would get back at night. If he was not there on time for the evening meal, she would put his dinner in the oven to keep warm, as he might not show up before nine o'clock.[37]

After supper, J. K. frequently retired to his library or even back to his office at the mill to continue work. He possessed a hungry mind. As if to make up for his lack of formal education, he vigorously read histories, trade journals, and newspapers.[38] He admitted, "I hate to go to bed early." Often his reading lamp burned until two o'clock the next morning as the entrepreneur caught up on the latest milling developments and current events.[39]

His sequestration served another purpose. Unable to leave the pressures of business at the office, Mullen often returned home tired and foul-tempered. At such times, his eldest daughter, Ella, remembered, "everybody in the house just sort of shut down."[40] His study was a place of refuge where he could go to unwind, but where everyone else passed on tiptoes.

Even in relaxation, Mullen favored diversions that brought together his family and social life under one roof. Temperate and an advocate of "innocent recreations," he spurned the smoky social and political clubs, taverns, and flesh palaces favored by many of his countrymen and business associates. He preferred instead to unwind in his own parlor. "My home is my club," he told friends.[41] His interests included reading, chess, and frequent Saturday- and Sunday-night poker games, all of which could be pursued in the comfortable confines of his home. He invited a small gathering of close friends to play whist and other card games "most every evening."[42] The local clergy, Protestant and Catholic, received standing invitations to Sunday dinner. Their conversation stimulated Mullen, who admired the variety of topics discussed, the depth of knowledge, and the moral atmosphere that the ecclesiastic gathering contributed to his home. The formal Sunday dinners would be remembered by his children as a weekly ordeal of enforced good behavior, to be avoided whenever possible.[43]

Mullen tried to make up for his long road trips by writing regularly to his "darling Kate." His surviving letters show his effort to be a loving husband and father from afar. He composed one such letter to Kate on an 1880 business trip to secure funds for the Hungarian Elevator. Writing from his cabin on the Hudson River packet, *Daniel Drew*, J. K. expressed his loneliness:

> You know Kate I cannot describe riches & elegance . . . but this steamer is rich in every part . . . Its furniture surpasses anything I ever imagined [but] more to me than all the rest of the world & among the riches & splendor of this elegant steamer the drawing room of which is a very palace . . . you are a magnificent work of art . . . Kate I somehow feel guilty tonight & have never been as lonesome in my life and just because there is so much here to enjoy & yet I am alone among all this throng. I know if you were here with me we would enjoy it all but as it is I cannot & have left it and come in to speak to you about it.[44]

J. K. acknowledged that whether he was home or away, it was Catherine who represented the domestic center of the household. From the beginning of their relationship, she shared his labors. She raised their daughters, operated a boardinghouse for their mill hands, oversaw a home crowded with extended family members, hosted an endless procession of priests, nuns, and businessmen, and counseled, cooked, laundered for, and made love to her loving, difficult husband. She somehow found time in between to cultivate her pet charities—especially those that helped Denver's needy children. As an officer of the St. Vincent's Orphanage Ladies Aid Society and the Denver Dorcas Society charitable sewing club and a fund-raiser for St. Joseph's Hospital, she set an example of family generosity. On one occasion, J. K. returned from work to discover his house stuffed with clothing, blankets, toys, and food collected by Kate for Denver's orphans.[45]

J. K. also depended on Kate to fulfill tasks for which he was ill-suited by his nature and by his cultural role in Victorian society. When she traveled alone, as she did frequently, he worried endlessly about her safety. "The next time you go visiting," he cautioned, "it must not be during the Spring floods when you can neither come Back or send Word . . . Perhaps you were all drowned in the Storm . . . " Failing to receive a prompt letter, he complained, "To tell the Truth—Kate this has been the Longest Week of my Life."[46] Life without her exposed his inadequacies as a housekeeper. When Kate took their first daughter to visit eastern relatives, the businessman listed the problems he faced around the house. After escorting his family to the train depot, he raced to the top of the nearest hill, hoping to wave the departing train out of sight. Arriving too late, he realized despondently that "Kate was gone for sure." He took the first of several suppers at his old bachelor digs in Williams's Boarding House. Returning home, he "pottered about" in the hen house, juggled his prize into the kitchen, and "flung the eggs" into an empty cradle. He overwatered the houseplants, creating a muddy mess on the living-room floor. Surrendering, he retired to the masculine cloister of his study, then back to the mill until late at night, leaving the cleanup for Kate's return.[47]

On the surface, the drive to succeed in business conflicted with Mullen's desire to enjoy a complete family life. Yet, the entrepreneur recognized no disparity between the two demands because he believed that both aspects achieved the same ends. A well-nurtured family was as much a social asset as any piece of mill equipment. As a tycoon, Mullen fondly looked back on the days when his daughter Ella "was all we had."[48] His belief was consistent with the Victorian-American dual culture of success, which legitimated the accumulation of wealth so long as it was used to support the fundamental values of religion, family, and philanthropy. Historian Richard M. Huber explains:

> Success writers [in the nineteenth century] almost always bounced back and forth between two types of success. The first was generally money; the second was final, ultimate, or "true success." "True success" was happiness, the joy of living, developing yourself by doing your best with the faculties that God has given you, leading a self-respecting life with a noble character, peace of mind, service to others, or the love and respect of family, friends, and community.[49]

The twin goals of success often clashed. Nevertheless, business-men worked hard to cultivate success at both ends. Although Mullen's family life suffered at the expense of his business activities, he tried to balance the respectable, but ultimately hollow, act of moneymaking with the deeper aspects of domestic life.

NOTES

1. Irvin G. Wyllie, *The Self-Made Man in America* (New York: The Free Press, 1954), 30.
2. Hasia R. Diner, *Erin's Daughters in America: Irish Immigrant Women in the Nineteenth Century* (Baltimore: Johns Hopkins University Press, 1983), 45.
3. J. K. Mullen, "The Family Register of John K. Mullen and Kate Theressa Smith, his wife," Weckbaugh family collection.
4. Charles W. Hurd, "J. K. Mullen, Milling Magnate of Colorado," *The Colorado Magazine* XXIX:2 (April 1952): 110.
5. *Denver Post*, March 26, 1925: 29.
6. William Newton Byers, *Encyclopedia of Biography of Colorado: History of Colorado* (Chicago: The Century Publishing and Engraving Co., 1901), 133.
7. Ibid., 133; Thomas J. Noel, *Colorado Catholicism and the Archdiocese of Denver, 1857–1989* (Niwot: University Press of Colorado, 1989), 17. The bell now rests at the Catholic diocesan center at the St. Thomas Seminary in Denver.
8. Hurd, 110.
9. Stan Hoig, *The Sand Creek Massacre* (Norman: University of Oklahoma Press, 1961), 174.
10. Hurd, 111.
11. Walter S. Weckbaugh, personal interview, July 21, 1997.
12. Samuel Bowles, cited in Carl Abbott, Stephen J. Leonard, and David McComb, *Colorado: A History of the Centennial State*, 3d ed. (Niwot: University Press of Colorado, 1994), 69–70.
13. Sandra L. Myers, *Westering Women and the Frontier Experience, 1800–1915* (Albuquerque: University of New Mexico Press, 1982), 186.
14. Noel, *Colorado Catholicism*, 301.
15. *Rocky Mountain News* (*RMN*), January 22, 1888: 4.
16. *RMN*, October 20, 1880: 3; January 22, 1888: 4.
17. J. K. Mullen, Letter to Frank W. Howbert, April 4, 1925, Mullen Foundation papers, Western History Dept., Denver Public Library, Denver, Colorado.
18. J. K. Mullen, "Statement concerning the individual business of J. K. Mullen," May 25, 1902, Mullen papers, Colorado Historical Society (CHS), Denver, Colorado.
19. Diner, 71.
20. J. K. Mullen, Letter to Ella M. Weckbaugh, May Dower, Catherine O'Connor, and Edith Malo, Denver, Colorado, 1928, Weckbaugh family collection (hereafter cited as Letter to his daughters); J. K. Mullen, Letter to Rt. Rev. Bishop Nicholas C. Matz, September 18, 1913, Rt. Rev. N. C. Matz papers, Archdiocese of Denver, Denver, Colorado (hereafter cited as Matz papers).

21. Diner, 46–47. While no national average exists, Diner cites local statistics such as in Buffalo, New York, where on the average, Irish men married at thirty-one, and only 8 percent of Irish women married before age thirty.
22. 1051 Ninth Street according to current enumeration. David J. Luebbers, "Directory of Ninth Street Historic Park, 1871–1900," unpublished manuscript (Dept. of Planning and Development, Auraria Higher Education Center, December 1977).
23. J. K. Mullen, Letter to C. S. Mullen, May 19, 1876, Weckbaugh family collection.
24. "Mullen Family Register," Weckbaugh family collection. The births were usually attended by the Sisters of Charity of Leavenworth, who traveled from home to home as midwives. By assisting in these births, the tireless sisters earned the gratitude of the Mullens, who repaid their debt with donations that helped establish St. Joseph's Hospital. W. S. Weckbaugh, personal interview, July 21, 1997.
25. "Mullen Family Register"; Elaine Tettemer Marshall, Letter to author, March 14, 1999. When the Mullen family transferred their plots from the abandoned Catholic cemetery in Denver to Mt. Olivet, Anne's remains were relocated. She is buried alongside her mother in an unmarked grave. Anne Weckbaugh, personal interview, February 6, 1998.
26. J. K. Mullen, Letter to C. S. Mullen, July 30, 1900, Mullen papers, CHS.
27. J. K. Mullen, Letter to C. S. Mullen, February 22, 1877, Mullen papers, CHS.
28. J. K. Mullen, Letter to C. S. Mullen, August 10, 1890, Mullen papers, CHS; W. S. Weckbaugh, personal interview, July 21, 1997.
29. W. S. Weckbaugh, personal interview, July 21, 1997.
30. Diner, 45.
31. Like D. W., Patrick H. Mullen's Colorado business career was sponsored by his brother. In 1875, P. H. set up another cooperage in North Denver, where he made flour barrels for J. K. Mullen. Mullen later appointed P. H. as an officer in the CM&E.
32. J. K. Mullen, Letter to Rev. Raymond J. Mullen, S. J., May 5, 1916, Mullen papers, CHS.
33. Ibid.; "Obituary of Dennis W. Mullen," *The Trail* IX:1 (June 1916): 29.
34. P. H. Mullin, Letters to J. K. Mullen, September 23, 1872; August 3, 1873, Weckbaugh family collection.
35. J. K. Mullen, Letter to his daughters, 1928; Mullen often failed to communicate this hospitality from behind his formidable reserve. Resident sons-in-law, like Eugene Weckbach and May's second husband, John L. Dower, squirmed under the disapproving stare of their father-in-law. Dower wrote, "We have been living in the same house at night and in sight of each other during the day for a period of years, and, strange to say, we are still strangers and far from understanding each other as we should, and I think this is a sad and deplorable reflection on us both." Dower, Letter to J. K. Mullen, June 5, 1926, John Kernan Mullen manuscript collection, MSS 705, CHS.
36. Hurd, 111.

37. Ibid., 110.
38. J. K. Mullen, Letter to Catherine S. Mullen, March 16, 1893, Mullen papers, CHS.
39. J. K. Mullen, Letter to Catherine S. Mullen, May 19, 1876, Weckbaugh family collection.
40. W. S. Weckbaugh, personal interview, July 21, 1997.
41. *Denver Post*, August 9, 1929: 4.
42. Hurd, 111; J. K. Mullen, Letter to his daughters, 1928; J. K. Mullen, Letter to George F. Cottrell, January 25, 1929, Weckbaugh family collection.
43. W. S. Weckbaugh, personal interview, July 21, 1997.
44. J. K. Mullen, Letter to Catherine S. Mullen, July 17, 1880, Mullen papers, CHS.
45. *RMN*, February 7, 1889: 6; *Denver Times*, December 6, 1901: 12; August 8, 1902: 3.
46. J. K. Mullen, Letter to Catherine S. Mullen, May 29, 1876, Mullen papers, CHS.
47. J. K. Mullen, Letter to Catherine S. Mullen, May 19, 1876, Weckbaugh family collection.
48. J. K. Mullen, Letter to Catherine S. Mullen, August 10, 1890, Mullen papers, CHS.
49. Richard M. Huber, *The American Idea of Success* (New York: McGraw-Hill, 1971), 97.

6

J. K. MULLEN AND COMPANY, 1875–1879

IN 1859, after carefully counting each of the seed grains on a stalk of wheat discovered growing errantly in an Denver garden, *Rocky Mountain News* editor William Byers concluded that the Pikes Peak region would one day be hailed as the "Garden of the World."[1] During the mid-1870s his jubilant prediction appeared within reach. Nature kindly sprinkled the plains with better-than-average rainfall each year from 1873 to 1885. Where nature failed, private and communal irrigation developers attempted to make up the difference. As a result, Colorado's rate of wheat production exploded between 1870 and 1890. The number of farms increased by 260 percent between 1870 and 1880 and again by 360 percent during the next ten years.[2] Although the wet years set the table for ultimate disappointment, in 1875 it seemed that the agricultural banquet would never end.

As Colorado sodbusters rushed to feast on the riches of golden grain, their overproduction drove down local wheat prices. In October 1874, the local wholesale price for wheat stood between $1.35 and $1.44 per bushel—slightly less than the national average price of $1.51. By July 1879, the local wholesale price of wheat had dropped to between 90 cents and $1, whereas the national average stood at about $1.22. The price of wheat pulled the price of flour down with it, but not nearly as precipitously. Flour that wholesaled locally between $3.75 and $4 per hundred-pound bag in October 1874 declined to between $2.65 and $3 in July 1879.[3] Grain speculators depended on local demand while millers gambled on the margin between wheat and flour prices for their profits. Only the owners of adequate large-scale storage

51

silos—which meant millers almost always and farmers almost never—could afford to wait for local price fluctuations to produce favorable futures estimates before unloading their grain supplies.

The expansion of wheat agriculture created a favorable climate for new grain brokers and flour millers. Between 1874 and 1878, the number of Denver flouring mills increased from three to six. The city mills alone produced between $250,000 and $300,000 in flour annually. Countryside mills, such as Littleton's Rough and Ready, flourished as well. A statewide increase from nineteen to thirty-four mills between 1877 and 1884 multiplied the pressure to perform efficiently, even as consumers enjoyed reduced prices.[4]

The expansion of Denver's flouring industry presented new chances for accomplished millers like J. K. Mullen. In 1875, J. K. was managing the Merchant's Mills—the mill where he had started for room and board—when just such an opportunity arose. Co-owner Charles R. Davis bought out Shackleton and offered the half-interest to Mullen. J. K. refused. As in Kansas, he colored his decision with his personal opinion of his boss, stating, "I didn't take kindly to Davis." Possibly, the idea of serving as Davis's junior partner did not sit well with Mullen's sense of independence.[5]

Once again, J. K. resigned. On July 9, 1876, with the help of his friend and attorney Thomas M. Patterson, Mullen drew up a one-year agreement of partnership with the veteran miller Theodore Seth.[6] Seth, the superior craftsman, oversaw the physical operations of the mill while Mullen focused on administration, capitalization, supply, sales, and mechanization. The partners split the initial capitalization costs of $8,000. Mullen turned to his wife and her family to help raise his portion.[7]

Mullen and Seth next leased the North Denver Star Mills, owned by O. L. Chrisman. Chrisman gave the partners a one-year term on the condition that the partners renovate the derelict mill. The improvements required Mullen's nearly round-the-clock presence. He sold his house at 339 Ninth Street and moved his extended family into a residence alongside the North Denver plant. The Star included its own boarding house, where Catherine, expecting their second daughter, cooked and cleaned for the mill hands. J. K.'s older brother, Patrick H. Mullen, arrived from New York to set up a barrel factory at Fifteenth and Wazee Streets. P. H. received exclusive contracts to craft flour barrels for his brother's firm.[8]

The partnership ran into financial difficulties. Following the overhaul, Seth came up short on the remainder of his investment. Mullen immediately exercised the contractual clause that allowed either party room to withdraw with ten days written notice. Seth refused to sell his shares of the company to J. K., but he also declined to buy Mullen's half. In order to meet their business expenses, the partners borrowed the balance of Seth's share. Mullen personally signed the loan and put up seventy-eight shares of his own stock from Union Savings and Loan as collateral. In return, Seth agreed to repay the debt along with the 18 percent interest.[9] Although Mullen risked his shares of the savings and loan, the agreement placed him in control of the company's future. During the nine months of actual operation, the partners quickly made up their expenses. At the end of the agreed-upon year and after paying off outstanding debts, Mullen and Seth divided $7,750 in profit. After some haggling, Seth sold Mullen his remaining interest for $1,000. He then withdrew to ventures in New Mexico, leaving Mullen in sole control of the company.

"I WAS THE COMPANY"

On July 10, 1877, just one month after his thirtieth birthday, Mullen became the sole proprietor of his firm. He counted among his assets $4,829 deposited at City National Bank; interest in the Union Savings and Loan Company; an accumulated stock of flour, grain, and feed; improvements on the Star Mill; and four lots of real estate on Fifteenth and Wewatta Streets, earmarked for future expansion. He also owned a lot and house on Ninth Street and a growing reputation in the local milling industry and Catholic community. Furthermore, he was free and clear of debt.

His choice of a new corporate name, J. K. Mullen and Company, reflected his aspirations. "I was the company," he declared, boasting that "no one in the world had an interest or invested any money in the business with me except my wife and her relatives."[10] He bolstered his family network by establishing his brother Patrick in a new barrel factory and bringing Dennis on as a mill hand. J. K. felt he needed to protect his younger brother from dissolution. "[Dennis] had got into bad company," J. K. worried, "and was drinking a little more than he should." Worse, "he got into politics and was hobnobbing with politicians."[11]

J. K. offered Dennis a sober alternative to the high life. "I said, 'D. W., if you quit that kind of business I will give you a working interest in this business of ours.'" He placed his sibling in an office job, raised his salary from $2 to $2.25 per day, and began pestering him to get married in the hope that he would settle down.[12] Over time, J. K. promoted his brother to manager of the Hungarian Mill. From this position of responsibility, Dennis created more problems for his brother later on.

Mullen, in turn, depended on the good graces of his own prosperous in-laws for additional investment capital. Instead of constructing new facilities, the entrepreneur squirreled away capital for further expansion by renovating existing mills. In March 1878, Mullen used his in-laws' capital and his own profits to lease the Ironclad and the Sigler Mills, both located in the yards behind Union Station. He also continued to acquire grain for future speculation. During one cold winter he scrambled to procure storage space for incoming grain even though the flume that powered the Star was frozen solid.[13] When the spring thaw unlocked mill races and drove up demand, he sold the surplus to his competitors at premium rates. His aggressive buying tactics paid off. His mills turned out so much profit that he offered double rent payments on the Star Mill.[14]

Mullen felt a great proprietary interest in the welfare of his company. He extended his personal working hours to the maximum in an effort to buy up all available stores of grain. Each harvest season took him on a far-flung circuit of Pueblo, La Veta, El Moro, Trinidad, and Longmont, Colorado, as well as to Grand Island, Nebraska. During one dry year, he personally hauled loads of wheat from Ephriam and Gunnison over a fifty-mile road to Nephi, Utah. The wholesaler in Nephi refused to receive his grain until J. K. loaned them the purchase price. His uncanny ability to sniff out wheat stores during periods of scarcity earned him a reputation as a wizard:

> Jim Richards was then operating the first mill that they built [in Utah] and he came over and begged me for a carload of the wheat . . . Richards was continually coming over and buying . . . sacks of flour . . . [he] wondered where in the world I got the wheat to make the flour.[15]

J. K. took pride in his personal involvement—a practice that he continued to cultivate as president of the Colorado Milling and Elevator Co. Mullen accompanied farmers into the fields during threshing season, personally inspected their crops, and persuaded them to sell to the CM&E on the bumpy buckboard ride home. The gregarious salesman suppressed a surprising degree of discomfort on these trips. He suffered from neuralgia, a condition brought on by damaged nerve endings acquired in an unrecorded accident. The disease produced excruciating pain that was aggravated by jolting wagon rides. In 1880, after a particularly agonizing trip up the deeply rutted road from the end of the railroad line in Granite to Leadville, he complained to his wife, "It is enough to kill anybody."[16]

Beginning in 1877, Leadville's rough roads funneled thousands of miners to the two-mile-high silver camp. Their demand for staple goods such as flour lifted J. K. Mullen & Co. to a new level of success. The contracts that J. K. secured in the booming city paid better than most Leadville silver mines. While surplus wheat stagnated in Denver at around $1.51 per bushel, the powdery white flour wholesaled in Leadville at $6 per hundred-pound bag.[17]

Mullen expanded quickly in order to keep up with the demand. Rather than take the costly and time-consuming step of building his own mill, he liquidated his lots on Fifteenth and Wewatta in order to purchase John W. Smith's West Denver Excelsior Mills, canal works, and 22,000 pounds of wheat "piled four or five feet deep" in the Excelsior elevator. On November 20, 1878, Mullen exchanged $10,000 in cash, $8,000 in refined flour, and $15,000 in four-year promissory notes for Smith's plant.[18] Although the notes drew 10 percent interest every three months and although they were not due until 1882, Mullen paid off each note ahead of schedule, retiring the last on May 20, 1880.[19]

Even with the new facilities, Mullen scrambled to keep up with the Leadville demand and outpace the competition. He incorporated efficient new milling techniques. The Excelsior was already a "big, substantial brick structure" powered by three turbines that dipped into the adjacent Smith Ditch. J. K. envisioned an even larger, state-of-the-art plant.[20] During the winter of 1878–1879 he made the last old-fashioned improvements to the Excelsior, adding two grinding burrs, enlarging the canal, and constructing a fourth overshot waterwheel and flume. Later that spring, he hired Milwaukee-based consultants and work crews from the American Middlings Purifier Company to enlarge the mill again.[21]

Along with the Milwaukee crews, Mullen hired William Dixon Gray to help modernize his mills. Gray, a Scottish consulting engineer who worked for the Milwaukee milling supplier Edward P. Allis & Co., had previously designed mills for Pillsbury and Washburn in Minneapolis. His innovations had already revolutionized the industry.[22] The Scotch engineer and the Irish financier became lifelong associates. Gray added ten new sets of burrs to the Excelsior and replaced fragile porcelain-jacketed grinders with a pair of long-lasting steel rollers designed to eliminate bran. The fully automated process promised to produce greater amounts of pure flour than had been previously considered possible.[23]

Two factors still challenged Mullen's ability to keep up with the Leadville demand. The first was power. With Gray's innovations, it was clear that the Excelsior's recently expanded mill race could still not draw enough water from the South Platte River to meet its growing energy requirements. Mullen traveled east, determined to find the tools to help out. On July 12, 1879, he bought a pair of boilers from his St. Louis "boiler man," John W. Wangler. A few days later, he purchased a 105-horsepower Harris-Corliss steam engine in Providence, Rhode Island.[24] The steam engine gave Mullen a temporary edge over many of his competitors, who still powered their mills from the Front Range's notoriously unreliable watercourses.

The second problem was capital. Despite his expressed aversion to debt, Mullen commonly relied on borrowing to fund his annual operations. He boasted that one of the keystones to his success was to buy his yearly supply of wheat during harvest time when abundant sources pushed grain prices to their lowest. To accomplish this, he borrowed his entire annual capital in advance. Many of his competitors who did not have access to similar credit were forced to renew their supply in the spring, when wheat prices were at a premium.[25]

Mullen secured credit by borrowing at higher rates than normal and paying promptly. He gambled that his deep wheat supplies and increased milling capacity would pay off the difference in the long run.[26] In order to expand, he borrowed $4,000 from City National Bank at an interest rate of 18 percent, borrowed more from his affluent in-laws, and put up shares of company stock as collateral for another note at his own Union Savings and Loan.[27] Fortunately, the Leadville demand held up through 1879 and 1880, allowing Mullen to quickly put these debts to bed.

The new mill necessitated another move and Kate Mullen found herself packing again. Their new two-story, twelve-room house at 1178 Ninth Street was at last a place where Kate could raise her family in relative tranquillity.[28] More importantly, after 1889, when J. K. Mullen quietly put the title in her name to guard against creditors, the house became her property and security. "The little house on Ninth Street" sheltered the Mullen family for twenty years. Over time, it became the family symbol of their struggling pioneer days. When they graduated into their "castle" in the Quality Hill district of Pennsylvania Street in 1898, the house on the corner of Ninth Street in the working-class neighborhood of West Denver would be fondly remembered by the entire family as the Mullen "homestead."

NOTES

1. *Rocky Mountain News* (*RMN*), October 27, 1859.
2. Carl Abbott, Stephen J. Leonard, and David McComb, *Colorado: A History of the Centennial State*, 3d ed. (Niwot: University Press of Colorado, 1994), 173, 393.
3. "Local Market Prices," *Colorado Farmer and Livestock Journal*, October 22, 1874; *RMN*, July 10, 1879; National averages: U.S. Dept. of Commerce, Bureau of the Census, *Historical Statistics of the United States, Colonial Times to the Present*, vol. 1 (Washington, D.C.: GPO, 1976), 208. One bushel of wheat weighed approximately sixty pounds. Two bushels of milled wheat produced about one hundred pounds of flour.
4. Corbett, Hoye, and Ballenger, *Denver City Directory*, 1874–1878, microfilm, Western History Dept., Denver Public Library (WHDDPL); Herbert E. Johnson, former general manager, Colorado Milling and Elevator Co., Letter to Guy Thomas, pres., Colorado Milling and Elevator Co., June 10, 1943, Herbert E. Johnson private manuscript collection, Denver, Colorado (hereafter cited as Johnson collection).
5. J. K. Mullen, Letter to Ella M. Weckbaugh, May Dower, Catherine O'Connor, and Edith Malo, Denver, Colorado, 1928, Weckbaugh family collection (hereafter cited as Letter to his daughters).
6. In a 1916 letter to his nephew Rev. Raymond Mullen, the miller referred to his habit of retaining papers and correspondence: "Tom Patterson drew up the contract. I have it in my files yet." J. K. Mullen, Letter to Rev. Raymond J. Mullen, S. J., May 5, 1916, Mullen papers, Colorado Historical Society (CHS).
7. J. K. Mullen, Letter to Raymond Mullen, May 5, 1916, Mullen Papers, CHS.
8. Ibid.; "Family Register of J. K. Mullen," Weckbaugh family collection, Denver, Colorado.
9. J. K. Mullen, Letter to his daughters, 1928; J. K. Mullen, "Statement concerning the individual business of J. K. Mullen," May 25, 1902, Mullen papers, CHS.

10. J. K. Mullen, Letter to his daughters, 1928; J. K. Mullen, Letter to Raymond Mullen, May 5, 1916, Mullen papers, CHS.

11. J. K. Mullen, Letter to John J. Mullen, June 1, 1926, Mullen papers, CHS.

12. Ibid.; Mullen took satisfaction when his brother finally married Anna Hughes of Oriskany Falls, New York, in May 1882: "I hold in my hand a letter he wrote to me from Oriskany Falls on June 3, 1882, in which he goes on to express his appreciation of what I had done for him, and to tell me that he realized the way he had previously acted and promised me from that time on he would never give me reason to complain. He said he had not drank anything for several months and did not intend to ever again." Mullen promptly paid for his brother's wedding suit, sent him $150 in travel money, and paid for jewelry that Dennis later presented to his bride. J. K. Mullen, Letter to Raymond Mullen, May 5, 1916, Mullen papers, CHS.

13. J. K. Mullen, Letter to Herbert E. Johnson, May 15, 1920, Johnson collection. "The dominant feature in the conduct of a business so far as I was individually concerned was to accumulate wheat in the early Fall . . . and pay less attention to the sale of flour."

14. J. K. Mullen, "Statement concerning the business of J. K Mullen," 2.

15. J. K. Mullen, Letter to H. E. Johnson, May 15, 1920, Johnson collection.

16. J. K. Mullen, Letter to C. S. Mullen, June 21, 1880, Mullen papers, CHS.

17. Market price, *RMN*, May 22 and June 12, 1879; Duane Smith, *Rocky Mountain Mining Camps: The Urban Frontier*, 2d ed. (Niwot: University Press of Colorado, 1992), 198.

18. J. K. Mullen, "Statement concerning the business of J. K. Mullen," 2; J. K. Mullen, Letter to his daughters, 1928.

19. J. K. Mullen, "Promissory Notes on Excelsior Mills," November 20, 1878, Mullen papers, CHS.

20. J. K. Mullen, Letter to A. J. Simonson, July 30, 1926, Mullen papers, CHS.

21. Charles W. Hurd, "J. K. Mullen, Milling Magnate of Colorado," *The Colorado Magazine* XXIX:2 (April 1952): 109.

22. Robert Murray Frame, "The Progressive Millers: A Cultural and Intellectual Portrait of the Flour Milling Industry, 1870–1930" (Ph.D. diss., University of Minnesota, 1980), 71.

23. Hurd, 109.

24. J. K. Mullen, "Statement concerning the business of J. K. Mullen," 2; J. K. Mullen, Letter to his daughters, 1928.

25. J. K. Mullen, Letter to H. E. Johnson, May 15, 1920, Johnson collection.

26. Ibid.

27. J. K. Mullen, Letter to his daughters, 1928.

28. *Relative* tranquillity. In order to accommodate the mill hands and visiting Milwaukee crews, Mullen bought the O. L. Shackleton residence and ran it as a boardinghouse. As at the Star Mill, Catherine cooked and cleaned for the laborers. J. K. Mullen, Letter to Raymond Mullen, May 5, 1916, Mullen papers, CHS.

7

THE PROGRESSIVE MILLER, 1880–1885

ON NEW YEAR'S DAY, 1880, a reporter for the *Rocky Mountain News* forwarded good tidings from the Excelsior Mills in West Denver:

> That splendid flour manufactory is in good order, and in full operation, with a very large stock of the staff of life on hand. The proprietors . . . have skill, experience, capital and other requisites for successful milling; in addition, they have perfect machinery and a mill with extraordinary capacity. The senior partner has been intimately connected with the mills of Denver for more than ten years.[1]

For Colorado's sodbusters and millers alike, these bulging stores of "the staff of life" signified the prosperity of the early 1880s. Between 1874 and 1884, local cultivators benefited from stable global wheat prices, a decade of above-average precipitation, and increased local demand generated by the Leadville and Aspen silver strikes of the late 1870s.[2] The *News* summarized figures compiled by the Colorado Agricultural College to illustrate the rise in wheat value. In 1878, Colorado farmers grew 1.25 million bushels of wheat worth $870,000. The following year, Colorado produced 1.5 million bushels of wheat worth $1.5 million dollars—a gross increase of 40 cents per bushel. During the same ten-year span, husbandmen enjoyed reduced storage and shipping rates brought about by increased milling and railroad competition. With a network of irrigation canals under development, the *News* predicted "a prominent increase" of wheat acreage for the coming years.

Underneath the confidence, problems lay ready to sprout. As sodbusters broke more of the plains to plant wheat, some observers noticed the first signs of soil exhaustion on existing fields. Only a handful of conservationists dared to pour cold water on the clamor for wheat production by suggesting diversification and crop rotation. At the same time, the growing mistrust between farmers and milling brokers crept toward open revolt. "There is always room for dispute," the *News* admitted, because grangers "very largely favor withholding the facts . . . in the fear that millers and middlemen will take advantage of them."[3] The paper chided farmers for allowing millers to monopolize storage facilities, thus letting the middlemen take advantage of short-term price fluctuations and futures speculation. Increasingly, discontented grangers grumbled about how they might increase their control of the wheat market.

Sharper competition unsettled the captains of the milling industry as well. Wheat prices remained high, holding down milling profits even as more flour manufacturers crowded into the state. The 1880 *Colorado Business Directory* listed twenty-six mills operating in Colorado—six of them in Denver. By 1884, the year the Colorado Milling and Elevator Company was founded, the number reached thirty-four. Certainly, farmers applauded the reduced rates that resulted from the increased competition among the mills, but the situation threatened the stability of established plants.

Mullen's Excelsior Mill prospered despite the new competition. Between November 1879 and November 1880, the Excelsior took in 10,825,284 pounds of wheat and sold 7,250,000 pounds of flour, causing a *News* correspondent to observe, "the intelligent reader can readily imagine the amount of capital used in such a business."[4] Such Excelsior brands as "Pride of Denver," "Silk Finish," "Hard to Beat," "Inter-Ocean," and others were traded as far away as Boston.[5] As a leader in the state milling industry, J. K. Mullen started planning the largest, most technologically advanced mill in the region to date—the Hungarian Mills. In the process, he began the transformation of Colorado's milling industry from a cluster of competing firms into a single corporation that would dominate the Rocky Mountain grain industry for the next sixty years.

PROGRESSIVE MILLING

The Leadville demand and the drive to modernize kept Mullen busy searching for more efficient sources of power. In 1879, he purchased the Platte & Denver Ditch Company, including the canal from which

A whiskered J. K. Mullen looks out from a photo c. 1880. J. K. first grew a beard in 1867. In the summer of 1898, the unacclimatized Coloradan shaved in order to cope with the oppressive heat of a Memphis sales trip. Courtesy, Western History Dept., Denver Public Library.

he first cleared winter ice. The summer of 1880 found him again pursuing newer and larger steam engines. He visited St. Louis and wrote back to his wife, "I suffered more from heat . . . than ever before in my life."[6] Traveling on to Indianapolis and Providence, he wrote back tersely, "Have not found anything in the shape of an engine that can be had in ninety days." Despite his schedule, he promised his wife that he would attend Mass each Sunday, "wherever I am."[7]

J. K.'s efforts to modernize his mills and increase the capacity of his plant took place within a national "progressive milling" movement.

During the 1870s and 1880s, milling engineers in the Midwest and Europe introduced several modern inventions and processes. Innovations such as the middlings purifier, porcelain and steel roller mills, and the gradual reduction of wheat through tiered roller mills revolutionized an industry that had seen no significant innovation since the 1790s.

The first two important developments of the 1870s—the middlings purifier and the roller process—took advantage of increased mechanization. Gritty stone-ground flour was high in nutritional content but both millers and consumers regarded the yellow tinge of leftover wheat germ, bran, and impurities as aesthetically unpleasing. Cleaning out the impurities was an expensive and time-consuming operation that most millers accomplished by hand. The purifier introduced large-scale automation to the cleaning process. Consumers appreciated the purer, whiter flour even if it lacked nutrition.[8]

Likewise, porcelain and, eventually, steel rollers replaced outdated grinding stones. Traditional flour mills harnessed the friction of revolving stone burrs to pulverize grain. While the time-honored burr system easily processed the softer spring varieties of wheat common in the East, hard winter wheats that adapted best to the arid western climates proved more resistant. On the first pass, burrs usually ground only three-quarters of the wheat into flour. "Middlings," the remaining unground grain, required a costly second pass through the stones. In the roller process, wheat descended through vertical tiers of rollers that pulverized the kernels more efficiently. Whereas stone-ground wheat required multiple passes through the grinders to produce pure flour, rollers contained several levels through which wheat passed, effectively creating higher grades of flour with fewer impurities and less leftover grain.[9]

A third innovation—the Hungarian process—promised to eclipse the former two. During the late 1870s, Austro-Hungarian millers in the milling center of Pest, Hungary, developed an automated combination of millstones and rollers that produced large quantities of clean flour as white as Rocky Mountain snow. Unlike previous processes, which "reduced the grain by bruising, grinding, and pulverizing," the Hungarian process involved the "gradual reduction" of wheat.[10] An intricate series of specialized rollers and cams applied incrementally increasing amounts of pressure to the wheat kernel. Each successive roller performed a specific function—gradually cracking and cleaning the wheat, peeling off the outer bran, and finally stripping away the inner layers. By introducing several steps in one machine, gradual reduction removed more impurities in fewer tries. The cheaper, high-quality flour produced by the Hungarian system caught the attention of the milling world.[11]

With the introduction of the Hungarian process and gradual-reduction milling, technicians led by Mullen's consulting engineer William Dixon Gray implemented a "great mill rebuilding and re-modeling program" between 1878 and 1882. Publicized by Gray, as well as by new milling handbooks such as James Abernathey's *Practical Hints on Mill Building* (1880) and progressive trade journals such as *The Northwestern Miller,* the innovations spread quickly beyond the Great Lakes region.

As historian Robert Murray Frame points out, industrial expansion changed the cultural outlook of the milling profession. The so-called progressive millers in Minneapolis and Milwaukee romanticized the new technology. They celebrated entrepreneurs who adopted new innovations while disparaging "old fashioned" millers.[12] Abernathey exalted the "enlightened" millers who adopted the Hungarian process ahead of "prejudice[d] and conservative" competitors. The *Northwestern Miller* disparaged "Stick-in-the-Mud" millers who "shut their ears to outside information and closed their eyes to progressive ideas [and are] waiting till the shadows have a little longer grown to pass into eternal commercial night."[13]

Trained in the preindustrial style, Mullen successfully made the transition to the new industrial reality. By embracing change, the entrepreneur affiliated himself with the progressive millers, whom the *Northwestern Miller* described as "manufacturer[s] of flour . . . dweller[s] in cities . . . and m[e]n of affairs."[14]

THE HUNGARIAN MILLS

Mullen, who read the journals and appreciated the booster spirit of the progressive milling movement, decided to investigate the new technologies for himself. In May 1881, he toured several Milwaukee plants that used the Hungarian system. The industrial city itself did not impress the miller. He declared that Milwaukee was a good place to do business, but the city's uniform grayness depressed him. "I wish I was out of here anyhow & back home," he wrote his wife.[15] The multilingual swirl of the city's eastern European immigrants bewildered and amused him:

> [There are] Dutch, Norwegians, Danes, Scandinavians, Polanders & Austrians. Some Hungarians. No Irish but me you bet! Such a blabbering you never did see *or hear* either . . . Every man you meet is a Dutchman & every woman a Dutchwoman & I suppose every girl is a Dutch girl but I don't meet any of them you know. The news boys yell out the news in their own or some foreign language.

The business at hand left little time for sightseeing. The veteran miller initially found Milwaukee's newspaper vendors and milling technicians equally incomprehensible. Mastery of the new technology demanded a daunting new understanding of specialization and organization techniques. Mullen grumbled about his new education, "I have been right busy since I came and am anxious to get away from here . . . There is so much difficulty in working in the systems & [it] requires so much study & labor that it crazes a fellow. I found another gray hair today in my head." He worried over the task of retooling his existing mill to the Hungarian system:

> Their system is so extensive & so intricate that it is very difficult to master and still more difficult to apply it to a mill that is using another system without first quitting out & leasing out the machinery now in use & replacing it in connection with the new that is to go in its place.

Trained as a traditional artisan-miller, he struggled with the complex new dynamics, anxious that his efforts would fail. Nevertheless, after inspecting the snow-white drifts of flour that poured from Milwaukee's rollers, he concluded that the potential results were worth the risk: "I feel well repaid already as the system of milling that . . . they call the Roller or Hungarian System is way ahead of anything I ever seen [*sic*] producing better flour & better yields than the burrs can possibly do."

Back in Denver with designs for the Hungarian system, Mullen undertook an ambitious plan of expansion. He proceeded in two directions, rehabilitating the Excelsior while at the same time purchasing land for a new facility. On July 31, 1881, the *Rocky Mountain News* printed a one-line notice that "Mullin [*sic*], the miller, is erecting an elevator on the west side." Two weeks later, Mullen received a permit to build a frame grain elevator, a twenty-six-by-sixty-foot brick warehouse, and a twenty-by-twenty-four-foot engine room worth $8,000 on the site of the Arbuckle Brothers coffee warehouse between Blake and Wazee Streets on Seventh.[16] In honor of the patent process that he hoped would win him the supreme spot among Colorado's millers, he christened the new structure the Hungarian Elevator.

By the first of January 1882, a *Rocky Mountain News* correspondent was able to describe the entrepreneur's progress. The Excelsior had resolved its power problems and was partially transformed to the Hungarian process: "These mills are run by an engine of one hundred and twenty-five horsepower with a water power of equal strength and a capacity of sixty thousand pounds of flour daily."[17] Likewise, the grain elevator and its accompanying feed mill occupied a thirty-foot frontage on Wazee Street. Served by a forty-five-horsepower elevator, it stood seventy feet deep, thirty feet high, and had the capacity to store sixty thousand bushels of wheat. The two-story warehouse had been expanded to sixty by sixty-two feet. A railroad siding served the buildings from the rear.[18]

Despite the rapid growth, J. K. Mullen and Co. still faced heavy competition from mills in Golden, Longmont, Loveland, Greeley, Fort Collins, and Trinidad. J. K.'s rivals also took advantage of the new milling developments. In fact, the Hungarian Elevator trailed its major Denver competitor, the Crescent Milling and Elevator Co., in the *Rocky Mountain News's* 1882 New Year's Day milling survey. The *News* pronounced the Crescent "the model of beauty and perfection . . . it has no superior anywhere [and] cost more money than any other mill of its size." Owned by a financial coalition led by the capitalist William Barth, the rival mill enjoyed a favorable location in the railyards along the South Platte River. It led all Denver mills in production, capacity, and revenue. Whereas Mullen averaged about $700,000 in business between 1881 and 1882, the Crescent Mills cleared over $1 million.[19]

Mullen fought back through diversification. He kept his elevator full by joining in partnership with wholesale grain dealer Lorin Butterfield, with whom he speculated on the booming wheat, hay, and feed markets. Meanwhile, armed with faith that the progressive milling movement would provide the competitive edge, he began consolidating lots to build a "monster" mill, in the model of the Washburn and Pillsbury mills in Minneapolis.[20]

Mullen's plans for expansion were delayed by a serious accident. On January 12, 1882, the entrepreneur returned from a trip out of town. As he rubbed down his favorite dray horse, the animal unexpectedly lashed out twice with its hind legs. The first blow shattered Mullen's jaw. The second delivered a glancing blow to the head that knocked the miller to the ground, unconscious. Family members discovered him and carried him into the house, where he regained partial consciousness. Hastily summoned doctors pronounced him "in a very dangerous condition" and proscribed bed rest for several weeks. J. K. recuperated in silence—his broken jaw made speech impossible.[21]

Although the accident delayed the start of construction, Mullen returned to work quickly. The invigorating pace of developments at the mill site seemed to spur his rapid recovery. In March he began purchasing the lots that surrounded his elevator. In May, he petitioned the Denver City Council for a Chicago, Burlington, and Quincy Railroad siding to the Hungarian Elevator.[22] By January 1883, he had paid out $3,500 for surrounding real estate and had sunk a 330-foot well to feed his steam boilers.[23] He broke ground on the Hungarian Mill in the first half of 1883. The timber frame mill, built at a cost of $128,000, opened in September and reached full production by November 1883.[24]

Financial as well as physical adversity tested the enterprising miller. Soon after completing the Hungarian Mills & Elevator, Mullen narrowly escaped a business blunder that left him vulnerable to his rivals at the Crescent Mills. The grain dealer had relied primarily on City National Bank for credit since he had formed J. K. Mullen and Co. In the early 1880s, the owners of the Crescent Mills, including William Barth and the "Denver merchant princes" Junius F. and J. Sidney Brown, assumed control of City National.[25] Despite the fact that his primary creditor was now also his primary competitor, Mullen negotiated an $80,000 loan from City National, having first received assurances that the bank's directors recognized no conflict of interest. Feeling secure by an initial payment of $28,000, J. K. traveled to Omaha to negotiate rates with the Union Pacific Railroad. In Omaha, he received a telegram notifying him that his remaining credit had been canceled. "You bet, I took the first train home," he later remembered. Mullen shared his hard-luck tale with Samuel Wood, president of First National Bank of Denver. Wood granted him enough credit to meet

The Hungarian Mills, Elevator, and Ware House, located between Seventh and Eighth Streets on Wazee Street was the core of Mullen's milling empire. Built on the site of the Arbuckle Brothers' coffee warehouse, the mill boasted a Denver and Rio Grande Railroad siding and a 150,000-bushel grain elevator. By 1887, its twenty-four sets of gradual reduction rolls and four stone grinders ran twenty-four hours a day, six days a week. Courtesy, Western History Dept., Denver Public Library.

his current obligations and so won over a new customer "that minute." J. K. never forgot the favor. In 1929, he wrote, "First National has taken care of me ever since, and has been loyal and helpful from that day to this."[26]

Perhaps it was understandable that the owners of the Crescent Mills would go out of their way to hamper their fiercest rival. With the construction of the Hungarian Mills, J. K. Mullen and Co. catapulted to the head of the Colorado milling industry. At the beginning of 1883, the Excelsior was only capable of producing five hundred 100-pound sacks of flour per day. By Christmas, the new steel rollers of the Hungarian churned out an additional twelve hundred sacks of Hungarian Patent, Pride of Denver, Charter Oak, Plymouth Rock, and Inter-Ocean brands daily. In the last four months of 1883, Mullen manufactured 2 million pounds of flour, worth $450,000. Added to grain sales, J. K. Mullen and Co. made nearly as much in the last quarter as in the first nine months of the year.[27]

When a September 1882 fire incinerated the Crescent Mills, J. K. Mullen and Co. stood alone as the leading flour producer in Colorado.[28] According to a *Rocky Mountain News* estimate, the Hungarian's output nearly matched the combined production of Denver's next three greatest mills—the Crescent, Charles Davis's West Denver, and the old Star Mills (now operated by Chrisman and Burnell).[29] Mullen enjoyed a happy financial outlook. "I didn't owe anybody a dollar," he boasted. By the summer of 1885, the Hungarian elevators fairly bulged. Mullen recalled:

> I had the elevator almost full of grain—so full that it was so difficult to invoice it that a disinterested committee of three directors was appointed in 1885 to go through the elevator and mark with paint the height of the surface of the grain in the bins. And then later on the same committee measured and accounted to me for the total amount of grain.[30]

After ten years of operation, J. K. Mullen and Co. owned two mills, two canals, three elevators, and various parcels of real estate. Its book accounts and grain stocks were worth $90,000. The company was free of debt, and, on the whole, solidly positioned to weather adversity.

Combined, J. K. Mullen and Co. and its competitors made Denver the leading mill city in the West. Denver's mills possessed the capacity to grind 3,300 100-pound sacks of flour per day. In 1883, they produced an estimated 432,000 sacks of flour worth $975,000, as well as bran, cornmeal, and feed worth $329,500. J. K. Mullen and Co. manufactured almost half of the total.[31] Colorado-ground flour fed Arizona silver miners, ranchers in Wyoming and New Mexico, Missouri roughnecks, and families in Boston, New York, and Philadelphia. Among Denver's manufactured products, flour milling ranked near the top of the *News*'s end-of-the-year list. Worth a combined $1,304,500, flour, bran, and meal was Denver's greatest product by value in 1883 (followed by machinery, iron, and brass works [$1,218,775], and railroad cars and rails [$993,125]). As an employer, Denver's flour-making industries ranked only seventh with 140 workers, but the industry ranked fourth in overall capital investment at $275,000, behind railroad cars and rails ($2,000,000), machinery ($779,000), and brewing ($550,000).[32]

To be sure, Colorado's mills were poorly regarded nationally, especially when compared with the giant mills of Minneapolis and Milwaukee. The twenty-four mills operating along the Falls of Saint Anthony in Minneapolis produced more than 2 million barrels of flour in 1880—over four times the combined Denver output.[33] By comparison, veteran CM&E officer Herbert E. Johnson recalled that only five mills in Colorado "could command sufficient capital to accumulate appreciable stocks of wheat . . . Many of [the others] only operated when water power was available."[34] Nevertheless, boosters looking for evidence of Denver's success could point to the smoky, churning mills as another pillar of Colorado's industrial progress.

NOTES

1. *Rocky Mountain News* (*RMN*), January 1, 1880: 17.
2. Carl Abbott, Stephen J. Leonard, and David McComb, *Colorado: A History of the Centennial State*, 3d ed. (Niwot: University Press of Colorado, 1994), 173.
3. *RMN*, January 1, 1880: 16.
4. *RMN*, January 1, 1881: 24; At the average published wholesale price of wheat and flour in 1880 (wheat: $1.94, and flour: $3.25), J. K. Mullen and Co. bought $210,010 worth of wheat from which it made $235,625.00 worth of flour. Since Mullen commonly bought wheat at a bulk discount as low as $.60 per pound, he probably cleared considerably more.
5. J. K. Mullen, Letter to Catherine S. Mullen, July 17, 1880, Mullen papers, Colorado Historical Society (CHS).
6. J. K. Mullen, Letter to Catherine S. Mullen, July 1 and 4, 1880, Mullen papers, CHS.
7. J. K. Mullen, Letter to Catherine S. Mullen, July 17, 1880, Mullen papers, CHS.
8. R. James Abernathey, *Practical Hints for Mill Building* (Moline, Ill.: R. James Abernathey, 1880), 225–226, microfilm copy, Auraria Library, Denver, Colorado; Robert Murray Frame, "The Progressive Millers: A Cultural and Intellectual Portrait of the Flour Milling Industry, 1870–1930" (Ph.D. diss., University of Minnesota, 1980), 39.
9. Abernathey, 224.
10. Ibid.
11. Ibid., 226–230.
12. Frame, xii.
13. Abernathey, 239; Frame, 170.
14. *Northwestern Miller*, cited in Frame, 159.
15. This and subsequent references regarding Milwaukee and learning the Hungarian system are cited from J. K. Mullen, Letter to Catherine S. Mullen, May 18, 1881, Mullen papers, CHS.

16. *RMN*, August 18, 1881: 4.

17. *RMN*, January 1, 1882: 13.

18. Ibid.

19. Ibid.

20. Frame, 94.

21. *RMN*, January 13, 1882: 8; January, 24, 1882: 1.

22. *RMN*, March 25, 1882: 7; May 6, 1882: 8; January 10, 1883: 3.

23. The well, located on the corner of Seventh Street and Auraria Parkway, still irrigates the Auraria Higher Education Center in Denver.

24. In later years, Mullen regretted his early faith in the unlimited access to resources, and the environmental devastation that businessmen like himself caused in the rush to build Denver: "The first water well we dug for boilers at the Hungarian gushered at 330 feet, the second one at 600, the third at 1200, and now we have to lift the water more than 3000 feet . . . The Hungarian Mills were built out of lumber on the Divide, within twenty-five or thirty miles of Denver. When you drive out there today in your automobile, there isn't a stick of timber in sight." J. K. Mullen, "Duties and Obligations of Merchants and Manufacturers," speech transcript, 1912, Weckbaugh family collection.

25. *RMN*, September 13, 1882: 4.

26. J. K. Mullen, Letter to George F. Cottrell, January 25, 1929, Weckbaugh family collection. Mullen returned the favor. In 1917 he became a director, and encouraged his wealthy friends to switch to and stay with First National.

27. *RMN*, December 25, 1883: 9.

28. *RMN*, September 13, 1882: 4.

29. *RMN*, December 25, 1883: 9.

30. J. K. Mullen, Letter to Maurice C. Dolan, April 19, 1927, Mullen papers, CHS.

31. The breakdown of Denver's flour production for 1883 (in 100-lb. sacks) is as follows:

Mill :	Mullen & Co.	Crescent	Davis	Star	Total
Cap./day	1,700	900	500	200	3,300
Cap./yr.	530,400	280,800	156,000	62,400	1,029,600
Actual	200,000	40,000	140,000	52,000	432,000
% of cap.	38%*	14%*	90%	84%	42%
Avg. net	$450,000	$90,000	$315,000	$118,125	$973,125

*The Hungarian Mills, with a capacity of 1,200 sacks, did not begin production until September 1883. Likewise, the Crescent Mills, which was rebuilt following the fire of 1882, only produced for the last quarter of 1883.

32. *RMN*, December 25, 1883: 9.

33. Frame, 94.

34. H. E. Johnson, Letter to Guy Thomas, June 10, 1943, Johnson collection.

8

THE LACE CURTAIN

Community Associations, 1880–1890

WHEN J. K. MULLEN ARRIVED IN DENVER IN 1871, he possessed little in the way of education or wealth to distinguish him from other work-ing-class Irish immigrants. When he died fifty-eight years later, he was memorialized as a multimillionaire, the president emeritus of a five-state milling conglomerate, a real estate mogul, bank director, promi-nent civic and religious patron, and scion of social reformers in Den-ver. In between these two events, his rise to wealth and prominence, tempered by his upbringing, affected his political, social, and eco-nomic outlook in many ways. The transformation can be traced in the social causes and organizations that interested Mullen over the course of his career. Throughout his life, an intertwining mixture of ethnicity, religion, and class identity guided J. K.'s social priorities. The propor-tions changed over time and through necessity. A captivation with radical politics gave way to more conservative yet socially progressive views. As a young mill hand, he devoured articles in the radical news-paper *The Irish World and Industrial Liberator* and cheered the victories of Democratic candidates.[1] As a middle-class mill manager and small-business owner, he served the local Democratic Party as a ward orga-nizer and election judge. As he moved into Colorado's financial elite, he backed away from active political participation, but he continued to support the progressive policies of his friend, Democratic senator Thomas M. Patterson. (In 1892, disgusted with "shameful" Republi-can bias, Mullen instructed his wife to "stop off all three of the Repub-lican papers & . . . subscribe for [Patterson's *Rocky Mountain*] *News*.")[2]

Success influenced Mullen to mix his progressive social views with a more conservative stance on business. He adopted a paternalistic attitude toward his employees and customers—going so far as to inform his managers that giving needy farmers the benefit of the doubt on financial differences was "the White Man's Burden."[3] By 1928, J. K., the paradigm of Irish immigration success and defender of the Catholic faith, unflinchingly supported conservative (albeit reform-minded) presidential candidate Herbert Hoover over the Democratic, antiprohibition, and Irish Catholic candidate, Alfred Smith.[4]

The transformation of values occurred as J. K. single-mindedly executed his escape from the working class into middle- and upper-class affluence. Wealth provided membership among Denver's business elite. As a result, J. K. shed many of his working-class immigrant sympathies in favor of the more progressive, acculturated, and middle-class values common to late-nineteenth-century Denver society. This tendency exhibited itself most visibly in the shift in Mullen's political and social affiliations between 1878 and 1885—the period roughly spanning the success of J. K. Mullen & Co. and the formation of the Colorado Milling and Elevator Company. During this time J. K. developed a form of paternalism toward his employees that combined equal parts of identification with and detachment from their working-class and ethnic identity.

"A PRACTICAL CATHOLIC OF GOOD MORAL CHARACTER"

Like many of his contemporaries, J. K. Mullen complemented his economic success by joining social and charitable organizations that offered chances for relaxation, companionship, and promotion of moral values. Victorian Americans in general and gregarious Irish-Americans in particular avidly organized, joined, or patronized ethnic clubs, political organizations, militias, and saloons. Mullen's social affiliations indicated the type of lifestyle J. K. valued.

As an entrepreneur, Mullen's middle-class status distinguished him from the majority of Denver's laboring-class Irish men and women. The establishment of the Excelsior and Hungarian mills solidified Mullen's position among Denver's Irish-American business community—the so-called lace-curtain Irish. This term, used primarily among Irish Americans, signified for the Irish the ability to afford ostentatious lace decorations often found in upper-class American homes. Although the term was (and is) considered pejorative by some, Irish lace symbolized respectability, comfort, and the escape from the working-class immigrant status of the "shanty," or working-class, Irish.[5] With his success in the milling business, Mullen joined the growing class of new Irish-American businessmen who were breaking into the American mainstream. After decades of intolerance the lace-curtain Irish finally began to achieve general acceptance based on their economic influence in American commercial life. Yet, the new ethnic middle class paid for acceptance in American society with increasing estrangement from the Irish working class. Historian Eric Foner explains:

> The "lace curtain" Irish were mostly merchants and professionals whose offices were located in modern downtown business districts catering to a non-Irish clientele. These lace curtain Irish enjoyed less political and social influence in the larger society than economic status . . . Their lives were far removed from those of the poorer countrymen.[6]

On Ninth Street, J. K. lived in a working-class neighborhood that included many Irish families. Yet, while he joined ethnic, religious, and secular organizations, he shunned the array of social, athletic, and drinking establishments preferred by Denver's Irish community. The capitalist either avoided or downplayed his support of working-class-oriented and extremist Irish or Irish-influenced organizations such as the nationalistic Fenians, the Ancient Order of Hibernians, the Shamrock Athletic Club, and the Knights of Labor.[7] Instead, he visibly affiliated with groups that espoused moderate, middle-class, or transdenominational values. His associations matched the self-consciousness of his social abilities. Awkward and reserved, Mullen shunned the social clubs of both his Irish and Protestant contemporaries. Instead, he looked for companions whose values encouraged restraint.

Restraint gave J. K. common cause with at least one working-class organization, the Knights of Labor, on one issue—temperance. Alcohol was central to Irish working-class community life. The immigrant saloon provided a familiar social atmosphere conducive to business, politics, and pleasure. Many reformers also believed that the liquor dispensed there was responsible for misery, irresponsibility, and abusive behavior.[8] Mullen, like the organizers of the trade-union movement, shunned the saloon as an enemy of productive, moral values. He signed his own temperance oath at the age of fourteen. Instructing abstinence in youngsters, J. K. cautioned, "When you come to a saloon, get off the sidewalk and go out in the street."[9]

J. K. had demonstrated that his belief in temperance transcended religious affiliation. In Kansas, he joined the Protestant Good Templars Society. The miller later cofounded and presided over the Denver chapter of a national Catholic temperance union, the St. Joseph's Catholic Total Abstinence Society. Established to support Catholic teetotalers and recovering alcoholics, the society boasted between fifty and sixty-five members.[10] If the officers reflected their membership, Irishmen represented a substantial portion of the society. Five of nine officers possessed Irish surnames in 1880, and four of eight in 1881. The July 15, 1880, issue of the *Rocky Mountain News* reported Mullen family influence in the organization:

> J. K. Mullen, the former president, who served two terms, declined a nomination because he did not believe in the third term. P. H. Mullen also declined because he believed in rotation in office. The society is in good standing, having nearly fifty members on the roll and about $1,000 in the treasury.[11]

The ex-president temporarily stepped down, but he was reelected six months later and became a trustee in 1883. Although no longer an officer, J. K. remained a "dry" throughout his life. Granddaughter-in-law Anne Weckbaugh recalled that the businessman offered $2,000 to each of his grandchildren if they abstained until the age of twenty-one.[12]

Mullen also helped organize an ethnic social club—the St. Patrick's Catholic Mutual Benevolent Society of Denver. J. K. served as the first president of this organization, which was founded on St. Patrick's Day, 1881. Like its namesake, Ireland's patron saint, the Benevolent Society tried to create a refined social environment for the surrounding Irish community. The society provided physical, spiritual, and social benefits to attract working-class and middle-class Irish members. Membership was open to Irish and Irish-American males between the ages of fourteen and sixty who "enjoy good health and [do] not have any disease calculated to impair health or shorten life." Applicants "must be practical Catholics, possessed of good moral character," with enough income to keep up with membership expenses.[13] Members paid an initiation fee of one dollar, monthly dues of twenty-five cents, and "spiritual dues" of twenty-five cents per year. Affiliates also participated in Communion together on the first Sunday following St. Patrick's Day and the first Sunday in August.[14]

In return, the society acted as a physical and spiritual insurance company. During illness, qualified members received weekly calls from the visitation committee, a five-dollar-per-week sickness benefit, and, if necessary, twenty-five dollars to cover funeral expenses. Members were assured of twelve masses per year recited for themselves and their families and the performance of a requiem mass for the repose of their souls upon their death. The society also sponsored social activities. Its members arranged dances, lectures, debates, and amusements, established a library, and organized "such other aids to mental improvement and innocent recreation as they may deem suitable."[15]

The St. Patrick's Benevolent Society may have emphasized its members' common Irish background, but it also encouraged acculturation with the American mainstream. The society attempted to bridge the gap of mixed Irish classes by stressing the common Americanism of its members. The society's constitutional preamble, with its references to the U.S. Constitution, echoed its American aspirations:

> We, the undersigned, Irish and Irish-American Catholics of the City of Denver, being desirous of securing to ourselves and our posterity the blessings of a more perfect union, with harmony of action in works of charity and benevolence, as well as in the encouragement of Christian education, so as to further elevate our social and moral standard in this community, do hereby ordain and establish the following Constitution . . .[16]

The St. Patrick Benevolent Society's appeal to a common nationalism across class boundaries fell on deaf ears. Even as entrepreneurs like Mullen embraced American ideals, their pro-American tone contrasted sharply with the rhetoric of working-class Irish nationalism. As it embraced temperance and middle-class reform, mainstream American culture alienated Irish ethnic and working-class institutions.

At the same time, corporate expansion and consolidation restricted opportunities for Irish laborers. Into the late 1870s and 1880s, working-class Irish immigrants saw themselves as exiles from the oppression of British imperialism. Now, Irish immigrants working in American factories felt increasingly threatened by another form of oppression—American industrialism. When faced with a choice between "lace-curtain," temperate reform, or standing with their working-class brothers and sisters against the "heartless speculators and rent-hounds" of both Ireland and America, Irish workers generally stood together in working-class solidarity.[17] Standing apart from their working-class brethren on this issue were up-and-coming Irish-American entrepreneurs such as J. K. Mullen.

POLITICS, CLASS, AND ETHNICITY

Mullen parted with the values of his working-class countryfolk in politics, as well. Although he chastised his brother Dennis for his political associations, J. K. participated in Democratic Party activities during the first three years of the 1880s—a period that coincided with his increased dependence on city permits for construction and right-of-way to his mills. The Democrats enjoyed traditional support from the Irish. J. K.'s personal affiliation with the Democratic Party stretched back to Oriskany Falls. Only later did the increasingly affluent businessman cast about for a more conservative alternative.

His later conservative political leanings contrasted sharply with the political interests of his youth. As a resident of Colorado Territory, Mullen was unable to vote in the national election of 1872. He nevertheless followed the campaign closely. The mill hand supported the Democratic candidate Horace Greeley over the Republican opponent Ulysses S. Grant.[18] He also entertained prolabor ideas gathered from Patrick Ford's radical newspaper, *The Irish World and Industrial Liberator*, "the voice of the politically conscious Irish-American working class," in the early 1870s.[19]

As a neighborhood business leader, J. K. became more involved in local political affairs during the election of 1880. He attended the First Ward caucus for the Arapahoe County convention with his brother Patrick.[20] Fellow West Denver ward members elected Mullen as one of two delegates to the state Democratic convention held in August. At the convention, he supported his friend, attorney and former U.S. representative Thomas M. Patterson, in a fiery denunciation of the Republican presidential candidate James Garfield, the "ensanguined garment" (bloody shirt) tactics of the Reconstruction Republicans, mistreatment of labor in the recent Leadville strike, and endorsement of the silver issue.[21]

In the 1881 Denver mayoral election, Mullen crossed political boundaries to demonstrate his commitment to Irish solidarity. The election saw Irish voters unite behind Robert Morris, a Protestant Irishman and Republican, to defeat hardware merchant George Tritch, a Democrat of German descent. Like Mullen, many Irish Democrats crossed the political line in "a unified frenzy" to elect their country-man—the last foreign-born mayor of Denver.[22] J. K., recently a Democratic ward delegate, praised the unification of diverse classes of Irishmen behind their countryman. Writing to the *Rocky Mountain News*, he asserted that Irish unification behind Morris was a reaction to intolerance among the native-born Protestant majority. "Oppression," he wrote, "has taught Irishmen to realize that in bickerings, in jealousies, and dissensions lies their greatest weakness."[23] Mullen criticized Protestant ministers who exhorted Protestant voters to boycott Morris on the erroneous grounds that he was a Catholic. The miller protested the "bigotry of a sect that would drag religion into a local contest" and claimed that "when the men . . . began to ignore and oppose [Morris] because of his birthplace, then the strong feelings, the warm sympathy . . . the close friendship and the high estimation in which he was held by his countrymen came to his support."[24]

In his 1985 study of western labor radicalism, historian David Brundage uses this letter to paint Mullen as an antilabor arch-conservative.[25] While his conclusion regarding sustained antilabor antagonism on Mullen's behalf is insupportable, the entrepreneur experimented with a series of political stances, some of which matched his affluence. In 1883, he spurned the boozy political atmosphere of the Graystone Democratic Club in favor of a "non-partisan . . . Committee of Seventy-Eight." This so-called citizen's party included such conservative business moguls as public-utility baron William Gray Evans, real estate developer William Barth, brewer Philip Zang, and hardware czar George Tritch. Under the leadership of these civic scions, the Committee of Seventy-Eight proposed to nominate a slate of "honest" candidates with the declared intention of reforming the Denver political machine.[26] How firmly J. K. backed the "nonpartisan" effort is uncertain. Just a few days later, Robert Speer, the kingpin of Denver's Democratic political machine, arranged for Mullen's appointment as an election judge in the First Ward.[27] The following year, Mullen joined the steering committee of a newly formed Prohibition Party, founded by a coalition of Protestant ministers and activists from the Women's Christian Temperance Union.[28] His flip-flops indicate that his loyalties were torn by his divided belief in the Democratic ethnic working-class values in which he grew up and the politics of acculturation and reform to which he aspired.

THE IRISH-AMERICAN LAND LEAGUE

That Mullen held political opinions that no longer mirrored those of the working-class Irish was most evident in his participation in the Irish-American Land League movement that swept the United States during the first half of the 1880s. The movement represented a conjunction of nationalistic interests between middle-class and working-class Irishmen. In 1880, the respected Irish parliamentarian Charles Stuart Parnell visited the United States to raise funds for a proposed land reform system in Ireland. Harnessing peaceful economic protests by western Irish tenant farmers, Parnell, a Protestant, united with radical Catholic nationalists Michael Davitt and John Devoy. The trio proposed to raise the necessary funds to buy out English landlords and redistribute the land to Irish farmers. The sophisticated Parnell met with great success in the United States as the Irish of all classes, as well as native-born Americans and even sympathetic non-Irish immigrant groups, flocked to support his plan.[29]

As the Land League movement spread across the United States, it crystallized tensions that divided different classes of Irish Americans. On one hand, the Land League rhetoric, as espoused by Patrick Ford in his popular New York paper, *The Irish World*, increased working-class awareness of unjust employer-employee relationships in the industrial world.[30] On the other hand, the nationalistic rhetoric served to unite Irish Americans in a common cause.

The Land League received mainstream support in America in part because it was represented by a respectable Protestant political leader and operated in the tradition of the nineteenth-century social reform movement. At the same time, it received working-class Irish support because it called for reform of an unjust class system. But as the Land League movement crossed class boundaries, it intensified the divisions among the American Irish. At the same time that Denver Irish voters united behind the election of their countryman Robert Morris, the Land League movement illuminated the class differences between the lace-curtain and shanty Irish. Their division lay in interpretation of the Land League rhetoric. While the Irish middle class adopted the respectable reform arguments of Parnell's non-Irish supporters, the working-class Irish used the Land League movement to call for radical social change. When the lace-curtain Irish failed to dominate the vision of their working-class brethren in the Land League movement, and as Eric Foner observed, the "ethnic nationalism" of Land League rhetoric failed to "unite the Irish working and middle classes at the expense of class identification across ethnic lines . . . the Land League experience widened the gap between the classes within the Irish community."[31]

When the movement reached Denver, Mullen jumped in squarely with the middle-class interests. Between 1881 and 1883, he served as Denver treasurer. He appeared prominently on committee panels and in Land League debates sponsored by Denver's Michael Davitt branch. In addition to making several donations (including $55 at a meeting in 1881), he organized a Christmas fund-raising ball in 1880, a picnic for twelve hundred Land League supporters in Morrison in May 1881, and several rallies.[32]

In the sensitive atmosphere of class division, Land League debates and speeches often cloaked class-based subtexts within nationalistic rhetoric. On October 17, 1881, for instance, the Davitt branch debated the following issue: "Resolved: That money exercises a greater influence in the world than intellectual culture." During the debate, a radical speaker illustrated the relationship between the moneyed interests who wielded "the power of gold [that] held Ireland in chains" and the "money-changers and Shylocks" who bought off "the representatives of the people" in America.[33] Mullen rebutted:

> Gold, I consider a secondary matter. The feeling for one's fellow man was foremost in the human breast, and greater than that entertained for money. Intellectual culture came from God, and therefore must be superior to gold, which, without culture and intellect was but of very little use to mankind.[34]

In his reply, the miller articulated his acceptance of the dual nature of success as defined by Victorian-American success advocates, who considered the acquisition of wealth as an empty gesture without the cultivation of moral character. Moreover, when the first speaker advocated raising funds for armed revolution, Mullen joined Land League president Robert Morris in reminding the gentleman that the league pursued "peace and good will." The members of the league promptly ejected the unidentified radical from the hall.[35]

LABOR RELATIONS

As an entrepreneur and prototypical "self-made man," it would be easy to paint Mullen as a staunch antilabor conservative. J. K.'s attitude toward labor defies such characterization. Labor historian David

Brundage portrayed Mullen as an artful underminer of labor organization within his firm. On the other hand, conservative historian Charles W. Hurd characterized Mullen as a benevolent father figure whose successful cultivation of company loyalty was rewarded by long periods of service among his workers. According to Hurd, the Colorado Milling and Elevator Company (CM&E) "was one big family, with Mr. Mullen at the head. He was like a father to his men."[36]

Mullen's correspondence indicates that the truth lies somewhere in between. J. K. referred paternalistically to the CM&E as "my child" and his employees as "my boys." He tried to judge his employees on the same standards of character that he perceived in himself. Especially in the management levels, the entrepreneur encouraged security of position and the belief that promotion occurred from within the ranks.[37] The result was that while some discontented employees grumbled, Mullen secured the loyalty of many others.

Still, Mullen unequivocally opposed organized labor. In an undated speech delivered to the Knights of Columbus, he drew an analogy that emphasized the importance of dutiful, nonstriking employees. The railroad worker who stops the train midway between destinations, he declared, should be fined for not carrying out his duty. "He could not in good health lay down his burden until he reached his destination—without incurring the penalty."[38] While almost no labor difficulties in Mullen's firms received publicity, an incident that occurred in February 1885 illustrates the businessman's idea of an appropriate penalty. When "one or two" discontented laborers attempted to seize the Hungarian Elevator, the miller fired them without comment, ejected them from the grounds, and continued operations uninterrupted. Significantly, both the Democratic *Rocky Mountain News* and the Knights of Labor chastised the discontented workers. The Knights disavowed them completely, promising not to "meddle where there is nothing at issue which in any way concerns them."[39]

J. K. developed a policy toward employee relations that was fairly liberal for his time. He successfully undermined labor discontent by awarding progressive incentives to his workers. In a 1924 letter to William S. Bunt, the manager of the CM&E mill in Claflin, Kansas, Mullen outlined his policy to motivate employees. He ordered Bunt to post a notice announcing that anyone was in line for promotion, based on "the satisfaction that their services give to the Company; and

Mill hands, clad in lily-white coveralls to hide ever-present flour dust, man the Boulder Milling and Elevator Company works. J. K. Mullen's relationship with his employees ranged from steadfast loyalty to persistent complaints of stinginess. Courtesy, Western History Dept., Denver Public Library.

depending also upon their honesty, their loyalty, their ability, their application to the business, their integrity, and their good character and clean living." He did in fact attempt to regulate his employees' off-duty behavior by demanding temperance and some form of religious affiliation. But he also made it clear that no employee was to be sanctioned for a particular religious denomination.

Mullen instructed his managers to pay their staff enough to meet their expenses adequately. "We don't expect you to hire your employees for the least possible amount," he informed Bunt. "We want to pay our employees sufficient compensation so that they can support themselves and their families in reasonable comfort." Nevertheless, he left the definition of "reasonable comfort" up to the manager. Anyone who remained discontented, he warned, could look elsewhere for employment.

Perhaps J. K. acted to head off discontent already present among his work force. To some mill hands, the miller had a reputation for stinginess. Denver city councilman Dennis Gallagher, a recipient of a Mullen scholarship to Catholic University and the grandson of a CM&E

mill hand, recalled that his grandparents considered Mullen's scholar-ships compensation for their low wages. J. K. joked about his own personal frugality, reminding his fashionable grandsons that he had never paid more than two dollars for a necktie.[40] He also believed that frugal wages promoted thrift:

> We live in an extravagant age; in a period of temptations and distractions . . . [if] a man made $50 a month he saved $10. If he made $75 he saved $25. When he began to make $100 a month he spent $100. When he began to make $125 he spent $150.[41]

Despite some dissatisfaction with, or perhaps because of, his wage policies, most employees were encouraged to believe in job security. The businessman urged his managers to maintain full employment during difficult economic times, even if it meant a short-term financial setback. "The services of a dissatisfied employee are very seldom help-ful to any industry," he counseled. He paid his workers during sick leaves of "a reasonable length," granted two weeks of paid vacation annually, and, of course, mandated labor-free Sundays.[42] Mullen insti-tuted a profit-sharing program with his employees in order to give them a working interest in the corporation and, in 1917, personally donated $11,000 to establish a $720-per-year pension fund for re-tired or incapacitated employees.[43]

His actions paid dividends in loyalty, particularly among Mullen's executive corps. Two career CM&E employees, Ralph W. Kelly and Herbert E. Johnson, represented best-case examples. Kelly joined the company as an eighteen-year-old stenographer in 1894. He moved up the ranks to accountant, auditor, and general auditor. By 1914, he was listed on the board of directors, where he served until his retirement in 1946.[44] Johnson was reassigned as a grain buyer in the San Luis Valley after the CM&E absorbed his employer, the Loveland Elevator, in the 1880s. In 1890, he supervised the startup Alamosa Mill. In 1895, he became general manager, responsible for the company's expansion into Idaho.[45] When Johnson retired in 1920, he wrote to his employer, "I shall always hold as one of my choicest possessions the deep and abid-ing friendship that I now feel for you. . . ."[46] Edmond M. Ryan, an-other junior associate who rose through the ranks, replaced Johnson as general manager.[47] J. K. benefited from this strong loyalty on the part of his junior executives even as he suffered from a tarnished reputation among his clients.

Mullen's paternalism sprang from many possible roots. Having grown up among the working class, he recognized an empathetic bond with his workers. He believed in the personal patronage typified by the political and business leaders of his childhood. His policies also reflected societal ideals, particularly of the employer-employee contract praised by many Protestant success writers of his time. In *The Self-Made Man in America*, Irvin G. Wyllie describes reciprocal obligations of the ideal employer and employee that mirror the policies that Mullen prescribed:

> The success cult insisted that the employees must identify themselves with their masters' interests, advancing those interests in every honorable way. Success philosophers [also] laid heavy obligations on employers ... This meant that the employer was to pay a living wage, enough to take care of every physical necessity and to assure peace of mind. Nor did glutted labor markets or the willingness of desperate men to work for less than a subsistence lessen the obligation.[48]

Wyllie also describes the "special obligation" of business owners to share the profits in good times. Mullen's agreement is indicated by a front-page article in the *Denver Times*, announcing a 10 percent wage increase at the Hungarian Mill. "Unusual prosperity should be visited upon the employees," declared company spokesman Dennis Mullen. "They have worked faithfully in the interest of the company, and it is nothing but fair that they should be given wages which will enable them to live comfortably."[49] The announcement, well received by the laborers, displayed Mullen's generosity as well as the necessity of publicizing its fulfillment.

J. K. rewarded loyalty and service. Nevertheless, he could no longer claim mutual identification with his working-class Irish employees. In politics, in business, and in society, his interests now coincided with Denver's upper class.

NOTES

1. P. H. Mullin, Letter to J. K. Mullen, March 16, 1873, Weckbaugh family collection.
2. J. K. Mullen, Letter to Catherine S. Mullen, March 16, 1892, Mullen papers, Colorado Historical Society (CHS).
3. J. K. Mullen, Letter to W. S. Bunt, Claflin Flour Mills, February 12, 1924, Weckbaugh family collection.
4. J. K. Mullen, Letter to Loyal L. Breckenridge, November 2, 1928, Mullen papers, CHS.

5. Eric Foner, *Politics and Ideology in the Age of the Civil War* (New York: Oxford University Press, 1980), 152.

6. Ibid.

7. Stephen J. Leonard, "Denver's Foreign Born Immigrants, 1859–1900" (Ph.D. diss., Claremont Graduate School, 1971), 143.

8. Thomas J. Noel, *The City and the Saloon, Denver, 1858–1916* (Lincoln: University of Nebraska Press, 1982), 58.

9. Charles W. Hurd, "J. K. Mullen, Milling Magnate of Colorado," *The Colorado Magazine* XXIX:2 (April 1952): 114.

10. Corbett, Hoye, and Ballenger, *Denver City Directory*, 1879, microfilm, Western History Dept., Denver Public Library, Denver, Colorado.

11. *Rocky Mountain* News (*RMN*), July 15, 1880: 5.

12. *RMN*, January 13, 1881: 1; January 14, 1883: 2; Foner, 151; Corbett, Hoye, and Ballenger, *Denver City Directory*, 1879; Anne Weckbaugh, personal interview, February 6, 1998.

13. "Constitution and By-Laws of the St. Patrick's Catholic Mutual Benevolent Society of Denver," Art. II, Sec. 1 (Denver: Labor Enquirer Printing House, 1881), Rt. Rev. John Henry Tihen, manuscript collection, Archdiocese of Denver archives.

14. Ibid., Art. III, IV.

15. Ibid. Art. V, IX.

16. Ibid.

17. Foner, 157–161; David M. Emmons, *The Butte Irish: Class and Ethnicity in an American Mining Town, 1875–1925* (Urbana: University of Illinois Press, 1989), 197–199; Thomas N. Brown, *Irish-American Nationalism, 1870–1890* (Philadelphia: J. B. Lippincott Co.), 53–56.

18. Patrick also described his habit of betting gallon kegs of beer on the voting practices of certain Oriskany Falls friends. P. H. teased, "Brother John . . . you men in the territories can not feel as much interest in Political affairs as if you had a voice in electing . . . either candidate." P. H. Mullin, Letter to J. K. Mullen, August 3, 1872, Weckbaugh family collection.

19. Foner, 157; P. H. Mullin, Letter to J. K. Mullen, March 16, 1873, Weckbaugh family collection.

20. Denver was part of Arapahoe County until local Progressives waged a successful campaign to separate the city from regional influences, creating Denver County in 1902. Stephen J. Leonard and Thomas J. Noel, *Denver: Mining Camp to Metropolis* (Niwot: University Press of Colorado, 1990), 129.

21. *RMN*, August 29, 1880: 1.

22. Leonard, 164.

23. *RMN*, November 11, 1881: 4.

24. Ibid.

25. David Brundage, *The Making of Western Labor Radicalism: Denver's Organized Workers, 1878–1905* (Urbana: University of Illinois Press, 1994), 78.

26. *RMN*, March 6, 1883: 4.

27. *RMN*, March 14, 1883: 8.

28. *RMN*, March 1, 1884: 1.
29. Brown, 103–105; Foner, 153–156.
30. Foner, 158.
31. Ibid., 195.
32. *RMN*, December 23, 1880: 3; July 19, 1881: 2; October 17, 1881: 6.
33. *RMN*, October 17, 1881: 6.
34. Ibid.
35. Ibid.
36. Hurd, 112.
37. Ibid.; J. K. Mullen, Letter to W. S. Bunt, Claflin Flour Mills, February 12, 1924, Weckbaugh family collection.
38. J. K. Mullen, "Our Duties as Catholic Citizens," handwritten manuscript, 1912, Mullen papers, CHS.
39. *RMN*, February 15, 1885: 8.
40. Dennis Gallagher, personal interview, November 24, 1997; "Necktie" joke, attributed by Anne Weckbaugh, personal interview, February 6, 1998.
41. Unattributed newspaper clipping, Katherine Mullen O'Connor scrapbook, Timothy O'Connor collection.
42. J. K. Mullen, Letter to W. S. Bunt, Claflin Flour Mills, February 12, 1924, Weckbaugh family collection.
43. Hurd, 117; CM&E, "Memorandum to the Board of Directors," September 19, 1919, Mullen papers, Western History Dept., Denver Public Library.
44. Hurd, 114.
45. Ibid., 113; H. E. Johnson, Letter to Guy Thomas, June 10, 1943, Johnson collection.
46. H. E. Johnson, Letter to J. K. Mullen, December 27, 1920, Johnson collection.
47. *Denver Post*, August 22, 1929: 1.
48. Irvin G. Wyllie, *The Self-Made Man in America* (New York: The Free Press, 1954), 82.
49. *Denver Times*, June 12, 1901: 1.

9

"I AM A LITTLE DAFFY ON THE SUBJECT OF GIVING"

Philanthropy, 1880–1929

THE SAME SUCCESS IDEOLOGY that encouraged the fair treatment of employees created in J. K. Mullen a strong sense of obligation to Denver's poor. As hard as he promoted his company, he continued to believe that philanthropy presented the truest path to spiritual and secular redemption. J. K., very often advised by his wife, Kate, gave away unrecorded thousands of dollars to religious, civic, social, and purely personal causes as a matter of course. Records of his public, private, and religious donations—from Christmastime collection-basket gifts of $5 to the $750,000 construction fund for the Catholic University Library—tally up to over $2.4 million, or about one-third of his net personal worth at the time of his death.[1] Added to that figure is an unknown amount that he gave in the form of personal gifts, tokens, checks, and cash handouts to charity, friends, and even deserving strangers. Together, these gifts summed up his belief that capitalists accumulated wealth in order to provide for the social good. Mullen instilled the value of stewardship in his children and grandchildren. By charging future generations with the maintenance of his social ideals, he ensured that his family would remain committed to philanthropy long after his passing.

The miller made his fortune during the great age of businessmen-philanthropists. To a large degree, he shared the ideals of industrial titans Andrew Carnegie and John D. Rockefeller regarding both economic order in the chaotic marketplace and social philanthropy. Strong cultural forces affected attitudes toward both the accumulation and distribution of wealth in nineteenth-century America. Success writers glorified the accumulation of capital—particularly when generated through the special talents of self-made men—as a trust to be used to benefit the public. Historian Irvin G. Wyllie writes that according to the doctrine of stewardship of wealth, capitalists were "under the obligation to preserve [wealth], enlarge it, and apply it to good works." In *The Gospel of Wealth*, Andrew Carnegie declared that "the man of wealth becomes the mere agent and trustee for his poorer brethren, bringing to their service his superior wisdom, experience, and ability to administer, doing for them better than they would or could do for themselves." Rockefeller concurred, stating, "I believe the power to make money is a gift of God . . . to be developed and used to the best of our ability for the good of mankind."[2] J. K. echoed both capitalists in his analysis of his own urge to give:

> Some of my good friends appear to think that I am a little daffy on the subject of giving away large amounts of money, but I have always felt that God Almighty had a purpose in giving me the opportunity to accumulate, and that he would hold me to a stern responsibility if I failed to do my duty.[3]

Like Carnegie and Rockefeller, Mullen saw himself as an enlightened steward of the public good.

The motivations that drove J. K. Mullen to give were complicated by social, cultural, and economic factors. As a boy, Mullen absorbed the example of two social benefactors who provided largesse on a local scale. In Ireland, J. K. grew up as a subject of a resident lord, much as Carnegie did in Scotland. The Earl of Clancarty was the eminent noble of the district that included Ballinasloe, Ireland. During the relatively prosperous pre-Famine era, the earl underwrote several projects that fostered the social well-being of the western Irish town. The Ballinasloe public enjoyed access to the earl's private art collection. Clancarty also maintained the wooded Garbally Park on his private estate for the public's enjoyment. The earl sponsored the Ballinasloe Horticultural Society, helped support the public schools and nursery, and encouraged the establishment of the Galway County Insane Asylum in Ballinasloe in 1833. This new institution adopted a reform philosophy, and inmates enjoyed an airy, clean, dignified refuge in fourteen acres of grounds enclosed for cultivation.[4]

J. K. never acknowledged the earl's influence over his own philanthropic affairs, but his later interest in the respectable care of orphans and the elderly, as manifested in the J. K. Mullen Home for the Aged and Home for Boys, echoed Clancarty's institutions. Other examples of his institutional philanthropy appear in his large, usually public donations to the Civic Center, the Denver Public Library, and the J. K. Mullen Library at the Catholic University of America in Washington, D.C. Over the years, John and Kate supported the St. Vincent de Paul Society, St. Joseph's Hospital, St. Vincent's Orphanage, the Sacred Heart Aid Society, Catholic Charities, and the Knights of Columbus, as well.[5]

Some of the philanthropist's larger donations served pragmatic ends. J. K. funded the *Broncho Buster* statue in Civic Center Park to offset questions about his patriotism and possible profiteering during the First World War[6] (see Chapter 14). Other projects were designed to make a moral point. J. K. followed through on his wife's donation of the family "homestead" at Ninth and Lawrence Streets with funds to build a church for the emerging St. Cajetan's parish[7] (see Chapter 18). Some endowments combined practical and moral ends. J. K. furnished the nondenominational University of Denver Chapel in order to promote religious toleration as well as to recruit the assistance of former Colorado governor and Denver University chancellor Henry A. Buchtel in his effort to remain on the U.S. Grain Production Board.[8] Whatever the reason behind the cause, most of his institutional charities were intended to improve the commercial, intellectual, social, or moral climate that he felt obligated to support.

A second type of charity reflected J. K.'s commitment to immediate personal assistance that was similar in style, but without the political motivation, to the Tammany methods of "help" that J. K. experienced in New York. This tendency is best represented by his alleged forays into Denver's poor immigrant neighborhoods, as described by C. W. Hurd. Armed with only a basket of fruit, the philanthropist supposedly visited the tumbledown shantytowns, knocking on doors, inquiring about the health of the occupants, and parting with money for bread or children's shoes, or just a simple hello.[9] The actual amount of these small personal donations is unrecoverable because of his insistence on anonymity for these types of contributions. The most complete surviving record for a single period of time appears in his personal ledger book for 1900–1905, which recorded Mullen's private charitable transactions. In the prosperous years between 1900 and 1903, his personal "help" amounted to an average of $1,722 annually, mostly in checks of $25, $50, or $100.[10]

The recipients of these small donations reflect Mullen's interest in an array of religious and social causes. Even in private, Mullen practiced ecumenical tolerance in his charity. During 1902, J. K. wrote checks to the Broadway Baptist Church ($50), the Eaton Baptist Church ($25), the Eaton Library ($50), the Home for Working Boys ($75), the Ancient Order of Hibernians ($200), the Oriskany (New York) Christian Association ($50), Sacred Heart College ($10), Associated Charities ($100), the Young Men's Christian Association ($25), and the Church of the Good Shepherd ($100).[11] Mullen was capable of promoting religious toleration on every level. This was evident not only in his small gift-giving practices but also by his 1925 charter endowment and appointment to the board of directors to the multidenominational Denver Foundation. J. K.'s contribution provided the initial support for this staple philanthropic fund.[12]

J. K. made a point of favoring diverse religious charities but his success bolstered his role as patron of the Denver Catholic diocese. The diocese constantly struggled with problems of finance, accumulating debt at an astonishing pace. To Denver's Catholic community, the successful and devout financier was an answer to a prayer. As early as 1876, Denver's first Catholic bishop, Joseph P. Machebeuf, included the miller in deliberations over the church's shaky finances.[13] Thereafter, J. K. provided financial assistance, land, time, and business advice generously. The markings in the 1902 ledger show that he produced his checkbook most frequently to support his own religion. Father William O'Ryan and St. Leo's Catholic Church received the greatest support in 1902—three checks amounting to $700. St. Leo's remained a favorite charity. The philanthropist set aside $50,000 worth of CM&E stocks in his will as a trust to benefit St. Leo's and the destitute family of his deceased Longmont milling associate, James W. Denio.[14]

The patron regularly supplied small gifts to struggling Denver parishioners and clergy members. His notes to Denver bishops Nicholas C. Matz or John Henry Tihen often included $100 checks, "to help you a little," or "from your old scolding friend."[15] Frequently, the layman covered the living expenses of parish priests when the diocese was unable to provide their wages. When Tihen apologized to the philanthropist for this state of affairs in 1928, Mullen expressed shock.

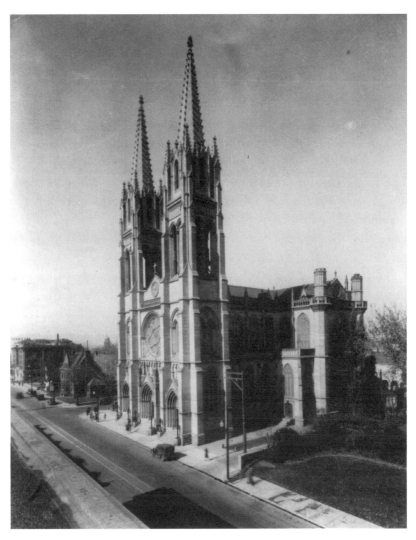

The temptation to exploit J. K. Mullen's pride in charity was sometimes more than local bishops could resist. While soliciting funds from Mullen, Bishop John Henry Tihen quoted remarks allegedly made by Grand Master Mason Ernest Morris at the dedication of the Scottish Rite Masonic Temple on Thirteenth and Grant Streets. Pointing at the nearby spires of the Immaculate Conception Cathedral (pictured), Morris declared: "Where that Cathedral over there shall long since have crumbled into dust this Cathedral shall still stand." Mullen refused the bait, replying that certain Masons were "the very best friends that I ever had in all my business career." He contributed anyway, but also made a special point of donating to Protestant charities. Courtesy, Western History Dept., Denver Public Library.

For over forty years, J. K. replied, he had quietly assisted cash-strapped parish priests. He offered a peek at the magnitude of his small gifts:

> I have taken the trouble to look back in my books in the last three or four years [since 1924–1925] and I find that during that time I have given to Priests . . . including just a few little checks to yourself, eighty-one checks . . . amounting to $10,255, and in all, I have given out during the time mentioned, more than five hundred checks for a total sum of $172,514.07. Not included is aid given directly to the poor in the form of cash, groceries, food and supplies, [amounting to] a very substantial additional sum.[16]

The role suited his upbringing to respect the clergy. When appropriate, he rewarded clergy members who eased the passages of his life. For example, when the Sisters of Charity midwifed John and Kate's five daughters, they were not forgotten when they came around to collect for the St. Joseph's Hospital fund.[17]

J. K. enjoyed a fringe benefit for his religious patronage—the ability to insinuate his opinion into local church affairs. As much as he perceived himself a defender of the local Catholic establishment, his generosity justified his role as the self-appointed tribune of Denver's lay Catholics. "I have reached the age," he wrote Bishop Tihen in the 1920s, "when it is no trouble whatever for me to give advice either to church or laity and to refuse to take any advice myself."[18] Bishops received Mullen money wrapped in strongly worded position papers on tolerance, on the behavior of errant priests, and on the fund-raising practices of the diocese. He used his influence to push his bishops toward ecumenism. In 1922, for instance, Bishop Tihen telegraphed a stirring appeal to the philanthropist, then on vacation in Atlantic City: "Denver needs you. It has always needed you. You have never been found wanting. Regis College needs a big man's example. All Denver looks to you." Evoking Mullen's recent ordination in the Papal Order of St. Gregory, Tihen encouraged the philanthropist to build "a Sir Knight and Countess Mullen Hall or Library or Science Hall or other Building."[19] J. K. tweaked the bishop by refusing the request. Because so many Protestants had already donated to the Regis Fund, the philanthropist replied, he was considering a contribution to the Protestant Iliff School of Theology instead. J. K. leveraged the bishop's appeal into a debate on the virtues of interdenominational fairness in which he emphasized the relative generosity of certain Protestant businessmen to Catholic charities. Ultimately, the philanthropist pledged

$15,000 to Regis, raised another $2,200 from the employees of his Denver mills—and pointedly donated $300 to the Iliff School.[20]

As Bishop Tihen could have attested, Mullen's control of the purse strings occasionally blinded him to the uncomfortable position of his supplicants. Accustomed to a certain amount of respect himself, J. K. occasionally overlooked the feelings of those for whom begging was a bitter pill to swallow. Father Bernard E. Naughten, manager of the Central City Catholic Men's Club, was one beneficiary who complained about Mullen's highhandedness. Having requested assistance from the philanthropist, Naughten received what he considered a terse and humiliating reply. "I never [before] found anyone who on account of their position of wealth expects me to 'cringe,'" he raged. "J. K. Mullen thinks he is important because of his money when it is an honor to be asked to help out." A very proud man, who wouldn't "knuckle down," Father Naughten reasoned that the only excuse for being treated so shabbily was that Mullen must have mistaken him for a Protestant minister instead of a Catholic priest.[21]

Father Matthew Smith, the editor of the *Denver Catholic Register*, also sparred with the financier over charity. Upon the recommendation of Bishop Tihen, Smith asked the philanthropist for an $18,000 loan to update printing equipment. Mullen, who disagreed with the way the newspaper had covered his opinions of church issues in the past, questioned the necessity of running a weekly Catholic paper at a loss. He suggested that Father Smith take a second job at another newspaper to make ends meet. "Why should you deliberately try to insult me?" Smith retorted, calling J. K.'s "sneering comments . . . the act of a cad" and a "first-class grouch." Smith promised to continue praying for Mullen, but vowed never "to bother you personally again."[22]

Despite occasional ruffled feathers, the many small checks Mullen wrote for the clergy, the groceries and clothing he bought for priests, nuns, or needy employees, his intervention in rent disputes, the funerals he financed for disgraced or forgotten priests, or his alleged forays under the viaducts in downtown Denver each generated gratitude that would have qualified him as a Tammany-era politician, had he been so inclined. Not cut from that cloth, he remained satisfied that his donations eased the way for others, cloaked him in respect and responsibility, and offset any spiritual conflicts that may have been attached to his sudden rise to wealth.

The philanthropist found the statement of one supplicant that "all the Catholics in Colorado know of Sir Knight John K. Mullen" to be uncomfortably true.[23] J. K.'s reputation for good works created a strong desire for anonymity. "It is not good form" to publicize his gifts, he wrote, in part because publicity encouraged a flood of applications "from many unworthy sources."[24] Like other well-known benefactors, he attracted unrealistic or unscrupulous solicitations. In 1923, Bishop Tihen forwarded Mullen's polite refusal of an application for $25,000 to start a Catholic mission in Central Africa. ("He says he can do nothing for Uganda.")[25] Closer to home, a Durango landowner named Richard McCloud solicited J. K. to buy six lots in Pagosa Springs in 1927. McCloud explained that although the town already had "a very nice . . . church," his property was "in a better location for the congregation than the present site." Once again, Mullen declined. With so many requests in the immediate region, he couldn't presently "entertain propositions such as yours from a distant territory."[26]

Mullen filtered out "unworthy sources" with standards common to givers of his era. His standards were codified in the admission requirements for the Home for the Aged. Although the institution pledged to practice "no discrimination nor preference . . . because of creed or nationality," elderly applicants needed to meet certain preconditions before acceptance:

> [They] must be well recommended, and not suffering from any disease; they must be citizens of Colorado and have lived here for one year previous to admission [Mullen wanted a five-year residency, but was dissuaded by the Little Sisters of the Poor]; they must be of Caucasian race; of good moral character; clean and neat in their personal habits.[27]

Like many successful Euro-Americans of his generation, J. K. failed to recognize the need to accommodate all races. Nevertheless, the principle of the deserving poor, a staple of American social philanthropy since the Puritans, served as a guidepost for his charity.[28] Widows, orphans, the aged, and those of "good moral character" temporarily down on their luck found a friend in Mullen. J. K. simply refused to subsidize those whom he considered shiftless, intemperate, or opportunistic—and, typical of many contemporary philanthropists, it never occurred to him to lend his support to non-Anglos in need.

When possible, Mullen profited from his own generosity while helping out friends who had fallen on hard times. In 1927, he traded living expenses to Horace Tabor's destitute widow, Baby Doe, in exchange for title to Leadville's celebrated Matchless Mine. Although he allowed her to occupy her shack, free from rent, for the rest of her life, friends speculated that Mullen would one day cash in on the rumored wealth of the Matchless.[29] Similar circumstances gripped an old family friend, Mary Elitch, in 1915. J. K.'s son-in-law/business manager, Oscar L. Malo, held a $20,000 mortgage to the struggling Elitch's Gardens. When the attraction went into receivership after the summer theater season of 1915, Mullen bought out the mortgage, taxes, and interest for $26,911.07. Two months later, he sold the property to John M. Mulvihill for $35,000 in notes. J. K. added three specifications into the contract to look after Mary Elitch—she would be allowed to stay in her on-site bungalow until she moved or passed away; the resort would pay for her utilities; and she would receive a $50-per-month stipend for life. Mulvihill agreed, and to J. K.'s admiration, retired the debt early, in 1927.[30]

As Mary Elitch's case suggests, Mullen remained comfortable with supporting the deserving poor. Not a man easily pushed into what he considered unworthy philanthropic projects, he nevertheless championed a wide range of social causes. His ability to transcend religious denomination, as well as his open generosity, earned him a reputation as one of Denver's greatest givers.

NOTES

1. Figures derived from newspaper clippings, financial statements, receipts, and private letters at the Archdiocese of Denver, Denver Public Library, State Historical Society of Colorado, and Weckbaugh family collection. Net worth of $6,262,177 reported to state inheritance tax department, cited in *Denver Post*, December 20, 1929. Including all CM&E assets, Mullen's net worth could be calculated as high as $25,000,000. *Denver Post*, August 14, 1929: 1.

2. Richard M. Huber, *The American Idea of Success* (New York: McGraw-Hill, 1971), 75–76; Irvin G. Wyllie, *The Self-Made Man in America* (New York: The Free Press, 1954), 88–89. Both Wyllie and Huber refer to the Calvinist precedents for considering the accumulation of wealth and notice the number of Protestant ministers who glorified self-help as a way to social enrichment. Wyllie, in attempting to explain why few Catholic priests published self-help books, notes that nineteenth-century urban Catholics had little chance of accumulating wealth and the cult of wealth contradicted "the church's traditional indictment of materialism" (p. 57). Undoubtedly, Mullen absorbed general ideas about the success cult from Protestant ministers of his acquaintance

but he also knew plenty of Catholic priests who could whisper specific wishes into his ear.

3. J. K. Mullen, Letter to Ella Mullen Weckbaugh, August 21, 1925, Weckbaugh family collection.

4. Samuel Lewis, *A Topographical Dictionary of Ireland*, vol. 1, 1837 (Reprint: London: Kennikat Press, 1970), 110.

5. Thomas J. Noel, *Colorado Catholicism and the Archdiocese of Denver, 1857–1989* (Niwot: University Press of Colorado, 1989), 106; Charles W. Hurd, "J. K. Mullen, Milling Magnate of Colorado," *The Colorado Magazine* XXIX:2 (April 1952): 115.

6. *Denver Post,* June 30, 1918: 15.

7. J. K. Mullen, Letter to Ella Mullen Weckbaugh, March 7, 1924, Weckbaugh family collection.

8. Mullen-Buchtel correspondence, December 3, 1917, to July 9, 1918, Weckbaugh family collection.

9. Hurd, 116.

10. J. K. Mullen, "Personal Ledger, 1900–1905," Mullen papers, Western History Dept., Denver Public Library (WHDDPL).

11. Ibid.

12. Thomas J. Noel, with Kevin E. Rucker and Stephen J. Leonard, *Colorado Givers: A History of Philanthropic Heroes* (Niwot: University Press of Colorado, 1998), 103; J. K. Mullen, "Personal Ledger, 1900–1905."

13 Noel, *Colorado Catholicism*, 39–40; Thomas Francis Feeley, "Leadership in the Early Colorado Catholic Church" (Ph.D. diss., University of Denver, 1973), 113.

14. J. K. Mullen, "Personal Ledger, 1900–1905"; *Denver Post*, December 30, 1929: 1.

15. J. K. Mullen, Letter to Rt. Rev. J. H. Tihen, August 22, 1928; Letter to Rt. Rev. N. C. Matz, April 2, 1915, both in Rt. Rev. J. H. Tihen papers, Archdiocese of Denver archives (hereafter referred to as Tihen papers).

16. J. K. Mullen, Letter to Rt. Rev. J. H. Tihen, April 24, 1929, Tihen papers.

17. W. S. Weckbaugh, personal interview, July 21, 1997.

18. J. K. Mullen, Letter to Rt. Rev. J. H. Tihen, 1922, Tihen papers.

19. Rt. Rev. J. H. Tihen, Telegram to J. K. Mullen, 1922, Tihen papers.

20. J. K. Mullen, Letters to Rt. Rev. J. H. Tihen, March 3, 1923; March 6, 1923; March 7, 1923; March 9, 1923, Tihen papers.

21. Rev. Bernard E. Naughten, Letter to Rev. Richard Brady, St. Mary's of the Assumption, Central City, February 28, 1913, Rt. Rev. Nicholas C. Matz manuscript collection, Archdiocese of Denver archives.

22. Rev. Matthew Smith, Letter to J. K. Mullen, May 1926, Tihen papers.

23. Richard McCloud, Letter to O. L. Malo, March 24, 1927, Mullen papers, WHDDPL.

24. J. K. Mullen, Letter to H. A. Buchtel, December 13, 1917, Weckbaugh family collection.

25. Rt. Rev. J. H. Tihen, Letter to John Forbes, January 23, 1923, Tihen papers.

26. R. McCloud, Letter to O. L. Malo, March 24, 1927; O. L. Malo, Letter to R. McCloud, March 28, 1927, Mullen papers, WHDDPL.
27. *Denver Post,* August 18, 1918: 5.
28. Paul Bernstein, *American Work Values: Their Origin and Development* (Albany: State University of New York, 1997), 248–250.
29. Hurd, 116. Neither Baby Doc, who died in 1936, nor Mullen ever benefited from the supposed treasures of the Matchless Mine. It remained a J. K. Mullen Investment Co. property until the family donated the surface rights to the Leadville Historical Society in the 1950s.
30. Edwin Lewis Levy, "Elitch's Gardens, Denver, Colorado: A History of the Oldest Summer Theatre in the United States" (Ph.D. diss., Columbia University, New York, 1960), 71.

10

THE COLORADO MILLING AND
ELEVATOR COMPANY, 1883–1886

DRY-LAND CASH FARMING WAS A CHANCY BUSINESS that was well characterized by historian Carl Abbott as "a serialized adventure in which the
same disaster occurred at the end of each episode."[1] Since the end of
the Civil War, high wheat prices had contributed to the expansion of
the frontier. Sodbusters who pushed west of the "water line" of the one
hundredth meridian into increasingly marginal land concentrated on
wheat production as "the most valuable and easily transported grain
product."[2] Despite attempts to persuade farmers to diversify, wheat
remained the monolith of western cash crops. This stubborn resistance
to diversification only intensified the suffering when depression and
drought caught up with the wheat industry in the 1880s. Farmers
hoping to cash in on the bonanza overproduced their crops and contributed to the decline of wheat prices. After briefly approaching $3
per bushel in 1877, the average national wholesale wheat price steadily
dropped.[3] By harvest time in 1884, Chicago prices fell so low that the
Rocky Mountain News reported, "Eighty cents for wheat has been talked
of as something which was a fanciful dream."[4]

If the average American farmer could still find a silver lining, it was
because the national price of wheat slumped gently. In Colorado, however, prices rose and fell at dizzying rates. The depressed mineral
economy and abundant supplies of Colorado wheat pushed the local
price 20 to 30 cents less per bushel than the national average of $2.20
in 1879. Grain prices rebounded during the Leadville and Aspen silver strikes. By 1880, Colorado grangers received from 75 cents to $1
more per bushel than the national average of $1.25.[5] Farmers enjoyed

higher-than-average local prices until production once again outpaced demand in 1882. Then, prices slipped dramatically. A sampling of wholesale wheat and flour quotations in the *Rocky Mountain News* shows that between 1882 and 1883, the average value of Colorado wheat dropped nearly 40 cents per bushel. The slide continued over the next five years until wheat had fallen from an 1882 high of $1.35 to about 77 cents in 1887.[6]

The devaluation chilled Colorado's farming community. Wheat, the *Colorado Farmer and Livestock Journal* reported, "has heretofore been the chief reliance from which to get money to buy our supplies, or to pay interest on debts, or purchase land or machinery."[7] As wheat prices slipped, farmers borrowed more, plunging into a spiral of over-production, deflation, and debt, the only remedy from which was still more overproduction.[8]

Colorado's thirty-four milling companies found that competition, reduced transportation costs, and the overabundance of wheat depressed flour prices as well. In 1874, Colorado flour was quoted at $4.38 per hundred pounds—only 80 percent of the average national price of $5.47.[9] As it had with the wheat market, the Leadville boom increased the local value of flour at a time when national prices plateaued. Similarly, flour dropped in value after the Leadville demand stabilized in 1882. In July, hundred-pound sacks of Colorado flour whole-saled at an average price of $3.47 or 75 percent of the national average of $4.60. One year later, the average price sagged to $2.55 or 65 per-cent of the national average of $3.95.[10] To overextended yeomen and millers alike, the uncertain situation of the early 1880s threatened economic ruin.

CONSOLIDATION OF COLORADO'S FLOURING MILLS

Colorado farmers helplessly watched the chance of redeeming their mortgages wither away with their crops in the arid summers of 1884 and 1885. The drought also weakened the economic prospects of Colorado's numerous small, financially unstable mills. Shackled by depressed flour prices, the scarcity of available wheat, and debts brought on by the rush to modernize, idle mills faced bankruptcy. Larger en-terprises, such as J. K. Mullen and Company, stood to benefit from an industry-wide shakeout. Mullen's business entered the recession on a solid foundation. In addition to the Excelsior, the Hungarian, two mill ditches, three elevators, and book accounts, the debt-free company owned a cash surplus of $90,000 in 1885.[11] The miller personally owed his company an additional $19,000—money borrowed to diversify into the booming cattle industry.[12] In all, his business appeared ready to weather an economic downturn.

Less stable mills prepared for the troubled economy by discussing consolidation. Colorado millers had previously experimented with the idea. In 1877, the milling industry organized a loose alliance called the Colorado Millers' Association and Millers' Mutual Protective Insurance Company (CMA). Meeting monthly at Denver's American Hotel, the CMA set regional milling policies, settled disputes among rival companies, and created a fund to offset fire and flood damages. The Colorado Grange and the proagrarian *Colorado Farmer and Livestock Journal* charged the CMA with a darker purpose. Critics charged that the so-called Wheat Ring conspired to fix grain prices to the advantage of local millers. Their fears were partially justified. The CMA collapsed in 1884, brought down by the stagnant economy and alleged corruption by unidentified members.[13]

Despite the demise of the CMA, the idea of combination continued to linger. Some millers continued to argue that consolidation was the only way to stave off economic disaster. As Mullen described the torpid situation soon after the formation of the Colorado Milling and Elevator Company:

> Many of the mills were about to be closed by the sheriff . . . The millers met and consulted with each other, and finally concluded that by bunching our property and working under one management we might be able to reduce expenses of manufacturing and . . . selling.[14]

From the businessmen's perspective, consolidation headed off chaotic competition in the marketplace, shored up weaker mills, and prevented potential panic. The option appealed to struggling owners looking to sell out but successful millers such as Mullen initially shied away from discussions about combination. The fiscally conservative businessman had entered the CMA reluctantly, believing his success as an independent operator would by compromised by association with his competitors. The advantages soon became apparent. Upon admittance to the CMA, his influence in the Wheat Ring increased. By 1881, J. K. served as an officer, influencing the purchasing and selling policies of his rivals.[15]

The farmers' fears of a flour mill trust were magnified by the formation of a new milling combination in late August 1885. Using the defunct Millers' Alliance as a springboard, several leading Front Range millers formed the Colorado Milling and Elevator Company (CM&E). The new conglomeration incorporated four of Denver's five largest mills. Charter members included major firms in Ft. Collins, Golden, and Greeley, as well as the two largest Longmont milling outfits.[16] Notably absent from the association were two prominent Ft. Collins companies, as well as the cooperative Farmers' Alliance Mill and landowner Benjamin F. Eaton's plant. On September 1, 1885, Mullen—"one of the last to consent to join" according to his longtime associate, Herbert E. Johnson—traded his mills to the CM&E in exchange for capital stock worth $75,000 on the Excelsior and $160,000 on the Hungarian. After some dickering, he split the stock with his brother Dennis on a three-to-one ratio. The founding members recognized the importance of their largest Denver partner by electing J. K. to the post of general manager. Whatever his initial qualms, "he went in wholeheartedly," in the words of a CM&E officer, to defend and promote the interests of the new flour trust.[17]

The company needed J. K.'s stability in order to survive. He later recalled, "The Colorado M. & E. Company didn't have a single dollar of working capital when they were organized."[18] The first company president, Bruce Johnson, invested less than promised. Some mill owners, distrusting the value of company stock, demanded cash payments for grain, horses, wagons, and even empty flour sacks. Without working capital, the fledgling company sold off $10,000 worth of stock in order to buy the Rock and Inter-Ocean mills outright. J. K. transferred $5,000 of his own stock to Charles R. Davis and Dickson & Webb as an inducement to join. The company found itself in immediate debt. Despite a loan by Mullen of his surplus $90,000 and loans from C. R. Davis and William Barth, the CM&E required additional loans from eastern financial houses. J. K. made the East Coast rounds, putting up personal property to secure loans from New York's Chemical Bank, the Traveler's Insurance Company in Hartford, and Fogg Brothers of Boston.[19]

Another challenge materialized closer to home. The consolidation of Colorado's milling industry may have appeared as an orderly transition from market chaos to the new CM&E shareholders but to

Colorado's embattled sodbusters the action threatened to undermine their already precarious autonomy as producers. Colorado's reform-minded agricultural institutions—the Grange, the Farmers' Alliance, and the *Colorado Farmer and Livestock Journal*—observed the formation of the CM&E with growing alarm.

AGRARIAN OPPOSITION

The rivalry between the sodbusters and milling companies transcended that of simple competitors. The dispute was grounded in control of a profitable cash commodity, in differing business and political ideologies, in rural versus urban orientation, and in the tensions of the Industrial Revolution. Farmers channeled their political outrage into the Colorado Grange Association and the Farmers' Alliance. Founded in 1867 by Oliver Hudson Kelley of the U.S. Department of Agriculture, the National Grange of the Patrons of Husbandry focused agrarian political and social discontent into the potent Populist movement. Through cooperation in business as well as politics, grangers successfully regulated railroad and milling monopolies in the West, South,

Stock certificate for the Colorado Milling and Elevator Company. Mullen's contribution of $325,000 worth of assets placed him in a dominant position regarding the future of the company. Courtesy, Timothy O'Connor collection.

and Midwest and raised the Department of Agriculture to a cabinet-level position. The Colorado Farmers' Alliance represented Colorado's most radical agricultural activists.[20]

The contrast between the flour manufacturer's preoccupation with industrialization and increasing agrarian discontent underscored the rift. At the same time that progressive flour barons read articles in the *Northwestern Miller* praising the modern, urban miller, Colorado grangers consumed articles criticizing milling industrialization. The main organ of Colorado agricultural discontent was John S. Stanger's *Colorado Farmer and Livestock Journal.* Stanger's editorials elevated rustic, rural yeomen over urban milling capitalists. The *Colorado Farmer* opined variations of this uniform theme: Automation, specialization, and industrialization all stole money away from the farmer. Faceless urban milling corporations undermined the yeoman ideal of freeholding, self-sufficient farmers. Industrialization introduced new methods to cheat grangers out of their hard-earned produce. The *Colorado Farmer* condemned the "vicious practice" of allowing millers to clean and grade the farmer's produce. Yeomen had no way to know when wheat was rejected or stolen outright when "the complicated machinery of a flour mill is beyond the ken of a quiet, simple farmer . . . There are too many temptations in the way to induce a little of the good wheat to stray into unknown paths or spouts."[21] "Clean your wheat at home," Stanger advised. "Never let a pound of it go through the millers' screens until it is theirs. If you do, you are served perfectly right if they rob you."[22]

Farmers shared the blame for the depressed agricultural economy; their decision to expand large-scale wheat production contributed to the overall drop in wheat prices. Nevertheless, reformers insisted that control of the hinterlands and the rights to the profits of labor were the issues at the heart of their struggle. Reformers argued that the prosperity of "the quiet, simple farmer" of yeoman ideology was smothered by incomprehensible systems of storage, transportation, capital, credit, and speculation.[23] Futures trading in distant commodity markets in Chicago, Omaha, Kansas City, and St. Louis largely determined the market value of both wheat and flour. Armed with capital, credit, favorable railroad rates, and the capacity to store their grain for future sale, city-oriented millers regularly played the markets with the crops they purchased from the farmer. Speculation was not even honest labor, Stanger complained. Unlike the producer, the urban miller "can afford to borrow money to carry wheat . . . Until somebody [else] builds elevators, farmers must expect millers to buy their wheat for speculation, as well as for legitimate milling."[24]

Worse, milling entrepreneurs manipulated transportation systems to exclude local husbandmen from the "legitimate milling" market altogether. Middlemen took advantage of regional price variations and inexpensive shipping rates to import cheap grain from Idaho, Utah, Kansas, and the Dakotas to the exclusion of Colorado farmers. Sodbusters, on the other hand, often could not afford the freight rates to sell to anyone but local dealers. Most sold their crop directly from harvest at the one time of the year when heavy supply forced local wheat prices down. Without expensive elevators or silos to store wheat until the price rebounded or the capital to ship their produce to competing dealers, farmers felt like shabby country cousins exploited by the milling industry.[25]

Unsurprisingly, the Farmers' Alliance and the *Colorado Farmer* took a dim view of milling consolidation. The milling pool, the *Farmer* charged, had always worked to hold the price of wheat down. Now they planned to establish a monopoly in order to drive flour prices back up. As if to confirm the Farmers' Alliance's worst fears, the price of flour immediately regained stability upon formation of the CM&E, while wheat continued to sink. Between July 1885 and July 1886, the average local price of wheat dropped from $1.38 per bushel to $1.23. During the same period, flour rose on average from $1.68 to $2.43.

The Farmers' Alliance angrily denounced the infant milling company. One alliance representative called Mullen, the general manager and chief spokesman of the CM&E, the "Jay Gould of the Colorado milling industry."[26] The farming cooperative announced a plan to expand its own mill into a network of mills and elevators in direct competition. Likewise, future Colorado governor Benjamin F. Eaton, hoping to take advantage of his rival's shaky public image, offered to buy wheat at higher prices than the CM&E was willing to pay.

Mullen addressed his critics bluntly at a Farmers' Alliance meeting in Fort Collins on January 2, 1886. "I am not present to apologize," he told an inhospitable audience:

> I now speak as Manager of the Colorado Milling and Elevator Company. We did not organize for the benefit of the farmers; but to benefit ourselves by protecting our own interests first, and next the interests of the farming

community . . . When we organized, the milling interests were in a very deplorable condition . . . and the milling business was in a much worse condition than the farmers could have possibly been. Milling property was standing idle two-thirds of the time . . . By bunching our property and working under one management we might be able to reduce expenses of manufacturing, and the expenses of selling . . . Besides this, we could obtain better railroad rates and better facilities for transportation. As a result of these many advantages we would be able to pay better prices for wheat to farmers than they have been receiving, and thereby induce them to raise wheat in greater quantities.[27]

Mullen explained to his audience that without cooperation from the Farmers' Alliance and organized labor "we do not expect to succeed, nor will we try." If they preferred, "we can easily . . . return to the old order of things, as they existed prior to the organization of this company." But he drew a grim picture of idle mills, depression, unemployment, and western yeomen at the mercy of big eastern firms and railroads as the result.

Mullen attempted to refocus the granger's contempt onto the railroads as a common enemy. Grain from the Far West passed through Colorado every day in route to eastern mills. If the Farmers' Alliance aligned with the CM&E, perhaps they could mutually pressure the railroads to require milling in transit, the practice of diverting western grain from lines between northern Colorado and the Missouri River to Denver for grinding at a rate of twenty-five cents per hundred pounds.[28] The resulting increase in volume would lower the unit cost of production and allow farmers to transport their grain at the same long-haul rate as the Far West. In turn, Mullen assured his audience, the CM&E would pass the savings on to the agricultural community. He concluded:

This is the way we must work together for mutual benefit, and if we can make this point I have every reason to believe that the unfortunate differences that have arisen will be overcome, and . . . you will realize that we are not as black as we have been painted . . . We ask this favor from you and hope you will give us a fair trial.[29]

The miller's candid talk backfired. Many farmers considered his speech patronizing, his offer self-serving, and his promises unconvincing. His assurance that "we have not . . . lowered the price of wheat or advanced the price of flour" contradicted recently published commodity rates. Although the central committee of the Farmers' Alliance jointly endorsed a petition requesting the Denver Chamber of Commerce to look into milling in transit, both Mullen and the CM&E underwent intense criticism from the more radical agrarian elements.[30]

Alliance spokesman H. Shull angrily responded to Mullen's speech. On January 28, he wrote the *Colorado Farmer*, "It has been the object and purpose of J. K. Mullen to secure complete control of the wheat and flour market of our state" since he built the Hungarian in 1883:

> To accomplish this purpose he has not hesitated to intimidate and bulldoze the weaker mills of the state by overbidding on wheat, and underselling on flour . . . [He] allays the fears, and blinds the farmers as to the real motives of his pool by fair promises and soft speeches, lest their wheat and patronage go to anti-alliance mills.

How, asked Shull, would "inducing" grangers to increase the supply of wheat help raise the selling price? How could rich urban millers be in "much worse condition" than the long-suffering farmers? Shull suggested:

> Now let Mr. Mullen buy 100 acres of land, buy his ditch stock, make the necessary improvements, and I will not insist upon the residence being as fine as the millers live in, hire his labor as cheap as he can get it, and sell his wheat . . . and compare the dividend with that of the milling business, and then tell us farmers which pays the best.

Shull dismissed Mullen's denial of conspiracy to control the market, his assurances of fair competition, and his pledge to cooperate with the Farmers' Alliance. "Mullen says when he goes fishing he tries to catch just as many as anyone else. Yes, and when he goes to talk to farmers, he baits his hook for suckers."[31]

Although he initially believed he was better off without the CM&E, J. K. showcased his organizational abilities in his rapid coordination of the member mills. At the same time, he bolstered the mistrust of a large part of his clientele with insincere assurances. In his defense, CM&E officer Herbert E. Johnson insisted that Mullen took the sodbuster's interest to heart when he joined the combination: "He once told me that one reason that he joined was that under the old system of senseless competition the Colorado farmers receive[ed] many times less for their wheat than they were entitled to receive."[32] Johnson further remembered that Mullen's first act as general manager was to raise the buying price of wheat nine cents above market values. J. K. appears to have deflected most of the criticism of this controversial issue from himself. He could easily have avoided further trouble by increasing his short-term buying price to compete with the nearby Eaton and Farmers' Alliance mills. His insistence, echoed by Johnson, that the elimination of "irresponsible" and "intolerable 'dog eat dog'" competition improved the farmers' negotiating position contradicted their perception of market economics. Mullen's assurances, along with the steady decline of wheat prices, created a long-burning antipathy among the wheat-growing community.[33]

Although the long-term recovery of the milling industry fulfilled Mullen's prediction that "by . . . working under one management we might be able to reduce expenses of manufacturing, and . . . selling [and] obtain better railroad rates and better facilities for transportation" the initial negative reaction instilled in the capitalist a desire to avoid repeating his early mistakes. J. K. instituted several measures designed to reestablish trust in his company. In order to provide a sense of local ownership, subsidiary mills acquired or opened by the CM&E were named for the community (e.g., La Junta Milling and Elevator Company, Alamosa Milling and Elevator Company). Local managers and key employees received stock in their own firms in order to create loyalty, proprietary interest, and local autonomy.[34] "We give to the Local Manager what might be considered full authority," Mullen boasted. Local managers were responsible for personnel, purchasing, and salary decisions. The general office set parameters for wheat buying and flour selling but expected local managers to use their heads regarding the local financial climate.[35]

Mullen also instituted a number of liberal policies designed to counteract the ill-will of farming communities. He reminded his managers that "farmers are . . . the hardest-working people and the poorest paid of any class in America."[36] He required employees to be courteous, accommodating, and scrupulously honest: "Any little thing that you can do to impress on the mind of the farming community the fact that you propose to pay them for every ounce that they deliver will be helpful." Anyone who short-weighted a sodbuster's load risked immediate termination, with the burden of innocence resting upon the accused. He ordered all CM&E managers to post comparative wheat quotations for their mill and local competitors prominently near the weigh scale. Moreover, managers were required to abrogate outstanding bills of less than $50 and instructed to provide their clients with low-interest loans during bad economic times. "You must always give the other party the benefit of the doubt," Mullen advised. "We prefer to suffer a financial loss at any time rather than have the name of being brought into the Courts."

Some lessons Mullen never learned. He never understood the reasons behind the revolt against milling consolidation, insisting that the new corporation would benefit the farmers by bringing order to the chaotic system. His effort to mollify the grangers stemmed in part from his perception of them as an honest, hard-working, but essentially suspicious lower class. In his estimation, he owed his clients fair treatment as any member of the elite owed consideration to the less fortunate. He advised, "You must assist [the farmers] if you expect them to assist you. That is the White Man's burden." This phrase, evocative of colonialism and patronage, was not likely to place him in high esteem with proud western yeomen who desired corporate charity even less than they wanted corporate domination of their livelihood.

Colorado's grangers never built up enough support to legally shackle the local milling industry. Instead, they used the formidable power of patronage as an outlet for their discontent. The Farmers' Alliance mill in Fort Collins, foundering at the time of the CM&E's inception, remained profitable for another thirty-five years. A second agrarian co-op, the Farmer's Milling and Elevator Company, opened in Longmont in 1886. Mullen grudgingly called this rival mill "one of the best—if not the best in northern Colorado" and gnashed his teeth when in 1906 the co-op built a concrete elevator in the CM&E's stronghold along the Twentieth Street viaduct in Denver.[37] A third Grange mill, the Farmer's Union (1915), "made very hard competition" as well, until agricultural recession in the early 1920s forced all three into CM&E hands. Among certain bitter farmers, Mullen's reputation as the "Jay Gould of Colorado milling" simmered until long after the First World War.

While J. K. avoided what, to him, would have been the most restrictive effects of Grange wrath, the mistrust that the CM&E engendered at its birth mirrored milling developments in other parts of North America. Mullen's public pronouncements of altruism largely succeeded in countering public criticism of his sharper practices but the CM&E was far from alone among flour companies who were criticized for their aggressive tactics. In other midwestern and southern

Mullen's critics wasted no time constructing rival milling companies. J. K. called the cooperative Longmont Farmer's Mill, established in 1886 and bought out by the CM&E in 1924, "the best in northern Colorado." Its Denver subsidiary, remodeled as the Flour Mill Lofts, remains as the only surviving downtown flour mill. Courtesy, Western History Dept., Denver Public Library.

states, Grange-dominated legislatures passed laws that set railroad rates, protected local farm products, and determined prices at the mill.[38] At the same time that the CM&E came under fire in Colorado, Canada's Ogilvie Milling Company was questioned for manipulating rebate rates with the Canadian Pacific Railroad, exploiting grading and cleaning processes, engineering regional wheat prices, and participating in grain speculation. As in Colorado, farmers responded by building rival co-ops and elevators.[39] What appeared to be orderly business to Mullen and his associates would ever be recognized as greed and exploitation by their clients.

NOTES

1. Carl Abbott, Stephen J. Leonard, and David McComb, *Colorado: A History of the Centennial State*, 3d ed. (Niwot: University Press of Colorado, 1994), 173.
2. Ibid.
3. C. Knick Harley, "Western Settlement and the Price of Wheat, 1872–1913," *Journal of Economic History* 38:4 (December 1978): 878; Franklin M. Fisher and Peter Temin, "Regional Specialization and the Supply of Wheat in the United States, 1867–1914," *Review of Economics and Statistics* 52:2 (1970): 143.

4. "The Fall in Wheat," *Rocky Mountain News* (*RMN*), August 12, 1884: 7.

5. *RMN*, July 10, 1879; January 1, 1880; April 21, 1880; June 1, 1880; *Colorado Farmer and Livestock Journal*, August 9, 1880; U.S. Dept. of Commerce, Bureau of the Census, "Prices and Price Indexes," *Historical Statistics of the United States, Colonial Times to 1970*, vol. 1 (Washington, D.C.: GPO, 1976), 208.

6. Prices taken from published commodities listings, *RMN*, September 3, 1874; October 1, 1875; July 15, 1876; January 16, 1877; July 15, 1878; July 10, 1879; August 9, 1880; September 8, 1881; July 27, 1882; July 3, 1883; July 16, 1884; July 11, 1885; July 16, 1886; July 16, 1887; July 17, 1888; July 8, 1889; July 12, 1890; July 11, 1893.

7. "Prices and Prospects," *Colorado Farmer and Livestock Journal*, August 11, 1879: 4.

8. Sean Dennis Cashman, *America in the Gilded Age*, 3d ed. (New York: New York University Press, 1993), 291–292.

9. *RMN*, September 3, 1874; U.S. Dept. of Commerce, *Historical Statistics*, 208.

10. *RMN*, July 27, 1882; July 3, 1883; Harley, 873.

11. Or, about ten times what he was worth when he formed Mullen and Seth in 1875. J. K. Mullen, Letter to Maurice C. Dolan, April 19, 1927, Mullen papers, Colorado Historical Society (CHS).

12. J. K. Mullen, "Statement of the Individual Business of J. K. Mullen," May 25, 1902, Mullen manuscript collection, MSS 705, CHS.

13. H. E. Johnson, Letter to Guy Thomas, June 10, 1943, Herbert E. Johnson manuscript collection.

14. "What the Millers Say," *Colorado Farmer and Livestock Journal*, January 7, 1886: 1.

15. *RMN*, January 21, 1881: 5.

16. *RMN*, August 29, 1885: 8.

17. H. E. Johnson, Letter to Guy Thomas, June 10, 1943.

18. J. K. Mullen, Letter to Maurice C. Dolan, April 19, 1927, Mullen manuscript collection, MSS 705, CHS.

19. Ibid. In a 1916 letter to Rev. Raymond Mullen, Mullen claimed the $5,000 worth of stock certificates went to Ben Hottel. It was more likely that the stocks went to Davis, Denio, and Webb because Hottel was an early supporter of consolidation, whereas Davis joined much later. Mullen manuscript collection, MSS 705, CHS.

20. Cashman, 316–317.

21. "Marketing Wheat," *Colorado Farmer and Livestock Journal*, August 21, 1879: 4.

22. "Selling Wheat," *Colorado Farmer and Livestock Journal*, September 4, 1879: 4.

23. Fisher and Temin, 143; Robert H. Wiebe, *The Search for Order, 1877–1920* (New York: Hill and Wang, 1967), 17.

24. *Colorado Farmer and Livestock Journal*, August 21, 1879: 4.

25. Cashman, 316; *Colorado Farmer and Livestock Journal*, September 4, 1879: 4; March 10, 1881: 4. According to Stanger, consumers also suffered from the greed of flour millers. The *Colorado Farmer* charged that Colorado millers mixed

inferior cheap Kansas wheat with superior Colorado varieties to "fraud and cheat" customers with "adulterated food," thereby "deceiving the buyer" and degrading the reputation of Colorado grain. At heart a booster, Stanger admitted that he preferred that millers keep their mills running on out-of-state grain than see them standing idle: "We would rather they should keep at work, and make the flour here rather than bring it from eastern mills."

26. "Farmers vs. Millers," *Colorado Farmer and Livestock Journal*, January 28, 1886: 1; Jay Gould was a ruthless New York financier who was notorious for his attempt to corner the gold market and monopolize railroads.

27. "What the Millers Say," 1.

28. "The Farmers and Millers," *Colorado Farmer and Livestock Journal*, January 14, 1886: 4.

29. "What the Millers Say," 1.

30. "The Farmers and Millers," 4. Their joint effort succeeded. By March, the railroad "pool" agreed "to allow each road to do as it pleas[ed] in the matter . . . the mills of Denver will have all the work they can do." *RMN*, March 14, 1886: 2.

31. "Farmers vs. Millers," 1.

32. H. E. Johnson, Letter to Guy Thomas, June 10, 1943.

33. Ibid.

34. J. K. Mullen, Letter to the stockholders of the Colorado Milling and Elevator Company, March 9, 1917, Weckbaugh family collection. In order to eliminate repetitive management bureaucracy as well as reduce liability, the company liquidated all CM&E subsidiaries and took over direct control of their operations in March 1917.

35. J. K. Mullen, Letter to Maurice C. Dolan, April 19, 1927, Mullen papers, CHS.

36. This and subsequent references to Mullen's company policies cited in J. K. Mullen, Letter to W. S. Bunt, mgr., Claflin Flour Mills, Claflin, Kansas, February 12, 1924, Weckbaugh family collection.

37. J. K. Mullen, Letter to Rt. Rev. J. H. Tihen, March 13, 1925. Rt. Rev. John Henry Tihen manuscript collection, Archdiocese of Denver archives. The Farmer's M&E (known to many old-time residents as the Pride of Denver), the last surviving downtown elevator, received new life as the luxury Flour Mill Lofts in 1999.

38. Wiebe, 8.

39. John Everitt, "The Early Development of the Flour Milling Industry on the Prairies," *Journal of Historical Geography* 19:3 (1993): 284.

11

DEALER OF GRAIN AND CATTLE, 1886–1895

FEW STORIES REINFORCE J. K. MULLEN'S REPUTATION FOR RESOURCEFULNESS in the face of commercial adversity like the legend of his quick action during the bank panic of 1893. On July 18, remembered by J. K. as the "black panic day," the capitalist observed "a long line of people" waiting to get into the First National Bank of Denver. C. W. Hurd related his version of events:

> A run was being made on the First National. It happened that [Mullen] had a considerable amount of money on hand for deposit. He hastily put it into two bags and took one of them and went downstairs. When some of the frightened ones saw him depositing his money they lost their fears and dropped out of line. He took down the other sack a few hours later and repeated the operation. It has been said that he saved the First National Bank of Denver that day.[1]

The story is probably apocryphal, or at least exaggerated—First National Bank historian Robert Pulcipher credits deep reserves of cash for helping keep the institution afloat during the disastrous summer of '93. While First National president David Moffat and the editors at the *Rocky Mountain News* praised commercial customers such as Mullen for keeping their heads during the panic, no contemporary account describes the flour miller's dramatic personal action.[2] The orderly line of patrons waiting to run the First National belies J. K.'s own recollection of the panic-driven mobs that collapsed twelve Colorado banks in mid-July. Furthermore, a review of Mullen's personal correspondence regarding the First National (where he assumed a director's chair in 1917) reveals a more conservative response. Similar stories circulated

113

about First National president David Moffat, City National president William Barth, Horace Tabor, and other Denver tycoons.[3] Nevertheless, the level-headedness and character that J. K. Mullen exercised in the tale were traits with which he most wished to be associated.

The economic crisis leading up to and during the panic of 1893 placed a severe fiscal strain on Mullen, as it did on many Colorado businessmen. The decade following the consolidation of the Colorado Milling and Elevator Company were difficult ones personally and financially. Far from solving the problems of competition, the CM&E struggled to move away from the mistrustful circumstances of its foundation. Mullen stretched his personal credit, already strained by the collapse of the Colorado cattle industry and aggressive acquisition of CM&E stock, to its utmost limit during the panic. The stress of his workload, increased travel, a financial quarrel with his brother Dennis, as well as the death of his youngest daughter began to tell both in his growing weariness and on the health of his wife, Kate. Finally, strife both within his own parish and in the growing tide of Protestant nativism forced Mullen to take a visible leadership role to bolster and protect Denver's Catholic community.

PERSONAL AND PROFESSIONAL DIFFICULTIES

Although the late 1880s were relatively prosperous times for Colorado agriculture, the Colorado Milling and Elevator Company continued to struggle financially. As grangers gained political momentum with the surging Populist Party, they were slow to resume trade with the new milling trust. Corporate expenses such as payroll, interest, and fixed dividends generated losses of more than $336,000 between the CM&E's first abbreviated fiscal year and the summer of 1889.[4] The losses scared away investors and required the company to make significant cutbacks.

By 1889, the CM&E owned nine mills, eight elevators, and eight warehouses in seven towns. Its combined grinding capacity was 5,800 sacks of flour per day. The firm could store more than 375,000 pounds of bran, 840,000 bushels of wheat, and 70,000 sacks of flour. Additionally, the long reach of the CM&E permitted Mullen to institute a simple policy of production and speculation for long-run success:

> Borrow money in the fall of the year, buy up wheat, put it into the elevators ... as near as possible to where it was grown, and hold it so that we always [have] our flour to sell and always get the benefit of the carrying charge.[5]

Even with this frugal policy, Mullen was forced to economize. The CM&E owed its investors regular fixed dividends that did not live up to the poor wheat market of the late 1880s. J. K. offered to liquidate his least-profitable mills to generate short-term revenue.[6] The CM&E also cut back on its labor force. Although in 1890 the $1.9 million worth of flour produced by Denver's mills still led all manufactures except smelting, the CM&E's 101 employees ranked just tenth.[7]

The early struggles of the CM&E benefited Mullen in at least one respect. Discouraged stockholders wishing to unload their shares found a ready buyer in the entrepreneur. The capitalist leveraged his personal assets heavily to purchase any CM&E stock that became available, usually below the $100 par value.[8] At the same time, Mullen asserted himself as the leader of the new company. He succeeded Bruce Johnson as company president in 1886, in part by stepping down as manager of the Hungarian Mills, appointing his brother Dennis to that post, and bolstering Dennis with a gift of five hundred shares of CM&E stock so that he would qualify for the electing board of directors.[9]

Elected with D. W.'s support, Mullen strove continuously for the next forty years to make his "child" the leading flour corporation in the West. J. K.'s fondness for that paternalistic term indicates that his interest was more than proprietary. He relied on the CM&E to guarantee a future for himself and his family. Like a proud but worried parent, he nurtured the company's interests and risked his personal assets to ensure its success. "No other Director or Manager endorsed a note of the Company but myself," he later declared. "Three different times every dollar's worth of property that I owned was endorsed over to our creditors." He also quietly covered his bets by secretly signing his house and other properties over to his wife in 1889 in order to protect his family in case he failed.[10]

The personal commitment drove Mullen to work harder than ever. He traveled extensively, writing back to his wife from such accommodations as the "abominable, but . . . cheap" Midland Hotel in Hutchison, Kansas. He journeyed to New York and Boston in search of capital; to the South on sales trips; to the Midwest to purchase equipment and gain technical expertise; to slop-filled Omaha stockyards to sell cattle and feed; to western farm towns to "wear down" wheat sellers in order to "buy as cheap as I can."[11] The lonely trips taxed his stamina. On a September 1886 machinery-purchasing swing through Springfield, Dayton, Cincinnati, Indianapolis, and Milwaukee, he wrote back to Kate, "I am tired of this life . . . I have not seen a paper from Denver or a person that I knew since I left but the only relief has been your . . . telegrams."[12]

Mullen battled loneliness on the road but, unlike many contemporaries, avoided the suggestion of impropriety. On an 1892 trip to Wisconsin he sampled a local St. Patrick's Day church service, writing home in an affected brogue: "'Twas pretty tough but 'twas a penance in a good cause and as it was St. Patrick's night I stuck it out."[13] After one particularly frustrating Christmas Eve spent hunting down carloads of grain in Fort Worth, Texas, the hungry, exhausted businessman wrote his wife, "It is the first Christmas I ever was away and I hope it will be the last."[14]

All the while, he expanded both his base of production and his markets. His financial situation eased significantly after 1890, when wholesalers in Texas, Georgia, Alabama, and Tennessee signed contracts for carloads of Colorado flour.[15] To help supply the southeastern market, Mullen opened new mills in southern Colorado. The Alamosa Mill (1890) in the San Luis Valley and the Lamar Mill (1892) along the Arkansas River were organized to take advantage of farmlands recently opened up by irrigation and agricultural rail centers.[16] At the Alamosa Mill, a shortage of trained laborers temporarily forced the visiting president to pitch in as a mill hand. He gleefully wrote back to his wife: "I have bought a pair of old overalls and am working my old trade again but don't know what they will pay me yet."[17]

Another distraction began during the late 1880s when Kate began to suffer from an unidentified chronic malady. Mullen and his wife shared a reticence regarding the exact nature of the illness. It was never specifically identified in their correspondence and seemed to defy diagnosis. For some years previously, Kate had quietly suffered from chronic pain. By 1886, waves of dizziness and weakness forced her into bed for extended periods. She repeatedly suffered from fits, endured "bad spells," slowly improved, and fell into sickness again. Following the death of her youngest daughter, Anne, in 1888, Kate deteriorated further. Visits to specialists and pharmacists and sojourns to health resorts in New York, New Jersey, and Manitou Springs appeared to have no effect.[18]

Kate's illness confounded J. K.'s desire to conquer all obstacles to his family's well-being. He constantly chided his wife to "rest and quit running around." In New York City, on a mission to secure elusive capital in the depression year of 1893, Mullen still found time to meet with a crosstown specialist who claimed to have a helpful tonic.[19] When the meeting failed to produce positive results, Mullen acknowledged the defeat of his will power: "I will see the doctor on my return & I will do all I can Kate & that is not much—I wish I could do more."[20] Despite the services of a resident doctor, spas, and familial solicitude, Mrs. Mullen suffered from bouts of her disease for the rest of her life.

CATTLE COMPANIES

Family concerns occupied Mullen's attention in other ways, particularly regarding the division of J. K. Mullen and Company assets with his brother Dennis. In July 1886, Mullen dissolved J. K. Mullen and Company. He split the assets of both the milling firm and his four South Platte River cattle companies with Dennis on a three-to-one ratio.[21] J. K. assumed several unpaid debts left over by the dissolution, including $900 entrusted to his care by the St. Joseph's Total Abstinence Society and about $1,800 due to the four cattle companies— the Weld County Land and Cattle Company, the Harmony Land and Cattle Company, the Riverside Stock and Ranching Company, and the Redstone and Buckhorn Land and Stock Company. Taking advantage of the booming cattle trade of the 1880s, Mullen and his brother had invested profitably with Denver contractor Charles D. McPhee in 1884. The investment provided a double boon in the form of exclusive feed contracts for the Hungarian and Excelsior Mills.[22]

The partition of the J. K. Mullen and Co. assets inaugurated a thirty-year spat between the brothers. J. K. assumed most of the responsibility for dividing the assets because, as he accused Dennis, "you never contributed one dollar or [did] a moment's work towards organizing them or attended a meeting, if you cared to." D. W., on the other hand, complained about this highhanded treatment, claiming that his older brother took over his shares without notification.[23]

As it did for investors around the world, Mullen's venture into the cattle business turned sour in the late 1880s. Weakened by a winter of severe snow and subzero temperatures, the entire Riverside herd perished in a February 1887 blizzard. J. K. stood good for both brothers' share of the loss to the amount of about $10,000. The action created additional tension. J. K. claimed he acted to protect his brother from the loss, while Dennis accused his brother of paying the entire expense in order to cut the younger sibling out of his rightful share of later profits. The series of disasters prolonged their fiscal troubles. The blizzard scared away some of their largest investors, leaving J. K. Mullen and C. D. McPhee in sole control of an empty ranch. Texas fever decimated the replacement herd. A cattle thief stole most of the survivors.[24]

Later, Mullen could afford to feel nostalgic about the difficulties involved in running cattle. In 1925, he and McPhee's son, William, redeemed a $500 debt for the Catholic church in Crook, Colorado—former headquarters of the Mullen-McPhee cattle companies. The philanthropist donated his share "in memory of the trials and difficulties that the Harmony Land & Cattle Company and Charlie and myself underwent."[25]

"THE BLACK PANIC" OF 1893

Mullen's trials on the cattle ranges paled in comparison to the disastrous events that threatened to bring down his empire in 1893. A depression sparked by a national bank panic hit Colorado particularly hard. The collapse of silver prices shattered the brittle edifice of overspeculation and undercapitalization that supported the state's farms, ranches, mines, and railroads. Within a year, hard-gained fortunes evaporated and thousands of unemployed workers left the state for brighter prospects elsewhere.

The panic hit Denver soon after Mullen returned from an unsuccessful attempt to secure a flour contract with the Bureau of Indian Affairs. He was unfamiliar with the intricacies of Washington deal making and vaguely uncomfortable with the glad-handing and under-the-table arrangements that accompanied the procurement of government contracts. Moreover, his side trip to his creditors in Boston, Hartford, and New York resulted in exhausting negotiations. "Times are not as good & money is tight & work scarcer," he wrote his wife.[26]

Conditions worsened on "the black panic day" of July 18, 1893, when mobs of depositors rushed the downtown Denver banks.[27] Far from racing out to stave off panic, Mullen watched the stampede from his third-floor office in the Tabor Block on Sixteenth and Larimer Streets. "The streets were jammed full of people," he recalled. "There was a run on every Bank in town. All kinds of business was [*sic*] at a standstill."[28]

Therefore, Mullen gaped when the young clothing-store clerk and future clothing baron George Cottrell entered to ask for a loan in order to cover a bid on a foreclosed clothier. "Why George, look out the window," J. K. exclaimed. "Don't you see there is a run on every bank in town? If I had money in the Bank today I wouldn't draw a check; I wouldn't dare take it out." Cottrell's audacity surprised the business-man, but the fact that the opportunistic young clothier banked on Mullen's support pleased the older capitalist to no end. Besides, J. K. considered his young protégé a worthy risk. A regular visitor at the Mullen household, Cottrell and his wife were whist partners and inti-mates in the private circle of Mullen friends and family. According to the financier, the clothier looked so glum that he relented. J. K. pur-chased the store from William D. Fisher in exchange for a promissory note at 10 percent. Mullen turned over the bill of sale to Cottrell in exchange for a note of his own. George established the Cottrell Cloth-ing Company, a major Denver menswear store into the mid-1990s. Leaving the clothier "as happy as a lark, I began to laugh about it," J. K. remembered.

Laughter was scarce in that panic year. On a trip to Eaton a few weeks later, J. K., who now advertised himself as a "dealer of land, grain, and cattle," discovered that the depression crippled all three. Debtors were unable to redeem their mortgages and he reported that "the mills are turning out badly this year."[29] His glum words, written on August 11, 1893, turned out to be prophetic. Three days later, at just before 1 A.M., a cinder from a passing train sparked a devastating fire on a loading platform at the Crescent Mill in Denver.

No menace disturbed the dreams of flour millers more than fire. Mill hands worked in an explosive haze of combustible flour dust, which coated their clothing and turned them into livid-eyed ghosts. Fueled by dust and dry timbers, the flames quickly skipped the Crescent's fire breaks, ignited the upper stories, and drove the night shift from the building. "The boys had all they could do to get out," Mullen reported the next day.[30] The fire department arrived, and, together with the mill crew, helplessly watched the Crescent burn

Sharp competition from the Crescent Flour Mills, located on Twentieth Street near the Union Pacific roundhouse, nearly sank J. K. Mullen during the 1870s. J. K. acquired the rival plant with the merger of the CM&E, but was nearly ruined again when the mill caught fire in 1893. Courtesy, Western History Dept., Denver Public Library.

"like a forced furnace."[31] The Silver Plume *Silver Standard* described the violent inferno:

> Seething flames were fanned from every side and the inside of the building was one great square mass of red flame . . . The heavy machinery fell with a loud report every few seconds as the floors gave way and metal was twisted from position. The walls began to rock to and fro from the great heat.

Unable to withstand the furious conflagration, one section of the wall collapsed, fracturing the skull of one fireman and slightly injuring another.

Only partially insured, the Crescent was completely destroyed. Mullen rushed back to Denver. He notified Kate, who had gone east to seek treatment for her illness. She was suffering through a very bad spell. Nevertheless, she worried about the accumulating expenses of her treatment. J. K. pooh-poohed her concern: "We will get through that all if we don't burn up some more mills." Still, "our loss is very heavy & it will be a big joke to settle with the Insurance Agency."[32] He complained of insomnia.

Fresh from the Crescent disaster, Mullen began an inspection tour of his mills. Each stop added to his despair. He gloomily wrote his wife from Fort Collins:

> We are not surprised the Longmont Elevator lost us $9,800 this year. Berthoud Elevator lost $4,300 & Loveland Elevator, $3,500 . . . So far our loss is over $30,000 this year. This added to our fire loss & the silver vote has gone against us too . . . P. S. Write oftener.[33]

By September, Mullen, known for his generosity to those in need, felt pinched. He vetoed Kate's suggestion that they provide foster care for an unnamed child of a down-and-out friend. Instead, he resolved to pay for the child's board until better times returned, explaining, "Everything is dead here yet & things don't look hopeful."[34] He also put the best face on adversity, encouraging Kate not to "scrimp" on herself or the children. "Get them everything they should have & let them run around all they want & don't you walk but get a carriage to take you around."[35] But he also swallowed his pride and took a $5,000 mortgage on the house at Ninth Street. The move was doubly humbling. In asking Kate to sign off on the note, J. K. acknowledged that she had unknowingly owned the house since 1889. She signed, but the revelation of his secret dependency made Mullen feel especially low.[36]

Two factors buoyed Mullen and the CM&E through this dark period. One was the productivity of the Alamosa Mill in the San Luis Valley. Defying the slump, the profitable mill provided capital for local expansion and kept the general CM&E fund from dropping too deeply into the red.[37] The second factor was Mullen's good credit. Ever since he had retired his debt on the Excelsior in 1880, he had struggled to maintain a pristine reputation for solvency. Initiative, C. W. Hurd explained, contributed to his "almost unlimited credit."[38] J. K. agreed, even if it required mortgaging his and his family's personal property "up to the neck."[39] His colleagues on the Chamber of Commerce, his banker David Moffat, and his East Coast mortgage companies did not wish to receive the black eye of a statewide industrial shutdown.[40] Instead, they preferred to extend his terms into the profitable long run. While other capitalists such as mining tycoon Horace Tabor, real estate baron Henry Brown, and railroad magnate John Evans

During the economic turmoil of the 1890s, the Colorado Milling and Elevator Company floated to prosperity on a smoky black cloud emanating from the Alamosa Mills. The visiting president of the CM&E found the plant short-handed during the harvest of 1890. He filled in, donning a pair of old overalls and helping out with the tasks normally assigned to apprentices. "Am working my old trade again," he gleefully wrote Kate, "but don't know what they will pay me yet." Courtesy, Western History Dept., Denver Public Library.

foundered in the fiscal tidal wave that overtook Colorado in the 1890s, J. K., aided by reputation, determination, and willpower, remained afloat until better times returned.[41]

WATERED-DOWN BIGOTRY:
THE CHALLENGE OF THE APA

The depression provided an additional headache for the Catholic businessman in the form of anti-Catholic harassment from the American Protective Association (APA). A quasi-secret organization that promoted the concept of "true Americanism," the APA traced a brief but bright arc through events surrounding the panic of 1893. The APA descended from earlier anti-immigrant organizations by appealing to Protestant Americans staggered by political strife, mining collapse, and agricultural failure. Organizers expanded the APA from its home in the Midwest by scapegoating Irish Catholics as minions of Roman despotism, destroyers of banks, and agents of labor strife. Members took an oath never to "employ a Roman Catholic in any capacity . . . enter into any agreement with a Roman Catholic to strike [or] vote for any Roman Catholic." The APA sponsored lectures by self-styled "ex-priests and 'escaped' nuns" who exposed titillating allegations of convent orgies and Catholic conspiracies to overthrow the government.[42]

Colorado experienced a brief but intense spasm of APA support. Members subscribed for a weekly dose of bigotry in the *Rocky Mountain American*. The organization allied with the local Republican party to influence political patronage. At its peak, the movement attracted Denver's mayor and a significant number of civic employees before, shaken by dissension, condemned by Colorado's oldest and most influential newspaper, the *Rocky Mountain News,* and undermined by the return to prosperity in the mid-1890s, local support rapidly trailed out.[43]

In part, supporters of the APA movement felt threatened by what historian Humphrey J. Desmond called "the growing social and industrial strength of Catholic Americans." Immigrants and their children were assuming leadership roles in business, politics, and labor "with not the slightest sense of inferiority."[44] As a result, the APA targeted prominent Catholic industrialists such as Mullen as the most visible representatives of the new social arrangement.

Their efforts fell short of total victory. An APA attempt to boycott CM&E mills failed when Mullen mistakenly received a letter destined for his rivals at the Longmont Farmer's Mill. Written, Mullen claimed, by "a prominent APA man," the letter promised to secure preferential business "because the Longmont Farmer's was an APA mill and our [Longmont Mill] was Catholic." J. K. contacted the author and solicited a retraction. He claimed that the anti-Catholic later became "one of the best friends that I have had for a great many years."[45]

The APA also made an effort to aggravate Mullen's cattle problems. In June 1891 the Mullen-McPhee herd was infected with cattle fever by steers recently imported from Texas by the Western Union Beef Company. The partners sued Western Union Beef for violating the recently implemented federal regulations regarding the transport of infected cattle. The case, which lasted three years, resulted in a dismissal.

That should have been the end of it, but just as J. K. made an inviting target of APA harassment, members of Colorado's Catholic community felt increasingly protective of their patron.[46] The case particularly concerned Father Thomas Malone, the editor of the *Colorado Catholic*. A staunch opponent of anti-Catholic bigotry, Malone was also sensitive to the fact that Mullen and McPhee had capitalized Colorado's first Catholic newspaper. Mullen, furthermore, was president of the *Colorado Catholic's* board of directors.[47] Using infiltrators to pierce the secrecy of the anti-Catholic society, Malone regularly exposed APA members in the pages of his newspaper. He now shared his lists with Mullen. J. K. introduced the lists in court and proved that several members of the jury were tainted by APA affiliation. His motion to appeal was duly approved.[48]

Although Mullen's victory proved the flimsiness of anti-Catholic activism by the APA, he ultimately lost his case. The state court of appeals, reflecting the probusiness orientation of Colorado government, ruled that regulations imposed by the United States secretary of agriculture had no more legal weight than "an expression of opinion." J. K.'s victory over bigotry busted over an issue of state's rights.[49]

Mullen's encounters with anti-Catholic bigotry support historian John Higham's argument that nativism usually appeared where economic and social conditions made conservatives fearful for their jobs and political power.[50] These conditions occurred wherever Mullen encountered intolerance, whether it was in the form of "Paddy-baiting" canal workers in Utica or a grain embargo by rural members of the Ku Klux Klan in the 1920s. The American Protective Association used the panic of 1893 to amplify its xenophobia into a national movement. Ironically, Mullen shared the same economic hardships as the APA conservatives who attacked him. Mullen easily survived the relatively weak threat of the APA. Later, he would find it more difficult to preserve his moral integrity as greater waves of intolerance washed over him.

NOTES

1. Charles W. Hurd, "J. K. Mullen, Milling Magnate of Colorado," *The Colorado Magazine* XXIX:2 (April 1952): 117.
2. *Rocky Mountain News (RMN)*, July 19, 1893: 2.
3. Leonard and Noel report that "[David] Moffat reputedly cashed in $2 million of his own securities . . . ordering his tellers to display mountains of cash. Trusting the First National, people took their money from other banks and deposited it with Moffat." Stephen J. Leonard and Thomas J. Noel, *Denver: Mining Camp to Metropolis* (Niwot: University Press of Colorado, 1990), 103.

Mullen related a similar story about William Barth at City National: "Barth got two or three police officers, and they had built a little platform out on the sidewalk in front of the Bank . . . and then he took a lot of money and piled it up out there by the side of the door where he entered the Bank, and he had those policemen watch it." J. K. Mullen, Letter to George F. Cottrell, January 25, 1929, Weckbaugh family collection.

4. Colorado Milling and Elevator Co. (CM&E), "Statement of Earnings and Disposition for the Years Ending July 31, 1889," Mullen manuscript collection, MSS 705 (hereafter cited as Mullen papers), Colorado Historical Society (CHS).

5. J. K. Mullen, Letter to Maurice C. Dolan, April 19, 1927, Mullen papers, CHS.

6. CM&E, "Statement of Earnings and Disposition."

7. David Brundage, *The Making of Working-Class Radicalism in the Mountain West: Denver, Colorado, 1880–1903* (Urbana: University of Illinois Press, 1994), 25.

8. J. K. Mullen, Letter to Ella M. Weckbaugh, May Dower, Catherine O'Connor, and Edith Malo, Denver, Colorado, 1928, Weckbaugh family collection. Mullen wrote his daughters that his goal was to attain majority ownership to provide for their future.

9. J. K. Mullen, Letter to Rev. Raymond Mullen, May 5, 1916, Mullen papers, CHS.

10. J. K. Mullen, Letter to Maurice C. Dolan, April 19, 1927, Mullen papers, CHS.

11. J. K. Mullen, Letters to Catherine S. Mullen, March 13, 1892; October 22, 1891; March 18, 1882, Mullen papers, CHS.

12. J. K. Mullen, Letter to Catherine S. Mullen, September 4, 1886, Mullen papers, CHS.

13. J. K. Mullen, Letter to Catherine S. Mullen, March 18, 1892, Mullen papers, CHS.

14. J. K. Mullen, Letter to Catherine S. Mullen, December 24, 1890, Mullen papers, CHS.

15. H. E. Johnson, Letter to Guy Thomas, June 10, 1943, Herbert E. Johnson collection.

16. Ibid. Irrigation played an indispensable role in the expansion of wheat agriculture and flour milling in Colorado. H. E. Johnson commented that a Colorado farmer in the 1880s "would have as soon planted bananas above his ditch line as to have sown wheat."

17. J. K. Mullen, Letter to Catherine S. Mullen, November 9, 1890, Mullen papers, CHS.

18. Ibid.; Catherine S. Mullen, Letters to J. K. Mullen, July 17, 1889; July 26, 1889, Mullen papers, CHS.

19. J. K. Mullen, Letter to Catherine S. Mullen, May 13, 1893, Mullen papers, CHS.

20. J. K. Mullen, Letter to Catherine S. Mullen, May 16, 1893, Mullen papers, CHS.

21. J. K. Mullen, "Article of Agreement Made and Entered Into This Twenty-fourth Day of July, A.D. 1886, Between John K. Mullen and Dennis W. Mullen," Mullen papers, CHS.

22. J. K. Mullen, Letter to Rev. Mayer, Crook, Colorado, August 21, 1925, Rt. Rev. John Henry Tihen manuscript collection, Archdiocese of Denver archives (hereafter cited as Tihen papers). C. D. McPhee and Mullen remained partners in Weld and Logan County cattle companies until they sold out in 1905. Together they built three irrigation canals from the Cache La Poudre River, Harmony Canals One, Two, and Three. As late as 1925, Mullen still owned "extensive lands" around Crook.

23. J. K. Mullen, "Statement Concerning the Individual Business of J. K. Mullen, May 23, 1902," Mullen papers, CHS.

24. Ibid.

25. J. K. Mullen, Letter to Rev. Mayer, Crook, Colorado, August 21, 1925, Tihen papers.

26. J. K. Mullen, Letter to Catherine S. Mullen, May 16, 1893, Mullen papers, CHS.

27. J. K. Mullen, Letter to George F. Cottrell, January 25, 1929, Weckbaugh family collection; see also Leonard and Noel, 103.

28. This and subsequent references to George Cottrell and the bank panic are cited in J. K. Mullen, Letter to George F. Cottrell, January 25, 1929.

29. J. K. Mullen, Letter to Catherine S. Mullen, August 11, 1993, Mullen papers, CHS.

30. J. K. Mullen, Letter to Catherine S. Mullen, August 14, 1893, Mullen papers, CHS.

31. This and the description of the Crescent Mill fire are cited in the Silver Plume, Colorado, *Silver Standard*, August 13, 1893: 1.

32. J. K. Mullen, Letter to Catherine S. Mullen, August 15, 1893, Mullen papers, CHS. The inadequate insurance discounts suspicion of arson on the behalf of the CM&E. According to the *Silver Standard*, the damages exceeded the mill's $107,000 insurance policy by $68,000. Flour mills everywhere were notoriously vulnerable to violent fires and the CM&E plants were no exception. Fires damaged the Crescent in 1882 and destroyed a warehouse at the Hungarian in 1899 (*Denver Times*, March 8, 1899: 1). A three-alarm fire destroyed the recently abandoned Eagle Mills in the winter of 1931, although firefighters managed to save the adjacent bran-filled warehouse (*Denver Post*, February 1, 1931: 1). The pioneer Longmont Mills succumbed to fire in 1934, and in 1952, a fire caused more than $1 million worth of damages to the Hungarian Mills (*Denver Post*, October 27, 1952: 1).

33. J. K. Mullen, Letter to Catherine S. Mullen, August 30, 1893, Mullen papers, CHS.

34. J. K. Mullen, Letter to Catherine S. Mullen, September 2, 1893, Mullen papers, CHS.

35. J. K. Mullen, Letter to Catherine S. Mullen, September 3, 1893, Mullen papers, CHS.

36. J. K. Mullen, Letter to Maurice C. Dolan, April 19, 1927, Mullen papers, CHS.

37. J. K. Mullen, Letter to Catherine S. Mullen, August 15, 1894, Mullen papers, CHS. High levels of wheat production and flour consumption in the San Luis

Valley created a bubble of temporary prosperity. By 1896, the CM&E's five San Luis–area mills handled over 1 million bushels of local wheat. As usual, the price for overproduction came due when alkali damaged the fertile San Luis soil. By 1943, only the Monte Vista Mill remained out of Mullen's southern holdings. H. E. Johnson, Letter to Guy Thomas, June 10, 1943, Johnson collection.

38. Hurd, 113.

39. J. K. Mullen, Letter to Catherine S. Mullen, August 15, 1894. It would be interesting to know how Mullen's professional creditors appraised the upstanding miller. An inquiry in the Dun and Bradstreet credit ledgers at the Baker Business Library in Cambridge, Massachusetts, revealed no mention of Mullen or his brothers. Dun and Bradstreet discontinued their handwritten credit reports in 1884, before Mullen achieved more than local reputation. Brent Sverdloff, Baker Business Library, Harvard University, Letter to author, May 6, 1997.

40. Lyle W. Dorsett, *The Queen City: A History of Denver* (Boulder: Pruett Publishing Co., 1977), 82.

41. Leonard and Noel, 102.

42. Humphrey J. Desmond, *The A.P.A. Movement* (New York: Arno Press and *New York Times,* 1969), 36–37, 52–53. See also: Leonard and Noel, 105; John Higham, *Strangers in the Land: Patterns in American Nativism, 1860–1925,* 2d ed. (New Brunswick: Rutgers University Press, 1988), 82–83.

43. Thomas J. Noel, *Colorado Catholicism and the Archdiocese of Denver, 1857–1989* (Niwot: University Press of Colorado, 1989), 79.

44. Desmond, 10.

45. J. K. Mullen, Letter to Rt. Rev. J. H. Tihen, March 13, 1925, Tihen papers.

46. Catherine S. Mullen, Letter to J. K. Mullen, July 21, 1889, Mullen papers, CHS.

47. Noel, *Colorado Catholicism,* 79; Mullen, along with stockholders McPhee, John Corcoran, John Conroy, and J. J. McGinnity, had paid off the initial debts of the *Colorado Catholic.* J. K. Mullen, Letter to Rev. Matthew Smith, December 7, 1927, Timothy O'Connor collection.

48. *Colorado Catholic,* March 15, 1894: 1.

49. *Mullen v Western Union Beef Co.,* 9 ColoApp 497 (1894).

50. Higham, iv.

12

THE CHURCH OF ST. LEO THE GREAT

St. Leo's was doomed from the beginning because it was built on a foundation of prejudice.

—FATHER ROBERT A. BANIGAN, final pastor of St. Leo's, 1965[1]

THE BARBS OF THE AMERICAN PROTECTIVE ASSOCIATION indicated the depth of J. K. Mullen's prestige in Colorado's Catholic community. Just as the economic troubles of the 1890s enhanced Mullen's reputation for business acumen, so the crisis brought into focus his role as lay leader of the Denver Catholic diocese. The Catholic church of St. Leo the Great was Mullen's first major philanthropic endowment. Although J. K. had long served as an advisor and benefactor of the Catholic community, the stringent climate of the 1890s brought about a fiscal crisis that both laypersons and ecclesiastics alike looked to the financier to resolve.

Like the church's namesake Leo, the warlike pontiff who chased Attila the Hun from Rome, St. Leo's seemed to invite conflict from the day it opened. Ethnic rivalry subverted the parish from the outset. In 1878, German immigrants built St. Elizabeth's, the first Catholic church in West Denver. The parish supported a German clergy who commonly held German-language services. As more Irish families settled in West Denver, the new parishioners faced the choice of sharing St. Elizabeth's with its German founders, traveling across the South Platte River to St. Patrick's in North Denver, or, like the Mullens, crossing Cherry Creek to worship in St. Mary's. Those who chose to worship in the German church discovered that different languages and customs created uncomfortable tension.[2]

For their part, the Irish possessed the intense pride of exiles. Free from the ethnic enclaves of the eastern seaboard, many of Denver's Irish and German Catholics socialized together and even intermarried occasionally. Other West Denver Irish defended themselves against perceived discrimination by looking down upon their German neighbors. Perceived prejudice offended Irish sensibilities. Worse, the brand of religion practiced by the German Catholics at St. Elizabeth's appeared strict to Irish eyes. When the Irish of West Denver decided that they were not welcome as worshippers in St. Elizabeth's, they constructed a separate parish a few blocks away.[3]

The result was St. Leo's, a squat brick structure shoehorned into a triangular lot on the corner of Tenth Street and West Colfax Avenue (this lot is now part of the Auraria Higher Education Campus). Imposing on the outside and cramped on the inside, St. Leo's still managed to provide a focal point for the Irish community in West Denver when it was completed in 1890. When parishioners solicited the patronage of Irish businessmen, Mullen rose to the occasion by donating land and contributing heavily to construction. Along with his brother Dennis, he accepted a seat on the board of trustees.[4]

Despite the support of the local parish, the red brick church seemed to lie under a cloud. Between 1888 and 1892, the new church needed a revolving door for its successive pastors. The founding father of St. Leo's, Father Patrick F. Carr, was promoted to the rectory of St. Mary's and assumed editorship of the *Colorado Catholic*. He was followed by Father William J. Howlett and in turn by Father William A. O'Ryan.[5] The constantly changing leadership contributed to a lack of direction during the church's formative years.

Money problems also troubled the parish. In early 1893, the trustees of St. Leo's, confident in the church's continued prosperity, took out a $17,000 mortgage from the Northwestern Life Insurance Company. One trustee, J. K. Mullen, protested. He pointed out that the church still owed approximately one-third of its original debt of $30,000. This new debt smacked of fiscal irresponsibility. When the board—including his own brother—overruled his objections, he resigned in protest.[6] True to Mullen's premonition, the depression undermined St. Leo's precarious debt structure. When, in June 1898, the trustees failed to redeem the mortgage, a United States marshal served foreclosure papers to Father O'Ryan on the church's doorstep. U.S. District

St. Leo's, a bulky Italianate church, sat on Colfax at Tenth Street. Dissension and intolerance doomed Mullen's first major philanthropic project. Today the site is occupied by the Technology Building of the Auraria Higher Education Center. Louis C. McClure photo. Courtesy, Western History Dept., Denver Public Library.

Court Judge Moses Hallet ordered the priest to pay $11,200 to the church's creditors within nine months or face eviction.[7] At almost the same moment, Bishop Matz exiled Father O'Ryan into penitent seclusion for inviting a rabbi and a Protestant minister to share his pulpit during Easter Mass. Matz, already unpopular with many Irish parishioners, further alienated the St. Leo's congregation by expressing a marked lack of sympathy regarding the fiscal affairs of the distressed church.[8]

The financial crisis and the exile of their pastor split the congregation. The outraged trustees, staunchly loyal to their Tipperary-born priest, advocated "open warfare with Bishop Matz." They met with the bishop in a bruising meeting. The trustees condemned Matz's treatment of their pastor. When the bishop sharply retorted that ecclesiastical administration was none of their concern, the trustees vowed to defy him. They declared their intention to buy lots in order to build a breakaway church.

Bishop Nicholas Chrystosom Matz, Mullen's close friend and foil, oversaw the explosive growth of Colorado's Catholic community during his twenty-eight-year term as bishop of Denver. Ethnic tensions caused many Irish-American priests and parishioners to criticize the French-born bishop. Controversy erupted between Matz and the Irish parishioners of St. Leo's in the 1890s and St. Patrick's in the 1900s. Mullen, too, lost patience with the bishop over the issue of tolerance. Courtesy, Thomas J. Noel collection.

Watching from the sidelines, J. K. Mullen felt simultaneously relieved not to be embroiled in a public fight with his friend, Matz, and concerned over the harmful disagreement. While antagonism deepened, negotiations between the church and the Northwestern Life Insurance Company faltered. As the mortgage deadline of March 14, 1899, approached, the chance of saving St. Leo's dwindled.

Because the trustees had acted irresponsibly in the first place, or perhaps because they had ignored his advice, Mullen resolved himself to the fact that St. Leo's was lost. Matz, on the other hand, indicated that he looked to the former trustee as the one person who could redeem the situation. In a March 9 interview with the *Denver Times*, Matz attempted to force Mullen's hand. He referred reporters to J. K. as the man most familiar with St. Leo's financial affairs. Nonplused, the financier pointed out that he was no longer a trustee and shrugged off inquiring reporters with the instruction, "Go see Bishop Matz. What he does not know is not worth knowing."

At first, Mullen absolved himself of what he considered unsound management. "I can only say one thing, and that is that I am satisfied that St. Leo's will pass into the hands of the Northwestern Life Insurance Company when the time of redemption expires."[9] Indeed, his prediction proved correct. On the eve of the deadline, the divided congregation and trustees were still bickering over which course to follow. O'Ryan's partisans called for building a new church nearby for their chastised pastor. Others argued that the parish should somehow pay off the original debts and recover St. Leo's.[10] The deadline lapsed in the midst of the debate. On March 14, 1899, the Northwestern Life Insurance Company took possession of St. Leo's. To the parish's great aggravation, the insurance company announced its intention to sell the church to an "interested congregation." Matz further raised the parishioners' ire by suggesting that the more disciplined Augustines or Franciscans could administer the new parish. Beaten, the trustees gave in. Led by Dennis Mullen, they implored J. K. and three unidentified "friends of the congregation" (including perhaps Verner Z. Reed, Dennis Sheedy, John F. Campion, Charles D. McPhee, or J. J. Brown) to repurchase St. Leo's. This time the miller assented. Within two weeks of the foreclosure Mullen and the congregation's "friends" added $10,000 to a hurried collection of $1,200 from the parishioners to redeem the beleaguered church.[11]

St. Leo's enjoyed the miller's support throughout the rest of his lifetime. He accepted reappointment as a trustee and negotiated new terms with the Northwestern Life Insurance Company, finally retiring the last of the debt in 1902.[12] After Mullen's death, the church received a combined monthly stipend of $150 from the estates of Mullen and Cripple Creek magnate Verner Z. Reed. The stipend represented almost the entire income of the struggling parish during the 1930s and 1940s.[13] Furthermore, Mullen's involvement with St. Leo's led directly to the resolution to similar cultural friction between Irish and Hispanic parishioners in the 1920s.

Unlike the Hispanic parish of St. Cajetan's, which thrived in West Denver, St. Leo's slowly declined. As the West Denver Irish population dwindled and Hispanics supported their new church, it became apparent that the same demographic surge that energized St. Cajetan's would devastate St. Leo's. The church's final pastor, Father Robert A. Banigan, blamed the loss of St. Leo's on intolerance. Criticizing St. Leo's Irish parishioners for relegating Spanish-speaking services to the church basement during the 1920s, Banigan claimed, "St. Leo's would never again be able to get [the Spanish-speaking Catholics'] support because memory of the days when they were confined to the basement would linger another generation."[14] The church struggled on until maintenance costs finally doomed the languishing parish. On the morning of February 28, 1965, Father Banigan announced "that it was better to shut down now instead of letting the elements, dust, wind, and snow damage it further. Old age just caught up with St. Leo's."[15] The church fell to the wrecking ball six weeks later. Ironically, if it had survived for only two more years, preservation efforts made on behalf of Auraria's surviving churches might have saved the brick chapel for rehabilitation on the Auraria campus. Today, it is just a footnote, its site occupied by the Auraria Campus Technology Building.

NOTES

1. *Denver Post*, May 22, 1965: 3B.
2. Thomas J. Noel, *Colorado Catholicism and the Archdiocese of Denver, 1857–1989* (Niwot: University Press of Colorado, 1989), 350.
3. Jason Krupar, "The Churches of Auraria," Rosmary Fetter, ed., pamphlet (Denver: Auraria Office of the EVOA, 1994); *Denver Post*, April 17, 1965: 6B; May 22, 1965: 3B.
4. Noel, *Colorado Catholicism*, 362.

5. *Denver Times*, September 5, 1892: 5; Noel, *Colorado Catholicism*, 79.

6. *Denver Times*, March 9, 1899: 8.

7. *Denver Times*, July 1, 1898: 2.

8. This and subsequent actions by St. Leo's parishioners cited in *Denver Times*, July 2, 1898: 6.

9. *Denver Times*, March 9, 1899: 8.

10. *Denver Times*, March 15, 1899: 6.

11. Krupar, "The Churches of Auraria"; Charles W. Hurd, "J. K. Mullen, Milling Magnate of Colorado," *The Colorado Magazine* XXIX:2 (April 1952): 111; *Denver Times*, March 9, 1899: 8; April 3, 1899: 6.

12. J. K. Mullen, Letter to Northwestern Life Insurance Co., 1902, St. Leo the Great Catholic Church manuscript collection, Archdiocese of Denver archives.

13. *Rocky Mountain News*, March 1, 1965.

14. *Denver Post*, May 22, 1965: 3B; Krupar, "The Churches of Auraria."

15. *Denver Post*, April 17, 1965: 6B; Krupar, "The Churches of Auraria."

13

THE MERCHANT PRINCE, 1895–1915

First in the Roll of Honor comes the Producer of the necessaries of life. Equally important . . . is the Distributor [but] in order that both a waste and a famine may be averted . . . the services of the Merchant are indispensable . . . It may well be said that he who fulfills this duty honorably has earned the title of Merchant Prince.

—J. K. MULLEN to the employees of the Mesa Milling and Elevator Co., Grand Junction, Colorado, September 10, 1912

WHEN ASKED TO SPEAK at the Mesa Mills company dinner of September 10, 1912, the president of the Colorado Milling and Elevator Company took a moment "to review the past and learn wisdom from the experience we have gained, that we . . . may avoid the many difficulties that accompany inexperience."[1] The struggles of the past reminded the entrepreneur that no future endeavors were certain. Still, J. K. Mullen could afford to look back with a sense of accomplishment over the years since the panic of 1893. Whereas the economic disaster ruined many of Colorado's mining millionaires, the agricultural capitalist emerged as one of Colorado's financial elite.[2]

Indeed, as agriculture replaced mining as the foundation of the state's economy, the CM&E expanded at a nimble pace. New European and domestic markets stabilized the price of American flour. Mullen used this demand to transform his "child" into the dominant milling company in the West. At age sixty-five, the entrepreneur felt vigorous—fit enough anyway to travel by automobile to his engagements in Grand Junction—fit enough, indeed, to have not missed an annual inspection tour of his far-flung mills in twenty-seven years. His stamina had been tempered during the lean years of the 1890s. In the healthy business climate of the early 1900s, entrepreneur and company flourished together. Only turmoil between J. K., his mature daughters, and his brother Dennis marred his complete tranquility.

"EVERY NEW TOWN WANTED A FLOUR MILL"[3]

One factor compensated for the losses of 1893—wholesale flour prices reached the bottom of their ten-year skid. Flour prices remained characteristically volatile, but on average they also rebounded more quickly than wheat. After 1894, expanding markets in England, Germany, Italy, and central Europe drove the average price of flour from its low point of $1.40 per hundred-pound bag to a 1909 high of $2.78.[4] While these prices didn't match the $4 and $5 highs of the 1870s and 1880s, they at least pushed flour above the break-even line. War demand drove flour prices even higher in the first two decades of the twentieth century until the commodity peaked at $11.58 per bag in 1920. The continued overproduction of wheat kept average grain prices relatively low. Flour dealers enjoyed a lucrative climate where wheat prices failed to grow in proportion to the price of flour.[5] Canny corporate mills bought low and sold high, retired their debts, and grew rich in the process. Such was the case with the CM&E. By following his long-standing policy of borrowing early, purchasing all available wheat at harvest time, and selling the surplus at a profit over the course of the year, Mullen turned his company around from the worst financial crisis of his tenure. Even during the depression of the 1890s he doubted that "there [had] been but two years in all that time . . . that the price of wheat didn't advance enough to pay the carrying charges many times over."[6]

As Colorado's economy recovered from the crash of the 1890s, J. K. interpreted the increase in international flour exports as a sign of revitalization. Beginning in 1895, the capitalist embarked on a campaign to dominate flour production in the West. He envisioned lines of CM&E mills, elevators, and warehouses that would acquire wheat and distribute flour from Missouri to Oregon. His plan started with the establishment of a modest mill in La Junta, Colorado. In 1903, J. K. returned to Kansas to build a successful mill in Hays. During the following years, the CM&E bought, built, or refurbished mills, elevators, and grain dealerships in Dodge City, Wilson, and Claflin, Kansas, as well as Springfield, Missouri. Closer to home, the CM&E established mills in Grand Junction and Pueblo in 1918–1919 and absorbed the competitive Farmer's Mill into its chain of Denver mills (the Crescent, Eagle, Excelsior, Roller, and Hungarian) in 1924.[7]

Also in 1895, the businessman directed his general manager, Herbert E. Johnson, to expand into Idaho. Over the next thirty years, Mullen and Johnson built or purchased mills in Idaho Falls, St. Anthony, Twin Falls, Burley, Wilson, Caldwell, and Pocatello. From there, the CM&E extended their grasp along newly irrigated sections of southern Idaho and Oregon. By constructing supporting elevators along the lush plains of the Snake River, the trust gained access to the softer varieties of wheat that still eluded Colorado husbandmen. Immediately following the First World War, the company expanded into Utah. J. K. bought the Husler Mill and three elevators in Salt Lake City and the W. O. Roy Grain Company and twelve elevators in northeast Utah and Idaho. The capitalist next connected the mills with networks of CM&E "warehouses and elevators at every station where deliveries of grain were sufficient to justify the investment."[8]

Herb Johnson remembered that by the early 1900s, "we were making a lot of money." He characterized Mullen's drive to expand as a compulsive aversion to idle investment capital: "Mr. Mullen was opposed to paying large dividends. He preferred to plow surplus funds back into the business." The CM&E's greatest challenge, Johnson recalled, was "the ever present problem of finding a place to invest surplus capital [where] earnings have been reasonably satisfactory." The rate of investment is indicated by the greater debts that the CM&E assumed. During the 1910s and 1920s, J. K. signed annual notes for over $3,000,000, then $5,000,000, then $10,000,000.[9]

Expansion into the Far West brought domination, but not monopoly. During the prosperous years of the First World War, fifty-seven grain-purchasing stations operated in Colorado alone. Twenty-three were CM&E plants. Farmer's cooperative associations operated an additional eight. Independent grain dealers and millers owned the rest. By 1928, the CM&E had moved closer to complete consolidation of the state milling industry. In that year, company president Oscar L. Malo boasted that the CM&E employed approximately 850 workers with a payroll amounting to "millions."[10]

At the same time, and in much the same manner, the businessman expanded his personal fortune. By 1900, he had amassed just under $1 million in investment capital. Four years later, the amount closed in on $1.25 million. Mullen sowed his revenues into Denver real estate, First National Bank of Denver stock, Weld and Logan County cattle ranches, Prowers County farms, and his pride and joy, the CM&E. To his immense satisfaction, he acquired a controlling interest in his "child" during the summer of 1904. It would remain one of the proudest moments of his life.[11]

He invested still more capital into expanded land, grain, and cattle holdings. With the partial recovery of the cattle industry after 1900, J. K. reinvested with Charles D. McPhee and his brother Patrick H. Mullen. By 1906, his holding company, the J. K. Mullen Land and Stock Company, owned shares in the Mitchell Stock and Produce Company and land and stock companies with names such as Tamarack, Plum Creek, Denver and Platte Valley, and Harmony. He also acquired eight Prowers County farms, which raised wheat, corn, sugar beets, and hogs. The diversity paid off. By 1905, Mullen was one of the largest private landowners in Colorado. Three years previously, despite personal interest payments of over $52,000, he netted almost $60,000 in dividends, rents, and salary.[12]

THE CASTLE ON QUALITY HILL

If Mullen's large new mills changed the appearance of the towns in which they were constructed, this was equally true of their effect on his West Denver neighborhood. Over the years, the community had become an industrial enclave surrounded by rail and lumber yards, an iron works, an open-air market, several breweries, and three smoky CM&E mills.[13] Those residents prosperous enough to escape to Denver's expanding suburbs did so with increasing frequency. By the end of the nineteenth century, Mullen was ready to join the flight. Although his monthly salary at the CM&E amounted to only $700, his investments catapulted him into a higher class, among whom a shabby West Denver address was no longer suitable. In 1898, he hired architects Aaron M. Gove and Thomas F. Walsh to design a three-story foursquare mansion on the affluent 900 block of Pennsylvania Street.[14] Much like its owner, the exterior of the gray brick house revealed an unassuming simplicity of form. Inside, a grand third-floor ballroom, a lush velvet pool table, and a central staircase adorned with polished mahogany rails invited appreciation of Mullen's wealth. To the perplexity of the family patriarch and his adult daughters, the banister also made an entertaining slide for three generations of children.[15]

The residence was located in a fashionable Capitol Hill neighborhood known as "Quality Hill." J. K.'s new neighbors included Denver's financial and political elite as well as such come-lately Irish millionaires as Thomas M. Patterson, John F. Campion, and John J. and Maggie "Molly" Brown. To the class-conscious Quality Hill society, Mullen and the Browns represented a new kind of millionaire—immigrants of working-class background, who, some critics thought, were attempting to buy their way into social acceptability. A tongue-in-cheek *Denver Times* article of June 26, 1901, parodied the stuffy nouveaux riche atmosphere of the neighborhood, where the "air of refinement hangs

John and Kate Mullen proudly pose in front of their recently completed "castle" at 896 Pennsylvania Street. The wide porch eaves served as a bicycle track for J. K.'s grandsons. J. K.'s daughter May occupied the house until her death in 1952. The American Humane Society kept offices in the home from 1952 until it was demolished in 1964. Courtesy, Weckbaugh family collection.

over the hill—an exclusive kind of air that isn't felt in the rest of the town." Quality Hill was where the ashman and the iceman charged double for their services, beggars and peddlers dared not tread, and signs of working-class or immigrant backgrounds were "buried in the [nearby] graveyard." Describing select homes with unflattering comparisons to their owners, the *Times* article depicted Mullen's "castle" as "a most forbidding house . . . built without a bend or curve to relieve its severe and imposing simplicity."

Indeed, the stiff, blocky mansion characterized the simplicity and exclusivity that appealed to the flour baron. He embellished on his privacy with $970 worth of door locks—his single largest household expense in 1900. In 1902, he purchased nineteen trees to screen his castle from both prying eyes and the unblinking Colorado sun.[16] Likewise, he bought up surrounding lots to discourage development and constructed houses for each of his daughters within one block of his own home.[17] The enclave of houses around Pennsylvania Street protected the tycoon somewhat from unwelcome neighbors while providing a measure of financial security for his daughters.

J. K.'s passion for control of his physical and financial environment led to a complete breakdown in his relationship with his brother Dennis in the early 1900s. Elected as a city alderman in the 1890s, Dennis (known to J. K. as "D. W." or "Denny") enjoyed more success in the Denver Democratic machine than in business.[18] While he managed the Hungarian Mill under his brother's watchful eye, Dennis suffered heavy financial losses in mining and commodity speculation throughout the 1890s. In 1898, the Arapahoe County sheriff confiscated his house to redeem a $20,000 lawsuit incurred in an ill-advised investment in a Helena, Montana, cemetery and streetcar association. Denny turned to his brother for help. In return for his aid, J. K. demanded and received from his younger sibling the five hundred shares of CM&E stock that he had given his brother to qualify him for the board of directors. Mullen then bought out the judgment for $3,500 and repurchased Denny's Tenth Street home and other property at a sheriff's auction. In order to regain his property, Dennis was forced to sign an agreement that gave J. K. a free hand in his future endeavors. Mullen kept track of his brother's investments through his contacts at First National Bank and continued to supervise Denny's business affairs.

The strain of his older brother's control embittered D. W. In 1899, he sued J. K. over one hundred shares of disputed CM&E stock. Dennis dropped the suit in 1902, but J. K.'s terms of reconciliation, which included an apology in the presence of both families and Denny's resignation from the Hungarian Mill, drove an icy wedge between the brothers and their families. On the following Christmas, J. K. Mullen received a package and card from John Mullen, Denny's son and J. K.'s namesake. Thinking it was a present, J. K. summoned his family together and opened it only to discover a box of cigars that he had earlier sent to John, returned, unopened, and unaccepted.[19]

Their affairs reached an unfortunate climax. Dennis, who unlike his brother was "never strong and rugged," slowly succumbed to heart disease in the spring of 1916. A widower since the previous February, he asked to see his brother throughout his illness. J. K.'s visits indicated a willingness to heal their old wounds. He brought Denny a customary box of cigars, held one to his invalid brother's mouth, and lit it as they reminisced about the past.[20]

As Dennis's health worsened, his family, fearing that J. K. would take advantage of his brother's illness to cheat them out of their few remaining stock shares, restricted Mullen's visitations. Rebuffed by Dennis's son Raymond, a Jesuit novitiate, J. K. allowed the bitterness of the previous twenty years to boil over. The furious letter that he dashed off to Raymond reveals a rare loss of composure caused by the anger and humiliation on both sides:

> I simply write to say that I felt so deeply pained at the most grievous insult that you gave me on Wednesday afternoon, May 3d at 4:30 P.M. that I thought it best to write the date and the very hour that you standing in the doorway of your father's house with the door partly open and I standing just outside but inside the outer screen door and begging you to allow me to see my sick brother was by you refused admittance. Not once did I ask . . . to see him but ten times and more did you refuse.

J. K. stood in the doorway, bickering with his nephew and choking back his temper: "I said he is my only brother and you should admit me to see him . . . I felt like putting my foot in the door and forcing my way in, but I tried to control myself and urged you in every possible way to . . . let me see him."

As if to persuade the reluctant seminarian, J. K. flourished a handful of stock certificates belonging to Dennis, on which he needed his younger brother's signature of transferal. Whether he meant to transfer them to Denny's family or to himself is unclear. Raymond sensed that his uncle intended to wrest the shares away from Dennis's control. Accordingly, he sent his uncle away. "And you studying to be a priest of the Holy Roman Catholic Church," Mullen sputtered,

> You should go down on your knees and beg your father's pardon and mine also . . . I arranged for him to come [to Denver] . . . When he had Typhoid Fever for seven weeks myself and wife slept on a mattress on the floor and gave him our only bed . . . I worked hard and cared for him and helped him to everything that he has and now you, his youngest child, says no you will not let me see him and he on his Death Bed and you pretending to be educating and fitting yourself for a priest . . . You are, in my opinion, as cold as a frog, and no warm blood in you. As soon as the certificates are properly endorsed I will transfer them [to you] and I will call and see my brother and bid him Good Bye.

It was not J. K.'s best moment. After he regained his composure to a degree, he excised the letter of the worst vitriol and sent Raymond a stiff, thirty-page history of the brothers' relationship. He dared Raymond to verify the facts of his story in available documentation, concluding,

> I am not begging your friendship . . . I have done nothing to be ashamed of and having lived in this city for 45 years, it is somewhat strange . . . that the only family I know of that was ever unfriendly to me and mine was my brother's family . . . Hoping that you will receive this letter in the good spirit in which it is written, I am *Respectfully Yours*, J. K. Mullen.

J. K. echoed his exasperation in dealing with other close friends and relations, including Baby Doe Tabor.[21] Under the circumstances, it is surprising that close friends and family would do business with him at all. Mullen's harsh treatment of Denny and his family cannot be explained away, but it may be interpreted. He loved Dennis, assuring Kate on one occasion that "he is as true as steel and has always been a good Brother to me." Yet he feared the effects that his brother's poor health, alcohol problems, and financial misadventures would eventually have on Dennis's wife and family. At the same time, it had been J. K. who assumed most of the risks in their early business endeavors. He refused to let Dennis, his sister-in-law, Anne, or his nephews claim one iota more than they were due. By attempting to restrain Dennis, Mullen believed that he was acting in his brother's interests. Ultimately, J. K. proved incapable of understanding the resentment generated by the constraints that he imposed on his brother. Mullen misjudged the one man whom he claimed to "know better than any one else" with tragic consequences.[22]

Ironically, most people who assessed the miller's character agreed that his greatest ability was an instinctive understanding of men. Charles W. Hurd, a family friend, wrote that Mullen "had a keen understanding of men and was always careful to pick the right man for the right place." Monsignor Hugh L. McMenamin, who knew J. K. as well as anyone, believed "the secret of Mr. Mullen's success lay . . . in his striking knowledge of men and in his rare judgement in selecting his assistants."[23] The characterization held true in business, where he repeatedly selected talented young men, cultivated their loyalty, and placed them in positions where it would benefit his interests the most. His talents translated poorly to his family life, where his blood relatives resisted bending to his will. He proved to be only slightly more effective in the evaluation of proper suitors for his daughters.

By now, the task of cultivating appropriate sons-in-law deeply preoccupied the aging capitalist. Now in their twenties, Ella, Katherine, Edith, and May attracted young suitors who recognized the ladies' many appealing features. In addition to being pretty, strong-willed, intelligent women, Mullen's daughters had the added advantage of a wealthy, generous father. As each married, J. K. presented the newlyweds with a government bond of $10,000, additional securities of $165,000 (with advice on how to manage them), and a large house near their parents' home on Pennsylvania Street. Furthermore, Mullen's prospective sons-in-law enjoyed access to investment capital, insurance against failure, and unique business opportunities.[24]

The following from a local gossip columnist illustrates the presumed advantages of a marriage into the Mullen clan:

> Ideal fathers-in-law are few and regrettably far between. So let us do honor to one right here in our midst . . . J. K. Mullen . . . has four daughters, all of whom have been sought for by throngs of suitors. Each of them is beautiful and a jewel . . . but their father is a whole casket of kohinoors [a mammoth diamond set into the Crown Jewels]. He has the ideas of the patriarchs of old. When the girls marry . . . a big inky deed is chucked after the bridal pair along with the old shoes [and] a Mullen mill is put at the disposal of any who do not prefer other business employment . . . Any time [Mullen] tires [of] piling up fortunes for himself, he can while away his time pitting a son-in-law against the odds he encountered while a lad. J. K. will probably have more fun seeing those boys try to show him what they

Oscar L. Malo mined lucrative business and benevolent deals for his father-in-law. Shown here donating Baby Doe Tabor's Matchless Mine cabin to the city of Leadville in 1953, Malo arranged the purchase of Mary Elitch's gardens for Mullen in 1912. He presided over the family foundation long after his associations with the Colorado Milling and Elevator Company ended. Courtesy, John F. Malo.

know about becoming millionaires than he would at a vaudeville show. He will never break his heart, however, if one of them never made a dollar, but if they lied or went back on a friend, it would be different. Young men who have the necessary backbone to face the patriarch and ask for a daughter are guaranteed a good friend in J. K., if they come into the family.[25]

Among his daughters' suitors Mullen hoped to find a surrogate son to control the guidelines of his business when he was gone. The man who best approached Mullen's expectations was Edith's fiancé, Oscar Louis Malo (1877–1964). Just prior to Edith's wedding, Mullen had converted most of his real estate assets into shares of J. K. Mullen Investment Company stock. He immediately turned over fifty shares to Malo and hired him as a clerk at the CM&E for $275 per month. Over time, Malo became Mullen's closest lieutenant in the milling industry. After briefly assuming the presidency of the company on Mullen's retirement, he became a formidable flour mill operator and investment banker in his own right.[26]

Ella Mullen Weckbaugh poses with her children, Joseph Kernan and Eleanore, c. 1916. Absent is father, Eugene. Ella, who never remarried following her divorce, made generous gifts to St. Joseph's Hospital in her parents' memory. The Catherine Smith Mullen Memorial Nurses Home and St. Joseph's nondenominational chapel reflected the ideals of piety, solace, and opportunity that J. K. instilled in his children. Courtesy, Weckbaugh family collection.

Some of his other daughters cultivated less fortunate matches that both lost J. K.'s money and "broke his heart" with other failings. In June 1903, Ella Mullen married Eugene Henry Weckbach in an "elaborate" wedding ceremony at St. Leo's Catholic Church.[27] Neither the officiation of Bishop Nicholas C. Matz nor a papal benediction from Pope Leo XII cemented the doomed relationship. Although from a distinguished family, the second-generation German from Nebraska appeared to lack the qualities of character that Mullen valued. A "dreamer" who lacked the natural aptitude for business that his successful brothers enjoyed, Gene fared poorly as manager of the Crescent Flour Mills. Unable to succeed in business, he focused his attention on the sporting pursuits enjoyed by many gentlemen of his class. Consequently, Gene, who at first lived with his wife in his new in-laws' home, encountered disapproval from his staid father-in-law.[28] Although presented with a beautiful pair of grandchildren—including the long-awaited male heir, Joseph Kernan Weckbaugh—J. K. grew increasingly impatient by his philandering son-in-law.

By 1912, Ella's patience wore out as well. Eventually, even Bishop Matz admitted to Ella that divorce "may be necessary for your own protection and that of your children."[29] Mullen presented Weckbach with a $15,000 check and a one-way ticket out of town. Eugene accepted the offer, but the money soon ran out. In later years, he depended on the secret support of his son, J. Kernan Weckbaugh.[30] Matz best summed up the sorry episode when he granted Ella permission to apply for a civil divorce in 1913. The bishop wrote that the "unfortunate wretch" had wasted his "chances for happiness and success."[31]

Other suitors, while handsome and socially appealing, turned out to be a mixed bag. In 1905, Connecticut attorney James Emerson O'Connor (1874–1918)—a "clean-cut type of Catholic gentleman," in the assessment of Father Hugh McMenamin—overwhelmed the objections of his potential father-in-law and married Katherine. O'Connor became a CM&E corporate attorney, a major organizer of the revitalized Cathedral Association, and a family confidant. These circumstances only increased the tragedy when James succumbed to syphilis at the age of forty-four.[32]

J. K. described May's first husband, Frank Louis Tettemer (1880–1912), as "the sweetest, gentlest, kindest man that I have ever met."[33] He, too, died prematurely after losing between thirty and forty thou-

The wedding party of J. K. Mullen's daughter Katherine and James Emerson O'Connor. Those who in J. K.'s opinion failed to demonstrate the necessary backbone endured glowering disapproval for any sleights of character. Mullen, for example, disparaged O'Connor as a product of "the effete east." Courtesy, Timothy O'Connor collection.

sand of J. K.'s dollars in the brick-making business. When May remarried to John Lawrence Dower (1867–1943), Mullen moved Malo out of the clerk's position and replaced him with his new son-in-law. Dower also received fifty shares of Mullen Investment Co. stock. Following J. K.'s death, Dower took over the CM&E and guided it through the Great Depression.[34]

Perhaps with good reason, J. K.'s sons-in-law found it difficult to break through their father-in-law's reserve and win his private trust and approval. His command of the family business made the jobs of his sons-in-law all the more difficult. Mullen complained that James E. O'Connor, a Yale graduate and a promising attorney, was a product of "the effete east." Likewise, John L. Dower complained,

> I have at different times tried to make suggestions to you but have never met with much success or attention, and your attitude has caused me to feel that you had neither confidence in nor regard for my opinions, my judgment or my motives.[35]

"Papa Mullen," charged the gossip maven, would find among his sons-in-law "no lack of material for strategic movements on the part of their domestic general." This, too, remained true. As distant as J. K. remained from his sons-in-law, he continued to entrust them with vital roles in the management of his company.

TYSON DINES

On at least one occasion, Mullen's unyielding demand for respect and occasional inability to show it for others landed him in a potentially fatal situation. In the summer of 1906, Kate's mortally ill older brother, Charles Smith, took up residence in the Mullens' Pennsylvania Street home. The end seemed near for Charley on July 30, when J. K. picked up his telephone receiver in order to summon help for Kate's dying brother. He discovered that Miss Virginia Dines, the teen-aged daughter of a neighbor, occupied the party line. When J. K. ordered the girl off the line, Virginia refused to budge. In exasperation, Mullen told her caller, Ellesworth Wood, that "Miss Dines is no lady or she would get off the line."[36]

Matters of honor were still not treated lightly in 1906. Miss Dines's father, Tyson S. Dines, was an attorney of sensitive Southern sensibilities—a compact bantamweight who retained proud memories of his family's Virginia heritage. Dines carried himself tightly, with his fists bunched, as if always ready to fight for his honor.[37] Hearing of this verbal assault on his daughter, the explosive solicitor stuffed a dog whip in one pocket and an automatic pistol in the other and stormed off to Mullen's house to extract satisfaction.

According to the evening edition of the *Denver Post*, J. K.'s son-in-law James O'Connor escorted Dines into Mullen's presence in the den. There, Dines brushed off attempts to talk the matter through. He instead launched himself at the older, smaller man. Pulling his dog whip, he slashed J. K. repeatedly across the shoulder, hands, and face, leaving swollen welts wherever he struck. Mullen swung back ineffectually—his flour-sack-hauling days were long behind him. Dines shoved him sprawling across a davenport, punching him in the body several times. The attorney next drew his pistol and waved it in Mullen's face, all the while shouting, "It is apology or death!" Finally, O'Connor and several female family members and guests wrenched Dines away from his victim. Adding to the bizarre din, Kate's sister, alone in her concern

The Denver Post *headline of July 30, 1906, read, "Tyson Dines Attacks J. K. Mullen with Whip." By reproducing sketches over photographs of Mullen's study, the* Denver Post *capitalized on the sensational confrontation between the flour miller and Tyson Dines. The normally reserved businessman bridled at this violation of his privacy. Clockwise, from upper left, J. K. Mullen, Catherine Smith Mullen, Mullen's library with superimposed sketch, Tyson Dines's residence, J. K. Mullen's residence, Virginia Dines, Tyson Dines, center. Courtesy, Colorado Historical Society.*

for the patient upstairs, stood in the doorway wailing, "For God's sake, don't do that. Stop! Charley's dead! Charley's dead!"

Having expelled the violent visitor from his home, Mullen retaliated through legal channels. He charged Dines with assault with intent to kill and sued the lawyer for $50,000. Dines escalated the absurdity with a theatrical lack of repentance. "I offer no apology," he told a *Post* reporter, "I have no regrets. Any man of character would probably have done the same as I did." In his deposition, reprinted in the October 7, 1906, issue of the *Denver Republican*, Dines condemned the "malicious, wicked, illegal, and insulting" treatment of his daughter and J. K.'s "vile and insulting language." He testified to the hearsay that Mullen "had thrown off his coat and rolled up his sleeves and . . . stated that he was able to whip the whole Dines and [Ellesworth] Wood families combined." Bringing a pistol because he feared for his life against such an ogre, Dines also admitted to carrying an "extremely light and pliable" dog whip. After enduring Mullen's verbal abuse, he struck the man "once or twice with the light leather lash." The result was that "both [Mullen] and son-in-law then attacked [the] defendant with their fists, wounding him in the face and hands," while Mullen's female family members "rushed into the room and attacked him with tongue and nails."

Ultimately, Dines admitted the speciousness of his story. In December, in a contrite letter to his victim sent through their mutual friend David H. Moffat, Dines communicated his "regret and remorse and desire to make amends . . . I frankly confess that the invasion of your home, the assault upon you . . . and the allegations made in my answer filed in your civil action . . . were without fact or foundation." He "humbly begged" Mullen's forgiveness, offered a complete and public apology, and submitted to redress for a sum of money to be arbitrated by Moffat.[38] After some negotiation, Mullen accepted Dines's apology and retraction. Dines paid the miller's legal and business fees (to the tune of $2,500) and amended his original apology, which suggested that J. K. had unintentionally insulted Virginia. "That is not sufficient, and not satisfactory," J. K. shot back. "I can only repeat; the apology must state definitely that I did not insult Miss Dines. That is a fact."[39] In return, J. K. promised to ask the district attorney to drop the criminal case. Dines, wishing to avoid criminal and civil charges, signed and returned the amended apology.

Although both sides considered the matter closed, the gentlemen's agreement ruffled the feathers of Denver's press. Several newspapers printed Tyson's apology alongside strong editorials condemning such agreements among Denver's elite as a "mockery" of justice. "[The Colorado State Prison in] Cañon City contains a hundred poor men, serving time for the same offense, who would be willing to apologize to get their freedom. They are wearing stripes."[40]

NOTES

1. J. K. Mullen, "The Policy of Our Company and the Dignity and Responsibility of a Merchant," typed speech transcript, September 10, 1912, Herbert E. Johnson collection.

2. Charles W. Hurd, "J. K. Mullen, Milling Magnate of Colorado," *The Colorado Magazine* XXIX:2 (April 1952): 116.

3. H. E. Johnson, Letter to Guy Thomas, June 10, 1943, Johnson collection.

4. C. Knick Harley, "Western Settlement and the Price of Wheat, 1872–1913," *Journal of Economic History* 38:4 (December 1978): 866; U. S. Dept. of Commerce, Bureau of the Census, "Immigrants by Country: 1820–1970," *Historical Statistics of the United States: Colonial Times to 1970,* vol. 1 (Washington, D.C.: GPO, 1976), 208.

5. Harley, 878.

6. J. K. Mullen, Letter to Maurice C. Dolan, April 19, 1927, Mullen manuscript collection, MSS 705 (hereafter cited as Mullen papers), Colorado Historical Society (CHS).

7. John Everitt, "The Early Development of the Flour Milling Industry on the Prairies," *Journal of Historical Geography* 19:3 (1993): 282; H. E. Johnson, Letter to Guy Thomas, June 10, 1943, Johnson collection; J. K. Mullen, Letter to Rt. Rev. J. H. Tihen, March 13, 1925, Rt. Rev. John Henry Tihen manuscript collection, Archdiocese of Denver archives (hereafter cited as Tihen papers).

8. This and subsequent Herbert E. Johnson quotes cited in H. E. Johnson, Letter to Guy Thomas, June 10, 1943.

9. J. K. Mullen, Letter to Rt. Rev. J. H. Tihen, October 17, 1922, Tihen papers.

10. *Denver Post,* August 10, 1918: 7; Oscar L. Malo, Circular No. 160 to District Managers, Managers, and Employees of the CM&E, December 18, 1928, Malo papers, Western History Dept., Denver Public Library (WHDDPL).

11. J. K. Mullen, Letter to Ella M. Weckbaugh, May Dower, Catherine O'Connor, and Edith Malo, Denver, Colorado, 1928, Weckbaugh family collection (hereafter cited as Letter to his daughters); J. K. Mullen, "Personal Ledger, 1900–1905," Mullen papers, WHDDPL.

12. This and subsequent references to Mullen's expenses and income for this period cited in J. K. Mullen, "Personal Ledger, 1900–1905."

13. Thomas J. Noel and Barbara S. Norgren, *Denver: The City Beautiful and Its Architects, 1893–1941* (Denver: Historic Denver, Inc., 1987), 8; "Bird's Eye

View of Denver, Colorado, 1908," map (Denver: Bird's Eye View Publishing Co., 1907).

14. Noel and Norgren, 202.

15. Walter S. Weckbaugh, personal interview, July 21, 1997; Timothy O'Connor, personal interview, December 11, 1997.

16. J. K. Mullen, "Personal Ledger, 1900–1905."

17. J. K. Mullen, Letter to his daughters, 1928, Weckbaugh family collection. The Mullen house at 896 Pennsylvania has been since demolished, but the French-style Eugene and Ella Mullen Weckbaugh home at 450 E. Ninth (1908), the Katherine Mullen O'Connor House at 895 Pennsylvania, and the Spanish revival–style Oscar and Edith Mullen Malo House at 500 E. Eighth (1921) still stand as examples of early-twentieth-century elite architecture in Denver. Noel and Norgren, 53, 59.

18. "Obituary of Dennis W. Mullen," *The Trail* IX:1 (June 1916): 29.

19. The disagreement may be traced in: T. J. O'Donnell, esq., Letters to J. K. Mullen, October 15, 1897; November 12, 1902; November 13, 1902; Milton Smith, esq., Letters to J. K. Mullen, August 24, 1898; August 29, 1898; August 30, 1898; September 4, 1898; J. K. Mullen, Letters to Rev. Raymond Mullen, May 5, 1916; December 1921; Letter to John J. Mullen, June 1, 1926; and Frank McLoon, Letter to J. K. Mullen, Oct. 2, 1921, Mullen papers, CHS.

20. This and subsequent quotations regarding the events surrounding the death of Dennis Mullen cited in J. K. Mullen, Letter to Rev. Raymond Mullen, May 5, 1916, Mullen papers, CHS. Dennis died "from heart disease, complicated by several attacks of apoplexy," on May 20, 1916, according to *The Trail* IX:1 (June 1926): 29.

21. J. K. Mullen, Letter to Rev. Matthew Smith, December 8, 1927, Timothy O'Connor collection, Denver, Colorado.

22. J. K. Mullen, Letter to Catherine S. Mullen, September 3, 1893, Mullen papers, CHS.

23. Hurd, 114; Rev. Hugh L. McMenamin, *Diamond Jubilee of the Cathedral Parish, Denver, Colorado* (Denver: Frank J. Wolf Printers, 1935), 95. See also H. E. Johnson, Letter to J. K. Mullen, December 27, 1920, Johnson collection, and for Mullen's own opinions regarding choosing assistants, "Responsibility of a Merchant," Johnson collection, and Letter to W. S. Bunt, Weckbaugh family collection.

24. J. K. Mullen, Letter to his daughters, 1928, Weckbaugh family collection; "Why Don't You Get a Father-in-Law Worth While? He's in Denver," unidentified, undated newspaper clipping, Sheila Sevier Collection, Denver, Colorado.

25. Unattributed newspaper clipping, Sheila Sevier collection.

26. Ibid.; LeRoy Hafen, ed., *Colorado and Its People: A Narrative and Topical History of the Centennial State* (New York: Lewis Historical Publishing Co., 1948), 591.

27. *Denver Republican*, June 14, 1903: 26. Ella changed the spelling of the family surname to "Weckbaugh" during the First World War.

28. Anne Weckbaugh, personal interview, February 6, 1998.

29. Rt. Rev. N. C. Matz, Letter to Ella Weckbaugh, January 27, 1913, Rt. Rev.

Nicholas C. Matz manuscript collection, Archdiocese of Denver archives (hereafter cited as Matz papers).

30. W. S. Weckbaugh, personal interview, July 21, 1997.
31. Rt. Rev. N. C. Matz, Letter to Ella Weckbaugh, January 27, 1913, Matz papers.
32. Rev. Hugh L. McMenamin, *The Pinnacled Glory of the West: Cathedral of the Immaculate Conception* (Denver: Smith-Brooks Printing, 1912), 151, 160; Timothy O'Connor, personal interview, December 4, 11, 1997.
33. J. K. Mullen, Letter to his daughters, 1928, Weckbaugh family collection.
34. Ibid.; Hafen, 446.
35. Mullen's opinion of O'Connor cited in unattributed newspaper clipping, Katherine Mullen O'Connor scrapbook, Timothy O'Connor collection, Denver, Colorado; John L. Dower, Letter to J. K. Mullen, June 5, 1926, Mullen papers, CHS.
36. This and subsequent details of the Tyson Dines incident cited in *Denver Post*, July 30, 1906: 1, 3.
37. *Denver Post*, March 28, 1929: 1.
38. T. S. Dines, Letter to J. K. Mullen, December 21, 1906, Weckbaugh family collection.
39. J. K. Mullen, Letter to David H. Moffat, December 20, 1906, Weckbaugh family collection.
40. Unattributed newspaper clipping, Katherine Mullen O'Connor scrapbook, Timothy O'Connor collection, Denver, Colorado.

14

THE IMMACULATE CONCEPTION CATHEDRAL

The Word Cathedral has always had for me a most wonderful significance and meaning.

—J. K. MULLEN, 1921[1]

WHEN NOT ATTENDING TO HIS RAMPANT BUSINESS INTERESTS or his distressed domestic life, J. K. Mullen made the completion of the Cathedral of the Immaculate Conception on Colfax and Logan a primary concern between 1906 and 1909. Father Hugh L. McMenamin, the cathedral's popular rector known as "Father Mac," praised the philanthropist as "a gentleman whose thoughts and dealings were so intimately bound up with Catholic life in general and with Cathedral Parish life in particular, that there would have been no Cathedral without him."[2] Since the establishment of St. Mary's Church in 1860, Denver Catholics maintained a cathedral parish without a cathedral. Mullen became involved in the affairs of the cathedral parish soon after his arrival in Denver, first as a Sunday school instructor, then as secretary of the cathedral parish committee. According to McMenamin, the philanthropist urged that a new cathedral be built to honor Bishop Machebeuf's golden jubilee in 1886. Although many Catholics shared his dream, the realization of a grand cathedral would take twenty years to materialize.

Others, including the Leadville mining magnates John F. Campion and John J. and Margaret Tobin "Molly" Brown, initially presented the cathedral parish with more money, but Mullen provided the lion's share of lay leadership regarding cathedral affairs. According to McMenamin, J. K. attended every important meeting regarding the future of the cathedral parish between 1876 and 1921. In 1895, Mullen, along with procathedral rector Michael F. Callanan, cattle and smelting capitalist Dennis Sheedy, lumber baron Charles D. McPhee, and others, arranged an exchange of diocese land between Lincoln and Sherman for twenty-two lots at the corner of Colfax and Logan.[3] In 1901, when Denver's leading Catholic businessmen purchased eight lots to round out the cathedral property, Mullen trailed both Campion and the Browns in donations to the cathedral fund. Campion and the Browns each gave $10,000 to Mullen's $3,000.[4] The Mullen family contributed in other ways. Kate and Ella served as co-vice-presidents of the cathedral fund-raising fairs of 1900 and 1902. (The fairs raised a combined $20,000 by raffling off, among other things, a Denver-made Eaton-McClintock "Gasomobile.") J. K.'s three younger daughters operated various concessions at the fair.[5]

Lubricated with cathedral fair money, excavation began in 1902. Work just as quickly ground to a halt when Father Callanan sank the $53,000 cathedral fund in Cripple Creek mining investments "of uncertain value."[6] Callanan turned over his personal property and meager salary to partially restore the loss. J. K. criticized Bishop Matz for retaining this "dishonest" priest whose error had set the cathedral drive back several years.[7] His judgment of Callanan was harsh. The priest was not the first investor to drop a fortune down a Colorado mine shaft. Still, the setback temporarily stymied cathedral construction. Enough money remained to dig the foundation but the task of raising an estimated $500,000 to finish the building discouraged even the most optimistic fund-raisers. Following the laying of the cornerstone on July 15, 1906, work ceased.

The stimulus to continue came in part from J. K.'s son-in-law James Emerson O'Connor. The young attorney organized a grass-roots campaign of affluent young Catholics to refill the parish coffers. His efforts, along with another fair, raised $26,000. This time, Matz appointed as treasurer a man proven reliable with church funds—J. K. Mullen.[8]

In May 1907, O'Connor and Bishop Matz summoned Denver's most prominent Catholic businessmen to a pair of meetings intended to restart the moribund drive. At these meetings Scottish and Irish business leaders such as clothier George Cottrell, undertaker William P. Horan, lumber and hardware barons John J. McGinnity and Charles

The twin-spired Immaculate Conception Cathedral included elements of French Gothic cathedrals in Chartres, Reims, and Bishop N. C. Matz's native Münster. Designed by Detroit architect Leon Coquard and finished by the Denver firm of Gove and Walsh, fund-raising limitations led the cathedral building committee to recommend a notable reduction of ornamentation from the initial drawings produced by Coquard in 1902. Courtesy, Western History Dept., Denver Public Library.

D. McPhee, and smelter operator Dennis Sheedy offered pledges that doubled the fund. Mullen led all donors with a contribution of $6,500. The financiers also reorganized the building committee consisting of Mullen, O'Connor, and McPhee, with John F. Campion succeeding the ailing Dennis Murtro as president.[9] Mullen was elected chairman of the new finance committee, which comprised the members of the building committee, as well as McGinnity, Sheedy, James Leonard, and others.[10] Along with the newly appointed rector, Father Hugh McMenamin, the cathedral building committee dedicated itself to cutting costs and raising the funds necessary to finish the church.[11]

The new building committee worked quickly to curtail expenses and expedite construction. Work had stalled due to the protracted absence of the project architect, Leon Coquard. Coquard's design for the cathedral, which drew on high French gothic style that he had learned in France, reminded Bishop Matz of his native cathedral in Münster. Although seriously ill, Coquard continued to approve design alterations from his native Detroit, where he had withdrawn for treatment. The long delays irritated the aggressive new building committee. Within a week of their organization, Mullen and the others offered to buy out Coquard's plans. The architect at first refused but reconsidered when the committee offered what the *Denver Catholic Register* called "a good round sum."[12]

The building committee turned over the plans to the Denver architectural firm of Aaron Gove and Thomas Walsh. These reputable architects, known for Denver's 1912 Union Station, the Sugar Building, and the Quality Hill homes of John Campion and Mullen, won the bid with the promise that they would reduce the estimated costs of construction by at least $50,000.[13] Despite a reduction in the cathedral ornamentation, the new architects disappointed the most ardent member of the building committee. As committee treasurer, J. K. Mullen drove a hard bargain with Gove and Walsh. His role on the committee, as he saw it, was not to glorify the church with expensive architecture. Instead, he explained, the committee "insists upon having a good job of work done for the least money that it could be done for."[14]

Mullen backed his insistence with regular inspections of the construction site. To the aggravation of the site supervisor, the sixty-year-old financier questioned the concrete integrity, ignored shouted warnings to avoid unsafe construction areas, and dragged his reluctant architects into the aeries of the cathedral towers. What he saw disappointed him. As he complained in a 1911 letter to Matz, "Gove & Walsh, have caused you and the Cathedral Association more trouble than any firm in the City of Denver." Provided beforehand with Coquard's plans, Gove and Walsh "did not put a scratch nor a line on the plans" that reduced expenses. Their bids on the stonework alone came in between $225,000 and $250,000—which Mullen believed included a kick-back to the new architects. He advanced the bid of an Irish stoneworker, John McLaughlin, over their architects' choice, the Italian contractor Frank Damascio. "We . . . forced this bid down the throats of Gove & Walsh, and we saved $37,000 by taking the bit in our mouth," Mullen declared with satisfaction.

Having received the final plans from these architects, Mullen rec-ommended—and received—their dismissal. In return, Mullen claimed that Gove and Walsh excluded subcontractors favored by the building committee on later projects. Mullen retaliated by suggesting that Matz overlook their bid on renovations to St. Joseph's Hospital.

Saving money on design and construction was one matter. Raising the funds was another. It fell to the business leaders on the committee to raise the bulk of the money. They did so in the approved manner—by signing notes for the expenses and saddling the church with future debt. In 1910, the Cathedral Association claimed assets worth over $336,000 against liabilities of $66,000 owed to the Denver National and German-American Banks. Mullen provided a personal loan of $11,000. The cathedral also owed his brother, city alderman Patrick H. Mullen, $1,500 and John F. Campion, $1,000.[15] By 1916, the Cathedral Association owed $207,000, the bulk of it in a mortgage held by the Massachusetts Mutual Life Insurance Company but also $7,500 each to Mullen and Campion.

Just as the fortunes of the cathedral appeared to smooth out, the cathedral's most active advocate abruptly resigned from the building committee. At issue was a matter of principle. In his Easter sermon of 1909, Bishop Matz charged that "not one Protestant minister in one hundred believed in the divinity of . . . Jesus Christ." Mullen found this accusation—delivered at a time when, as historian Thomas J. Noel has written, "most Catholics at best believed that Protestants were bound for limbo, if not hell"—to be objectionable.[16] As Mullen communicated to his friend Matz:

> God alone knows the inmost thoughts of a Human Mind and . . . I think
> it not only presumptuous and ridiculous but also unchristian for any one
> & above all a Bishop . . . to publicly dispute their statements . . . Many of
> my best Friends are among the Protestant Clergy & I would believe their
> Statements as quick as your own & I could not in Justice to myself and
> family stay on the Building Committee another day if I knew our Bishop
> was guilty of such intolerance and Bigotry so please deny it.[17]

J. K. had long felt strongly about issues of tolerance. Just as importantly, he worried the damage Matz's inflammatory statement might
have on the good will of the Protestant business community.

Matz, one of the most dogged if not the most diplomatic of Colorado church leaders, found himself in the difficult position of having
to defend his principles while not offending his most important patron. His polite but firm reply failed to mollify Mullen. The conclusion—"believe me, my dear Mr. Mullen, as a religious issue, Protestantism is dead"—alarmed the philanthropist further.[18] J. K. responded
respectfully at first, then picked up speed:

> It is presumptuous in a layman to in anywise enter into a controversy with
> [his bishop]. I doubt if anyone has or can have greater regard or respect for
> church authority . . . than the writer . . . but your conclusion is to my mind
> so repugnant . . . that I am shocked beyond expression and feel that it is my
> bounden duty to protest.[19]

The real issue, he continued, was not the health of Protestantism but
rather intolerance. Intolerance, he concluded, represented "too much
doctrine and not enough Christianity," and he repeated, "I would not
care to remain on the Cathedral Building Committee for 24 hours if I
learned . . . you had made the statement as quoted."[20]

It was an ingrained habit for Mullen to question this bishop whom he
had known so long. "I write and talk plainly to Church authorities and
other people seem afraid to do so," he observed to Matz's successor, Bishop
John Henry Tihen.[21] Mullen adhered to the Irish cultural respect of the
clergy but also recognized their human failings, displaying, in his
words, "a proper reverence for the Priesthood, whether worthy or unworthy."[22] As a lay sponsor and personal friend of the clergyman, he
felt entitled to speak forcefully, if deferentially, on strongly held issues. Calling himself "your old scolding friend" and reminding the
bishop repeatedly of his friendship and respect, he nevertheless un-
failingly pointed out the differences between his principles and Matz's
rhetoric.[23] When the bishop refused to bend, J. K. lashed out privately:

I suppose that being born with original sin means that we all have a mean streak in us that should be washed out & if so I need another sousing because I believe it is next thing to wrong if not absolutely wrong to sacrifice and build a church that will be pointed at as a tribute and a memorial to a man [Matz] that has not the first principle of what I consider Christianity . . . & of whom not a man, woman, or child speaks one kind word. Those engaged in the building of the Cathedral are doing a good work because they are actuated by a love of God & our holy religion & they so manifest themselves but I am one of these that believe our Savior is more easily found in the Lowly Churches than in the Lofty Cathedrals . . . The three great virtues, Charity, Love, and Forbearance . . . are seldom found in the high places & certainly not with our most Rev. Bishop.[24]

J. K. understood that, despite their moral leadership, priests sometimes succumbed to human failings. As president of the *Colorado Catholic* in 1890, Mullen had locked out the newspaper's staff and confronted the editor, Father Patrick Carr, when the priest profited on an unauthorized sale of the newspaper to another clergyman for $3,000. Scandalized by this act of venality, Mullen suppressed it from the public record for thirty-seven years.[25] Nevertheless, he often privately criticized Catholic authorities more harshly for their failings, particularly regarding intolerance, than he did intolerant elements of Protestant society.

Mullen considered it his duty to speak out in favor of tolerance for three reasons. The first was that he believed in the principle of tolerance taught in the New Testament. According to C. W. Hurd, Mullen tried to live by the Biblical passages of the Sermon on the Mount, which encouraged men and women to love their enemies, treat each other kindly, and pray for their persecutors. Mullen declared his creed to a CM&E employee with less discretion, "I firmly believe that the untutored Indian [who] has never heard the name of Our Lord and Savior, Jesus Christ, will, if he lives a half decent life, find eternal rest."[26] More pragmatically, J. K. understood that intolerance tended to swing both ways. During periods of insecurity and nativism such as occurred in the 1890s and would come again with the Ku Klux Klan in the 1920s, Matz's anti-Protestant statements could damage the reputation of all Catholics. As he had since his years as an inexperienced mill hand in Kansas, Mullen developed close bonds with Protestant clergymen and lay leaders. Their influence was reflected not only in his manner of thinking about interdenominational issues but also in his sense of

Father Hugh L. McMenamin, popular rector of the Immaculate Conception Cathedral, c. 1910. Courtesy, Thomas J. Noel collection.

financial dependence on the goodwill of the Protestant community. Moreover, J. K. possessed the strength of character and financial wherewithal to back his opinions with action. When Matz declined to

The Shadow of the Debt

*"Have you never remarked the influence of a shadow?" asked
Father McMenamin in his fund-raising letters. "Have you
never noted that shadows breathe sickness, disease, death? . . .
'THE SHADOW OF DEBT SHALL DISAPPEAR!'"
Courtesy, Archdiocese of Denver.*

retract the statement, Mullen resigned from the building committee
in June 1909.[27]

Once off the building committee, Mullen allowed himself to be
convinced by Father McMenamin to remain active as an undesignated
steward of the cathedral. The unfinished structure still carried annual
interest payments of more than $30,000. With the skill of a born
showman, McMenamin revived the interest of the parishioners in the
fortunes of the struggling cathedral. Potential donors received a sketch
of the cathedral shrouded in darkness. The accompanying letter asked

parishioners: "Have you never remarked the influence of a shadow? Have you never noted that shadows breathe sickness, disease, death? . . . Let this be our firm resolve—'THE SHADOW OF DEBT SHALL DISAPPEAR!' "[28]

When McMenamin pledged interior furnishings to wealthy donors, the Mullen family single-handedly retired a year's worth of interest. John and Kate underwrote the marble communion rail to be placed in front of the altar and a spectacular Bavarian stained-glass window depicting the Council of Ephisus in the transept.[29] Daughter Ella sponsored the Sacred Heart statue, while Katherine and James O'Connor provided a window depicting the Visitation of Mary. Mr. and Mrs. Patrick Mullen presented the Nativity. The family of Dennis Mullen subscribed for an Old Testament scene, the Sacrifice of Melchisedech.[30]

McMenamin's efforts raised enough money to pay the annual interest, as well as retiring nearly half the debt between the dedication of the cathedral in 1912 and 1920. In the meantime, Mullen began to recognize his personal responsibility to retire the remaining amount. Although he had resigned from the cathedral building committee, he had carried the burden of the cathedral parish for too many years to set it down so close to completion. In 1914, he set aside $110,000 worth of government bonds—supposedly raised through a penny-a-pound surcharge on CM&E flour—in a trust.[31] Designated to redeem the mortgage held by the Massachusetts Mutual Life Insurance Company, the trust accumulated interest for seven years. The extent to which Mullen personalized the debt became evident when he refused to pool his assets with an independent fund drive begun by William D. McPhee, Mr. and Mrs. Verner Z. Reed, and others.[32] When McMenamin proposed the surplus of the combined accounts be spent on construction of a cathedral high school, Mullen refused to allow his fund to be used on any endeavor that did not retire the construction debt.[33]

On Consecration Day, October 23, 1921, Mullen forwarded his congratulations to Father Mac from Washington, D.C., where he had gone to discuss the endowment of a new library building:

> Next to the Beautiful and Inspiring Word Mother, the Word Cathedral has always had for me a most wonderful significance and meaning . . . The Dedication of our Denver Cathedral was beautiful beyond expression but its Consecration to the worship of Almighty God FREE FROM ALL WORLDLY OBLIGATIONS [Mullen's emphasis] will be an inspiration to all who have the great privilege of being present . . . YOU it was who

planned and worked and prayed and begged continuously from before the first stone was laid until its completion and from its completion until its entire indebtedness was paid.[34]

His letter, exuberant with the emotion of the moment, relays his identification with the project in the emphasized phrases. "YOU it was," he reminded Father Mac in Irish vernacular, who spearheaded the movement. But he also nudged Father Mac to remember who released the cathedral "FROM ALL WORLDLY OBLIGATIONS."

To the philanthropist's great pleasure, his efforts received recognition from no less than the Vatican. In August, word reached Mullen that Pope Benedict XV was considering him for one of the highest lay honors of the church—membership in the Order of St. Gregory.[35] Just prior to the cathedral's consecration, Mullen's ordination was confirmed by a telegram from Bishop Tihen in Rome. "There . . . must be some mistake about it," J. K. at first replied. Nevertheless, he beamed at the

"The Pinnacled Glory of the West." The Immaculate Conception Cathedral, sans windows, stands near completion in 1910. Mullen closely identified with the drive to build what were, to him, grain elevators for the soul. Louis McClure photo. Courtesy, Western History Dept., Denver Public Library.

honor bestowed on his family, his community, and himself, promising "that I will endeavor to so live the remainder of my days that the Holy Father, Yourself [Tihen], the church, or my Friends will have no occasion to feel that I have brought either disgrace or discredit to the title."[36]

Indeed, there is every indication that Mullen expected his family to continue the legacy of cathedral stewardship. He instilled in his family a proprietary sentiment that survived his passing. In 1928, Oscar and Edith Mullen Malo constructed the Oscar Malo Jr. Memorial Hall in honor of their recently deceased son. This combined theater-gymnasium at 1825 Logan complimented the nearby Cathedral High School at 1854 Grant Street.[37]

In 1997 and 1998, the Immaculate Conception Cathedral underwent renovations aimed at restoring many of its original elements. The traditional struggle for construction funds continues as the parish faces challenges from time and nature. On June 21, 1997, a bolt of lightning shattered the cathedral's eastern spire, sending stones tumbling to the street below and closing Colfax Avenue for six weeks. When engineers inspected the damage, they discovered the entire 2,700 pound weight of the pinnacle resting on "one little brick." The pinnacle, wrapped in a heavy plastic brace, took two weeks to remove. Although the accident temporarily diminished cathedral attendance and reduced collections by 50 percent, Archbishop Charles Chaput committed to rebuilding in the original Indiana limestone. Architect David Owen Tryba, responsible for renovations to the interior and exterior of the cathedral, fully restored the tower by the summer of 1998.[38]

If the supposedly apocryphal account of the penny-per-bag rate hike is true, J. K. could not have picked a more propitious time to be generous with the assets of the Colorado Milling and Elevator Company. The war in Europe, which began in 1914, created a golden boom for American wheat farmers and flour millers. J. K. would ride the swell to new levels of affluence, only to see much of his prestige come undone in the war-generated climate of withdrawal and intolerance.

NOTES

1. J. K. Mullen, Letter to Rev. H. L. McMenamin, October 21, 1921, Immaculate Conception Cathedral papers, Archdiocese of Denver archives, Denver, Colorado (hereafter cited as Cathedral papers).
2. This and subsequent references to Mullen's involvement in early cathedral parish affairs cited in Rev. Hugh L. McMenamin, *Diamond Jubilee of the*

Cathedral Parish, Denver, Colorado (Denver: Frank J. Wolf Printers, 1935), 93, 95–96.

3. Rt. Rev. N. C. Matz, "Circular Letter," March 28, 1895, Cathedral papers.
4. "Immaculate Conception Cathedral, General Financial Statement, 1901," Cathedral papers.
5. "Cathedral Building Fund Fair, November 27–December 13, 1902, at Coliseum Hall," Souvenir Program, Cathedral papers.
6. "General Financial Statement, Immaculate Conception Cathedral, 1903," Cathedral papers.
7. Ibid.; J. K. Mullen, Letter to Rt. Rev. N. C. Matz, October 9, 1903, Rt. Rev. Nicholas C. Matz manuscript collection, Archdiodese of Denver archives (hereafter cited as Matz papers).
8. McMenamin, *Diamond Jubilee*, 37–38.
9. Rev. Hugh L. McMenamin, *The Pinnacled Glory of the West: Cathedral of the Immaculate Conception* (Denver: Smith-Brooks Printing, 1912), 158.
10. *Denver Post*, June 9, 1907.
11. Thomas J. Noel, *Colorado Catholicism and the Archdiocese of Denver, 1857–1989* (Niwot: University Press of Colorado, 1989), 65.
12. *Denver Catholic Register* (*DCR*), May 16, 1907: 1.
13. Thomas J. Noel and Barbara S. Norgren, *Denver: The City Beautiful and Its Architects, 1893–1941* (Denver: Historic Denver, Inc., 1987), 202.
14. This and Mullen's subsequent complaints about Gove & Walsh cited in J. K. Mullen, Letter to Rt. Rev. N. C. Matz, July 14, 1911, Matz papers.
15. "Financial Statement of the Immaculate Conception Cathedral Association," September 24, 1910, Cathedral papers.
16. J. K. Mullen, Letter to Rt. Rev. N. C. Matz, April 12, 1909, Matz papers; Thomas J. Noel, with Kevin E. Rucker and Stephen J. Leonard, *Colorado Givers: A History of Philanthropic Heroes* (Niwot: University Press of Colorado, 1998), 70.
17. J. K. Mullen, Letter to Rt. Rev. N. C. Matz, April 12, 1909, Matz papers.
18. Rt. Rev. N. C. Matz, Letter to J. K. Mullen, April 21, 1909, Matz papers.
19. J. K. Mullen, Letter to Rt. Rev. N. C. Matz, May 2, 1909, Matz papers.
20. Ibid.
21. J. K. Mullen, Letter to Rt. Rev. N. C. Matz, May 2, 1909, Matz papers.
22. J. K. Mullen, Letter to Rt. Rev. J. H. Tihen, February 4, 1928, Rt. Rev. John Henry Tihen manuscript collection, Archdiodese of Denver archives (hereafter cited as Tihen papers). Mullen expressed this opinion when he offered to pay for the burial of the "mentally unbalanced" Father Michael Culkin. For Irish opinions of the clergy, see Andrew M. Greeley, *That Most Distressful Nation: The Taming of the American Irish* (Chicago: Quadrangle Books, 1972), 85.
23. J. K. Mullen, Letter to Rt. Rev. N. C. Matz, April 2, 1915, Tihen papers.
24. J. K. Mullen, Letter to Rev. H. L. McMenamin, June 30, 1909, Tihen papers.
25. J. K. Mullen, Letter to Rev. Matthew Smith, December 7, 1927, Timothy O'Connor collection, Denver, Colorado.

26. Charles W. Hurd, "J. K. Mullen, Milling Magnate of Colorado," *The Colorado Magazine* XXIX:2 (April 1952): 118; J. K. Mullen, Letter to L. L. Breckenridge, November 5, 1928, John Kernan Mullen manuscript collection, MSS 705 (hereafter cited as Mullen papers), Colorado Historical Society (CHS).

27. *Denver Post*, June 4, 1909: 15.

28. Rev. H. L. McMenamin, "The Shadow of Debt," circular, December 19, 1915, Cathedral papers.

29. The communion rail was relocated in accordance with Vatican II guidelines in the mid-1970s despite a lawsuit to restrain the action by Mullen's granddaughter Eleanore Mullen Weckbaugh. It now rests in the cathedral foyer. Noel, *Colorado Catholicism*, 217.

30. McMenamin, *Diamond Jubilee*, 59–60. Melchisedech was a priest-king in the Old Testament to whom the prophet Abraham paid tribute (Gen. 14:18–20, Heb. 7:1–21).

31. Noel, *Colorado Catholicism*, 316. The source of this claim, J. K. Mullen's barber, is questionable but Mullen was not above using his mills to further Catholic ends (see Chapter 13 herein and J. K. Mullen, Letter to Rt. Rev. J. Henry Tihen, March 7, 1923, Tihen papers), nor was he known for keeping flour prices down. If this claim can be believed, Mullen cleared the debt by selling only 1,100 one-hundred-pound bags of flour. A penny-per-pound surcharge and the resulting increase of $1.00 per cwt. would have invited unfavorable criticism. Based on the CM&E production rates at the time, an increase of a penny per ten pounds (11,000 bags) or a penny per hundred pounds (110,000 bags) would have been less noticeable but still enough to raise the construction relief fund.

32. J. K. Mullen, Letter to Rev. H. L. McMenamin, July 8, 1921, Cathedral papers.

33. McMenamin, *Diamond Jubilee*, 61.

34. J. K. Mullen, Letter to Rev. H. L. McMenamin, October 21, 1921, Cathedral papers.

35. *Rocky Mountain News*, August 7, 1921: 1.

36. J. K. Mullen, Letter to Rt. Rev. J. H. Tihen, 1921, Tihen papers.

37. Noel, *Colorado Catholicism*, 217.

38. *Denver Post*, July 19, 1997: 3B; July 20, 1997: 5.

15

THE ENEMY MILLER, 1914–1919

To the ears of American wheat processors, the muted rumblings of the Great War sounded like the ring of golden good fortune. As armies sowed European wheat fields with the ghastly seed of death, wheat prices, which had only grudgingly advanced since the depression of 1893, skyrocketed to record levels in American commodities markets. The increased demand benefited Colorado's farmers, but it was Colorado's leading flour supplier who stood to gain the most financially and politically from the distant catastrophe. As the war drums beat closer to home and America began mobilizing to enter the fight, political leaders naturally invited the industrialist to join the wartime advisory councils both in Colorado and in the national capital. J. K. felt that his contributions to the war effort as chairman of the Colorado Council of Defense and as a member of the U.S. Council of Defense and the U.S. Grain Corporation solidified his role as a member of the national business elite. To his astonishment, public criticism brought about by Colorado Milling and Elevator Company price manipulation and public relations blunders, and intensified by the dogmatic wartime climate, elicited questions about J. K.'s patriotism. By the end of the war, Mullen would have to scramble to retain his public prestige.

WARTIME WHEAT REGULATIONS

In Denver, Mullen's place in the councils of local decisionmakers testified to the security of his political and financial connections. As a member of the Denver Board of Trade; vice-president and member, along with

Anne Evans, Rabbi William S. Friedman, and Judge A. Moore Berry, of the City and County of Denver Library Commission; and, after 1917, a director of the First National Bank of Denver, he hobnobbed with newspaper publishers, financiers, reformers, clergymen, and politicians from both major parties.

When America entered the war in April 1917, J. K. found ready employment as a "dollar-a-year man"—a business leader who advised the government out of patriotic spirit. Governor Julius Gunter appointed Mullen as chairman of the Colorado Council of Defense. Soon after, President Woodrow Wilson selected the miller as a member of the prestigious U. S. Council of National Defense—a committee charged with no less a task than "the coordination of industries and resources for the national security and welfare . . . of the nation."[1] Wilson also assigned the miller to the U.S. Grain Corporation, one of a number of "collective" bureaucracies created to coordinate American war production. Headed by the popular former Belgian Relief Commissioner Herbert Hoover, the U.S. Grain Corporation distributed grain supplies to Allied armies and promoted home-front conservation through voluntary "wheatless" days. It attempted to stimulate wheat production by urging farmers to "Plant More Wheat!" and suggesting that "Wheat Will Win the War!" Most importantly, it suppressed speculation and price gouging by regulating the prices and levels of national wheat reserves. The term "profiteer" became a dirty, if not treasonous, label. Production and consumption would be guaranteed through voluntary self-sacrifice.[2]

The concept of self-sacrifice—deliberate delay of self-gratification and profit taking until it was over, "over there"—took time to germinate among many wheat speculators. War, combined with poor harvests in 1916 and 1917, pushed the wholesale price of wheat and flour to new highs in unregulated commodities markets. By May 1917, wheat bought for $1.44 per bushel in the fall of 1916 sold for $3.45 per bushel in Chicago. The bonanza produced an estimated profit of $50 million per month for American speculators, jobbers, and millers, although farmers and consumers saw little of the windfall.[3] At the CM&E, Mullen and the board of directors rewarded their employees for the boom by establishing a $140,000 pension fund from "the Company surplus" in September 1917. Augmented with $10,000 from Mullen's personal savings, the pension awarded retired or incapacitated employees of twenty years' service with an annual stipend of up to $720.[4]

This El Dorado of wheat speculation was marred by nationwide accusations of price gouging. Locally, the *Denver Post* renewed the old complaint that "the Mullen trust" paid too little for its clients' wheat harvests and sold its flour too dear. Spokesmen for the CM&E blamed the increased price of Chicago wheat for the markup. The *Post* countered that Colorado farmers could sell their wheat in Chicago for twenty-six cents per hundred pounds more than CM&E buyers were offering in Denver, freight included. Since Colorado husbandmen depended on western markets to consume their wheat, they appeared to be at the mercy of "arbitrary" pricing decisions made by the CM&E.[5]

J. K. used his new influence to undercut some of the grumbling. Three days before the United States entered the war, Mullen, acting in conjunction with his role as chairman of the state council for war preparedness, released spring wheat seed to farmers at the previous year's

The flood of prosperity created by an expanded Homestead Act and high wartime prices left wheat producers such as this Western Slope farmer wading in profits. The speculative boom tempted middlemen around the country to circumvent wartime price regulations. Louis C. McClure photo. Courtesy, Western History Dept., Denver Public Library.

noninflated prices. The CM&E stood to lose $100,000 but the gesture, intended to kick-start the American war production effort, was praised by the *Post* as "a patriotic policy" in line with the spirit of wartime cooperation.[6] The *Post*'s good opinion quickly soured in light of revelations regarding Mullen's alleged manipulation of wheat regulations from his seat on the state defense production council.

The emergency demand for flour created nearly irresistible temptations for gouging throughout the country. In order to control prices, the U.S. Food Administration sponsored legislation that granted the U.S. Grain Corporation a purchasing monopoly on wheat. Congress fixed the wholesale price of wheat at $2.20 per bushel, but lax enforcement, combined with complicated and sometimes contradictory production, ratio, substitution, and grading regulations, led to mistakes and abuses nationwide. Mills all around the country, including the mills of the CM&E, paid minor fines for running afoul of the rules. In 1918, for example, the CM&E's Husler Mill in Salt Lake City was cited for adding an improper amount of wheat flour to its barley mixture—allowed under an older set of rules but recently banned. The Food Administration dropped the charges against the CM&E and issued a letter of thanks "for their efforts to cooperate with the government in carrying out its food regulations."[7] On the darker side, millers commonly relied on outright trickery to evade the regulations. In his history of the U.S. Grain Corporation, former Food Administration attorney William C. Mullendore reported, "Some millers attempted to evade the limitations by setting up separate jobbing departments . . . Cost reports were . . . padded, salaries were increased, [and] excessive depreciation figures were included."[8]

Abuses were widespread. In Colorado, the CM&E squeezed out an extra profit by paying farmers the federally regulated price less the cost of freighting the wheat to Chicago. Although local wheat was processed in local mills, the corporation defended its practice by arguing that, technically, wheat could only be redeemed for the federal price on the Chicago Grain Exchange. The twenty-nine-cent-per-hundred-pound difference between Colorado and Chicago prices, spokesmen argued, merely represented the break-even point of shipping. In reality, the CM&E pocketed the difference. The following year, the government issued lower price restrictions. The CM&E refigured its buying prices to offset freight rates to Jacksonville, Florida—

the farthest possible continental destination. The rate discount was merely a phantom bookkeeping trick that maintained profit levels. To the outrage of angry farmers, both schemes received the official sanction of the state food administrator as well as Mullen's state council of defense. Farmers did not hesitate to point out the conflict of interest.[9]

Schemes such as the rate loophole seemed more egregious because the Wilson administration food councils supposedly represented a noble alliance of government and private industry for the public good. Instead, Mullen's conflicting roles as president of the CM&E and chairman of the Colorado Defense Council appeared to represent collusion between government and business. Colorado tillers shared the concerns of a Wisconsin farmer who complained that the defense councils were packed with "the same class of people who have incurred . . . ill will in former times . . . representatives of a business system . . . who now under the guise of Patriotism are trying to ram down the farmers' throats things they hardly dared before."[10]

Although Mullen was in a position to make a policy that appeased his critics, he continued to make highhanded pronouncements, which his opponents happily used against him. Attempting to reassure wary consumers about the volatile flour market, he declared, "I control the price of flour in Colorado." Negotiating a price on the highest grade of flour (soon to be banned by new Food Administration regulations), he remarked, "I won't allow the stores to sell my fancy flour at a profit of less than 50 cents."[11] Both statements, appearing in local newspapers without context, cast the capitalist in an arrogant light. Worse, his declarations could be made to appear treasonous. In December 1917, the state legislature locked seed prices at prewar rates—a gesture that J. K. had made on his own nine months earlier. When Mullen complained about the usurpation of the market, state attorney general Leslie E. Hubbard branded the miller as an "arch-traitor" whose self-interest undermined the very soldiers on the front. "If the sacrifices of our boys in arms, ready to throw themselves like chaff into the burning hell of war, is not to be in vain . . . unjust profiteering must stop."

To J. K.'s surprise, the critical arrows began finding their mark. The *Denver Post* revived the farmer's old objection to "docking" wheat by up to 30 percent during cleaning:

> Just what amount is deducted is wholly up to the "trust." The farmer never
> knows how much dirt and wastage there was in his grain—except what the

"trust's" statement tells him . . . and they can "soak him" for whatever they please.

Angry farmers, this time joined by housewives fed up with rising flour and bakery prices, boycotted CM&E flour. They also petitioned Governor Gunter to remove Mullen from the Colorado Defense Council. The U.S. Food Administration summoned the industrialist to Washington to defend his actions. Word reached Denver that President Wilson was considering removing Mullen from the U.S. Council of National Defense.[12]

Closer to home, Mullen faced a commercial backlash from the heirs of the Grange. The Farmer's Co-Operative and Educational Union erected a competitive mill at Millikin, planned another in Longmont, and opened thirty-six elevators statewide. Co-op spokesman Dr. William R. Collicott denounced the "Mullen mills . . . practice of purchasing cracked and shriveled wheat from the farmers at the lowest possible price [and] later dispos[ing of it] at the prices of A No. 1 wheat." Collicott looked to mining unions for inspiration, going so far as to call for check weighmen in CM&E mills.[13]

"We are going to cut out . . . the milling trust," Collicott confidently predicted. He found allies in Henry H. Tammen and Frederick G. Bonfils, the controversial owners of the *Denver Post*. When it boosted circulation, the publishers perceived enemies to American values behind every bush. Traitors did not require Teutonic ancestry, although Germans absorbed a large amount of discrimination. Instead, the opportunistic publishers castigated anyone who failed to conform to standards of "100-percent Americanism."[14] The two archetypal traitors slinking behind a stalwart but oblivious American sentinel in a January 17, 1918, political cartoon showed that the *Post* recognized no distinction between the bomb-throwing "German Spy" and a fat, money bag–toting "War Profiteer." Mullen's manipulation of grain and flour prices during the national crisis justly deserved criticism. The *Post*, in the supernationalistic climate of the war, transformed the gouging issue into a more sinister question of loyalty.

The editors at the *Post* crucified Mullen. Any given evening, the miller might cringe to read such banners as: "Mullen Grabs Chance to Dip into Pockets of Flour Consumers: Finds Opportunity to Gather Few Extra Dimes While Food Board's Hands Are Tied with Making Rates—Fine Brand of Patriotism." Combining jingoism and investigative

WEATHER FORECAST.
Tonight and Friday, Fair; Not Much Change in Temperature.

THE DENVER POST

POPULATION DENVER.
Census, 1910..............213,381
U. S. Census, estimate, 1917.268,439

3D EDITION
14 PAGES

★ THE BEST NEWSPAPER IN THE U. S. A. ★

2¢ BY NEWSBOYS.
5¢ ON TRAINS.

DENVER. COLO.. THURSDAY. JANUARY 17. 1918.

WAR PROFITEER

GERMAN SPY

TWO CHIEF ENEMIES BEHIND THE AMERICAN LINES!

"*Two Chief Enemies Behind the American Lines!*" The Denver Post *identified moneybag-toting capitalists and bomb-throwing traitors as co-conspirators in the assault on democracy. To Mullen's discomfort,* the Post *made an example of his exploitation of loopholes to illustrate that wartime profiteering equaled treason. Courtesy, Colorado Historical Society.*

reporting, the ensuing article capped justifiable criticisms with charges of disloyalty. J. K.'s actions were characterized as "a sample of the brand of patriotism and the kind of treatment which the milling trust . . . is according patriots of Colorado whose sons are sacrificing their lives in the cause of freedom."[15] When Mullen was summoned before the U.S. Food Board, the *Post* editorialized:

> The food administration has been able . . . to divide all the millers of the United States . . . into just two classes: American millers and enemy millers; those who are serving Uncle Sam and those who are working for the Kaiser . . . Some of these enemy millers are not subjects of the German imperial government; some of them even profess, in words, to oppose it, while in deeds they . . . faithfully serve the Kaiser in every revolution of the rolls with which they produce flour.

"No one wants to do the trust or Mullen any harm," the *Post* primly concluded. Neither did they want the miller to turn traitor "as a result of his mistaken independence."[16]

While Bonfils and Tammen shook the stick of conformity at the milling capitalist, Mullen protested about his inability either to justify fair charges or to rebut false ones. He complained that reporters either misquoted him or failed to look deeply at the complicated nuances of wartime regulations. In order to maintain a continuity of quality and price, for instance, wartime food-production regulations permitted the milling of only a single midgrade flour. After the war, federal regulations controlling wheat, bran, and flour grades and prices were rescinded and millers resumed making high-quality baker's flour. Mullen tried to explain to an inattentive *Post* reporter that although the market price for midgrade flour had dropped, his mills were now producing a line of higher-quality flour that raised the overall average price of CM&E products. The next day, he read the headline: "Consumers Gouged . . . Flour Should Drop 17 Cents Under Former Rules But Not a Cent Reduction Comes." The body of the article failed to mention his explanation. He complained to Bonfils, "The *Post* again presents this matter in a false light to our detriment and holds us up as gouging the community . . . Do you think that's a fair treatment? . . . Isn't it about time to let up?"[17]

Frustrated when his responses were turned against him, Mullen at first offered stony silence to the reporters, then, when badgered for a quote on Christmas Eve, 1917, he publicly turned the other cheek:

"Oh Yes! You go back to Harry Tammen and tell him that J. K. said that he wished him good health, a long life, and a Merry Christmas. That's all the statement I care to make."[18]

RESTITUTION: THE *BRONCHO BUSTER* AND THE UNIVERSITY OF DENVER CHAPEL

His light handling of the situation belied the depth to which Mullen was stung by the charges of disloyalty. He scrambled to repair his damaged reputation through a burst of civic charity. In 1918, he helped found an "Americanization Committee" answerable to the Colorado Council for Defense and contributed funds "for the furtherance of this most worthy object."[19] He also looked to his long friendship with Denver mayor Robert Speer to provide a handy outlet for high-profile public philanthropy. Mayor Speer was a powerful ally who owed J. K. much. During the 1880s, Mullen had served as an election judge in Speer's nascent political machine. In 1907, J. K. sat on an "independent committee" of capitalists who had rubber-stamped Speer's controversial Civic Center project—which razed three city blocks to make way for a colonnade-flanked promenade between the state capitol and a proposed City and County Building. After helping smooth the way for the construction of the Carnegie Library in the Civic Center Plaza, J. K. also donated to Mayor Speer's Denver Public Library book fund in 1917.[20]

The Civic Center master plan called for a sculpture garden in the central "Plaza of the Past." Intended to, in the words of Speer's promotional magazine *Denver Municipal Facts*, "preserve the picturesque atmosphere of the frontier," the planned sculpture garden would feature bronze versions of Alexander Phimister Proctor's sculptures *Equestrian Indian* and *Broncho Buster* to replace plaster models that were already crumbling in the vacant plaza. In 1918, Mullen and CM&E director Stephen Knight agreed to underwrite these suitably patriotic works for $15,000 each. Proctor, the sculptor, recalled that "Mullen said that he would donate the cowboy, and Knight agreed to donate the Indian." The *Post* guardedly praised Mullen's and Knight's generosity but took a cut at Mullen by pointing out that the model for the *Broncho Buster* was an accused horse thief, whose release Proctor had arranged long enough to finish the piece.[21]

Political motivations brought on by the *Post*'s criticism also spurred one of J. K.'s most high-minded religious endowments. In December

Mullen's gift of the romantic Broncho Buster *statue to Civic Center Plaza, one of the most visible symbols of Denver's pioneer heritage, coincided with wartime accusations of profiteering and disloyalty. In his memoir,* Sculptor in Buckskins, *A. Phimister Proctor recalled that "Mullen said that he would donate the cowboy, and Knight agreed to donate the Indian." The* Post *guardedly praised Mullen's civic virtue but took the opportunity to point out that the statue's model stood accused of horse theft. Louis C. McClure photo. Courtesy, Western History Dept., Denver Public Library.*

1917, as the profiteering scandal threatened J. K.'s position on the U.S. Council of Defense, the philanthropist committed $16,000 to furnish an interdenominational chapel at the Methodist-leaning University of Denver. Mullen made the donation as a gesture of ecumenical tolerance. He emphasized his point by commissioning an electrically lit bronze plaque from Tiffany's of New York, which read:

> This room was finished and furnished by J. K. Mullen, of Denver, Colorado, a Roman Catholic, in the hope that religious prejudices may vanish from the life of all Christian bodies.[22]

The timing of the gift also indicates the extent to which Mullen used his patronage to influence political favor. J. K.'s donation coincided with his summons to Washington to defend his actions to the Food Administration and President Woodrow Wilson. His gift won the gratitude of DU chancellor and former Colorado governor Henry A. Buchtel—a man with powerful connections in the national capital. Buchtel accordingly presented President Wilson with a voucher of Mullen's character:

> We in these parts never pay any attention to any attack which is made upon any one by the *Denver Post*. Mr. Mullen is a man of incorruptible integrity. No one here or anywhere has given himself more completely to the service of his country than has this man of superior character.

Buchtel shared with Wilson the text of the bronze plaque at DU, concluding, "this tells Mullen's story."[23]

The gift revealed an interesting blend of high-minded idealism and political pragmatism. Mullen stipulated that the donation was to remain secret until the chapel was completed in order to prevent the press from speculating about his motives. Shunning any display of ostentation at this politically sensitive time ("I very much dislike any appearance of show," he remarked), Mullen refused front-row seats at the dedication ceremony.[24] With the help of Buchtel and Catholic University chancellor Bishop Thomas Shahan, he quietly retained his seat on the U.S. Council of National Defense.[25]

Accusations of wartime profiteering sputtered into 1919, as the *Denver Post* speculated about secret CM&E control of local baking companies—charges that caused competing bakeries to pull CM&E flour from their shelves in protest. In fact, CM&E director Stephen Knight maintained a financial stake in the Campbell-Sell and Macklem Baking Companies, but Mullen took out a full-page ad in the *Post* to deny investing in bakeries either personally or on behalf of the milling company.[26]

As if to prove his patriotism during the Great War, the flour baron afterwards displayed the certificate of appreciation he received from the president for his work on the council. The certificate symbolized his hard-earned status as a member of the financial elite, won at the price of further estrangement from the yeomen with whom he traded. To J. K., vindication continued to require the creation of sensitive endowments. One of his greatest, the Mullen Home for the Aged, spanned the same period.

NOTES

1. United States Council of National Defense, "Certificate of Acknowledgment to J. K. Mullen," June 28, 1919, Weckbaugh family collection.
2. Robert G. Athearn, *The Mythic West in Twentieth-Century America* (Lawrence: University Press of Kansas, 1986), 39; David M. Kennedy, *Over Here: The First World War and American Society* (New York: Oxford University Press, 1980), 119: Ellis Wayne Hawley, *The Great War and the Search for Modern Order: A History of the American People and Their Institutions, 1917–1933* (New York: St. Martin's Press, 1979), 23–26.
3. William C. Mullendore, *History of the United States Food Administration, 1917–1919* (Stanford: Stanford University Press, 1941), 123.
4. Colorado Milling and Elevator Co., "Memorandum to the Board of Directors," September 1919, Mullen papers, Western History Dept., Denver Public Library (WHDDPL).
5. *Denver Post*, August 10, 1918: 7.
6. *Denver Post*, April 13, 1917: 18.
7. *Denver Post*, September 13, 1918: 8; "J. K. Mullen Mill Cleared of Charge," unattributed, undated clipping, Weckbaugh family collection.
8. Mullendore, 127–129, 147.
9. *Denver Post*, August 10, 1918: 7.
10. Cited in Kennedy, 120.
11. This quote, as well as the profiteering claims, Leslie Hubbard's remarks, and the public reaction, cited in the *Denver Post*, December 10, 1917: 5.
12. *Denver Post*, September 13, 1918: 7; December 21, 1917: 24; Henry A. Buchtel, Letter to President Woodrow Wilson, December 24, 1917, Weckbaugh family collection.
13. *Denver Post*, January 22, 1918: 1.
14. Stephen J. Leonard and Thomas J. Noel, *Denver: Mining Camp to Metropolis* (Niwot: University Press of Colorado, 1990), 186–187; John Higham, *Strangers in the Land: Patterns of American Nativism, 1860–1925*, 2d ed. (New Brunswick: Rutgers University Press, 1988), 204.

15. *Denver Post*, August 10, 1918: 7.
16. *Denver Post*, December 21, 1917: 24.
17. J. K. Mullen, Letter to Frederick G. Bonfils, December 24, 1918, Weckbaugh family collection.
18. *Denver Post*, December 21, 1917: 24; J. K. Mullen, Letter to F. G. Bonfils and Harry H. Tammen, December 14, 1917, Weckbaugh family collection.
19. J. K. Mullen, Letter to Henry A. Buchtel, July 9, 1918, Weckbaugh family collection.
20. *Rocky Mountain News*, March 14, 1883: 8; *Municipal Facts* (Denver: City and County of Denver), February 12, 1910; January 14, 1911; October 1918.
21. *Municipal Facts*, October 1918; April 1919; A. Phimister Proctor, *Sculptor in Buckskin*, Hester E. Proctor, ed. (Norman: University of Oklahoma Press, 1971), 175; Thomas J. Noel and Barbara S. Norgren, *Denver: The City Beautiful and Its Architects, 1893–1941* (Denver: Historic Denver, Inc., 1987), 142; *Denver Post*, June 30, 1918: 15.
22. H. A. Buchtel, Letter to President Woodrow Wilson, December 24, 1917, Weckbaugh family collection.
23. Ibid.
24. J. K. Mullen, Letter to H. A. Buchtel, December 14, 1917, Weckbaugh family collection.
25. Rt. Rev. Thomas J. Shahan, Letter to H. A. Buchtel, December 23, 1917, Weckbaugh family collection. In his own letter to Secretary Joseph P. Tumulty, Shahan deplored the "stigmatization" of Mullen's family by the *Post*: "It hurts me . . . that in the evening of his life he should be subject to these attacks in this city . . . of which he is the chief citizen." Shahan, Letter to Tumulty, December 23, 1917, Rt. Rev. John Henry Tihen manuscript collection, Archdiocese of Denver archives.
26. *Denver Post*, April 23, 1919: 13, 18.

16

THE J. K. MULLEN HOME FOR THE AGED

> Myself and my wife lived here for a great many years. When we came, there were no old people, we were all young and because of this we consider ourselves pioneers . . . We wanted, before we passed away, to leave something in the nature of a memorial.
>
> —J. K. MULLEN, 1916[1]

"WHEN WE CAME . . . WE WERE ALL YOUNG." By 1910, the generation who had grown up with Denver could no longer claim that distinction. Mullen perceived the gradual passing of the frontier in the diminishing numbers of his peers. In 1912, the sixty-five-year-old capitalist reflected that four of the nine founders of the Colorado Milling and Elevator Company were deceased. Those remaining, he felt, should "put their house in order, for the time approaches when they shall also pay the debt of Nature."[2] Nature tried to claim J. K. himself in March 1913, when the capitalist refused treatment for an inflamed appendix until it became septic. He survived—without benefit of antibiotics—but not before family members summoned Father William O'Ryan to administer last rites.[3] For nearly eight weeks, the flour baron lingered near death, oblivious to all news of the outside world. Recovering, he endured an even greater emotional shock. His surviving older brother, Patrick, had suffered a fatal stroke. J. K.'s family withheld the news fearing its effect on the ailing miller. Still too critically ill to leave his own bed, J. K. had to be restrained from rushing to his deceased brother. He nevertheless insisted on being carefully transported by ambulance and stretcher to where Patrick lay in state. The two siblings lay together silently for a time, one bound for the grave and the other nearly so. Finally, J. K. placed his hand against his brother's face and tearfully bade his brother farewell.[4]

The invalid businessman had plenty of time to ponder ways to preserve his legacy as one of Denver's diminishing population of pioneers. His own prospects were secure, yet conditions among Denver's poor aged population disturbed him. "I don't believe," he told a reporter, "there is anything sadder than the sight of an old man, deserted, friendless, penniless, alone in the world."[5] He rededicated himself to a project, begun two years before when he had first met Mother Germaine, the Mother Provincial of the Little Sisters of the Poor, of Palatine, Illinois.

Founded in 1839 by Jeanne Jugan of Brittany, France, the Little Sisters of the Poor dedicated themselves to this simple, praiseworthy mission:

> To obtain for the poor old people a little peace, calm and happiness in their old age, to keep them from dangerous occasions and all earthly cares . . . and thus prepare them for a happy death.[6]

Mullen agreed with the Mother Provincial that Denver needed a home that provided dignified care for the elderly. Together, the philanthropist, Bishop Matz, and Mother Germaine began looking for a site. As early as 1911, they inspected a large, weedy block located between Quebec and Syracuse Streets on East Montview Boulevard. J. K. foresaw problems. The sandy, unirrigated lots were far from the city center, distant from the nearest streetcar line, and "extravagantly" priced. The north half of the block belonged to friends of the Catholic diocese—John F. Campion and Dennis Sullivan—but the other half belonged to non-Catholic developers who it was believed opposed the construction of a Catholic rest home. Mullen anticipated difficult purchasing negotiations with the owners of these lots. He also worried that "the Sister does not realize the difficulty she will encounter out here . . . to either cultivate or beautify a big piece of ground."[7]

Nevertheless, the drab realities gave way to an overwhelming vision of this monument to Catholic generosity. According to Matz, Mullen strode the barren grounds, declaring: "I want a house here where everyone coming out on this magnificent boulevard might see it and take an object lesson on the charity of Catholics . . . on behalf of the aged poor who of all the poor are the most abandoned."[8] Accordingly, Mullen purchased half the block and opened negotiations for the rest, only to be informed by Matz that the Little Sisters were unable to organize a Denver rest home until 1915 or 1916. "I paid a big price for the half block," he complained. In order to avoid an additional tax

A pioneer enjoys the view from the newly completed J. K. Mullen Home for the Aged in 1918. Operated since its opening by the Little Sisters of the Poor, the institution remains the national model of dignified care of the elderly despite the fact that all funding comes from donations. Courtesy, Western History Dept., Denver Public Library.

burden, he withdrew his offer on the remaining lots until the Little Sisters organized the means to return.[9]

Momentum had shifted to his side, however. Working under the misunderstanding that Mullen had already purchased the Montview property, Mother Germaine convinced her Superior General to open the new home two years early, in 1913. Her enthusiasm, Matz's desire that "immediate steps be taken," and Mullen's life-threatening appendicitis granted an impetus. Objecting local landowners provided an obstacle. Opponents argued that the proposed Catholic rest home would reduce the value of their property. A sympathetic city council agreed, passing an ordinance that "prohibited the construction of buildings of this kind . . . when located along the line of a boulevard" without the written consent of adjacent property owners.[10]

At first, Mullen indicated a willingness to fight the naysayers, but after receiving placatory advice from Cardinal John Farley of New York, he changed his mind:

> I was never entirely satisfied that the location was the best . . . and . . . I did not want to excite the ill will or antipathy of any portion of the community . . . I am quite sure that I could have the ordinance repealed . . . but I prefer to avoid it . . . if the parties interested would purchase the block from me.[11]

Other locations made better financial sense. J. K. had worried that the Montview site was too distant from downtown. Exposed to the prairie, the proposed home would require the "very considerable" extra expenses in heating coal and irrigation ditches to make the sandy soil bloom.[12] Added to that were the inflated prices of the east Denver streetcar suburbs. "I can go outside of the town, probably somewhere on the north side . . . and buy fifteen to twenty acres for what this Block . . . would cost me," he lamented.[13] The larger space would have room for a chapel, an irrigation ditch, and gardens. More importantly, Mullen could control adjacent parcels in order to prevent further restrictions.

Accordingly, J. K. abandoned the lot in east Denver and focused instead on negotiations to the north. Health problems, delays in the city council, and J. K.'s work on the defense boards delayed the project for two more years. In late August 1916, Mullen procured a new location on West Twenty-Eighth and Thirtieth between Lowell Boulevard and Newton Street for about $50,000. The site was the home of Denver real-estate developer and tree farmer Hiram G. Wolff.[14] A former nursery, the irrigated, tree-lined, ten-acre lot provided a stark contrast

As this c. 1920 photo suggests, Mullen encouraged Colorado's pioneers to continue their self-sufficient practices by planting vegetable gardens at the Mullen Home for the Aged. Today, residents repose under shade trees on the landscaped grounds. Courtesy, Western History Dept., Denver Public Library.

to the arid block in east Denver. "It is the finest plot of ground in the city," Mullen wrote.[15]

Again, local opponents tried to block the rest home. When rumors of the proposed sale circulated, "protestants" from North Denver acquired "several hundred" signatures on petitions opposing the erection of such an institution. Mayor Robert Speer, a longtime friend and political ally of the capitalist, outmaneuvered the city council. He calmly informed the protesters that because "no application [for a construction permit] had been made to the city," the city had no legal grounds to act.[16] The outcry increased J. K.'s caution. He asked all involved parties to preserve silence about their plans "until after the real estate transfer . . . becomes a matter of public record."[17] The backlash, bolstered by Mother Germaine's advice and his own principles, influenced Mullen's decision to scrap the idea of a Catholics-only rest home and open the facility to all denominations. His draft conveyance—handwritten on the backs of CM&E accounting sheets—demonstrates

A collection of Denver pioneers resided at the J. K. Mullen Home for the Aged. Segregated by gender and initially restricted to whites, the institution nevertheless pioneered the removal of social barriers based on creed. Courtesy, Thomas J. Noel collection.

the change of heart. Under qualifications for admission, Mullen struck out the phrase "Catholic" and replaced it with "without restriction as to sex, religion, or nationality."[18] His concession represented a concrete, if limited, application of his principles of tolerance. While accepting diverse creeds and gender, both the first and final drafts specifically excluded nonwhites. As an attempt to sever the lines of discrimination, the effort is laudable, but still constrained by the racist assumptions of Mullen's generation.

Mullen, Mother Germaine, and Catholic diocesan attorney John H. Reddin hammered the philanthropist's scribbled expectations into a final agreement. Mullen suggested that the board of incorporators include five "prominent Catholics" and two "highly respected, liberal Protestants" who would all quietly resign "at the first meeting of the board" in favor of the Little Sisters.[19] Mother Germaine thanked Mullen for his "very practical" suggestion, but informed him that the "spirit and rules" of the Little Sisters prevented lay people from joining the organizing body.[20] In keeping with his preference for pioneers, he also favored a residency requirement of five years for qualified applicants.

Both Reddin and Mother Germaine convinced him to lower his restrictive standard to a one-year residency requirement.[21]

Nevertheless, the trio agreed on the basic terms. For the sum of one dollar, Mullen promised to turn the property over to an incorporated body of Little Sisters. He pledged an additional $150,000 for the development of the building and grounds in return for a prominently displayed tablet commemorating "The J. K. Mullen and Family Memorial Home for the Aged People of Colorado to the Little Sisters of the Poor."[22] On August 30, the site was ready for occupancy by Mother Germaine and her assistants. The first five sisters—Germaine, Justine, Elisabeth, Marie Wilfride, and Dominique—arrived on September 12, 1916, and set up their headquarters in the old Wolff laundry building.[23] The next day, they incorporated as the Little Sisters of the Poor of Denver, Colorado. On September 16, the Little Sisters received title to half of the Wolff lot, although Mullen withheld fifteen acres, deeding it to St. Vincent's Orphanage in 1919.[24]

Mullen reserved the right to supervise construction of the home. In that capacity, he hired architect Harry James Manning and the Dunn and Gibson Construction Company to design and build the rest home. Manning designed a four-story, neoclassical, brick and terra cotta structure that incorporated "boarding rooms for 150 people, a health clinic, a dining room, library, recreation rooms, and a chapel."[25] Even the *Denver Post* temporarily relinquished its concurrent campaign against the capitalist to call the building "a fitting testimonial to the fine spirit of the donor."[26] The complex overran cost estimates by $37,638, which the philanthropist paid without his customary complaints.[27]

When Bishop Tihen dedicated the home on September 1, 1918, two thousand people, including Governor Julius F. Gunter and the new Denver mayor, William F. R. Mills, braved a thundershower to compliment Mullen for his charity.[28] Their congratulations paled beside that of the grateful residents who rose one by one to shake the beaming philanthropist's hand and offer the benediction, "God Bless you, Mr. Mullen."[29]

As J. K. would have wanted it, support continues to come from the family via the Mullen and Weckbaugh Foundations. In accordance with their patriarch's wishes, the family constructed a stable, as well as a clubhouse, suitable to "smoke and yarn, play cribbage and bridge, or send billiard balls darting across green tables," in 1932.[30] During the Depression, the Mullen Home provided unprecedented security for elderly housewives who often lacked the retirement pensions available to their husbands. In 1935, Bishop Urban J. Vehr dedicated a statue of the Sacred Heart in the memory of the late Katherine O'Connor. The Mullen Foundation donated $450,000 for the $1.2-million, three-story Mullen Home Annex on Thirtieth Avenue and Mead Street, which opened in 1973.[31]

Most of the praise for the success of the Mullen Home goes to the generations of loving nuns who daily serve the elderly residents. Over the years, the Little Sisters of the Poor have continued the tradition of providing dignified, comfortable care for the elderly. The Mullen Home has become the modern standard by which other rest homes are measured. It successfully caters to the needs of its residents despite the fact that the sisters solicit their operational funds, as well as most of their supplies, through donations. Denver grocery chains, produce companies, and packing plants provide much of the food consumed by the

In 1973, the J. K. Mullen Foundation added to their legacy at the Mullen Home for the Aged by donating $450,000 for the $1.2-million, three-story Mullen Home Annex on Thirtieth Avenue and Meade Street. James Baca photo. Courtesy, Western History Dept., Denver Public Library.

residents. Still other gifts arrive through the good offices of St. Joseph, the Little Sisters' patron saint, who resides in the home's basement kitchen. By tradition, residents place small offerings of items they desire at the statue's feet. When a Coors distributor noticed an empty beer bottle resting against the stature, he ensured that the residents would never run out of the local brew.[32] Faith, and the unending labor of the Mullen Home's tireless caregivers, engenders success. Starting at 5:15 A. M., the sisters serve food, clean bathrooms, arrange activities, perform therapy, and oversee administration duties in addition to their daily devotions. "Such work isn't odious," claimed one Little Sister in a 1989 interview. "On the contrary, there is a beauty in it."[33]

NOTES

1. J. K. Mullen, Letter to Sister Germaine, Mother Provincial, Little Sisters of the Poor, August 30, 1916, Mullen papers, Western History Dept., Denver Public Library (WHDDPL).
2. J. K. Mullen, "The Policy of Our Company and the Dignity and Responsibility of a Merchant," typed speech transcript, September 10, 1912, Herbert E. Johnson manuscript collection (hereafter cited as Johnson collection).
3. *Denver Post,* March 7, 1913: 1.
4. *Denver Times,* May 1, 1913: 1; unattributed newspaper clippings, Katherine Mullen O'Connor scrapbook, Timothy O'Connor collection.
5. Ibid.
6. "The Little Sisters of the Poor," booklet (London: Burns, Oates, and Washbourne, Ltd.), Little Sisters of the Poor/Home for the Aged papers, Archdiocese of Denver archives.
7. J. K. Mullen, Letter to Rt. Rev. N. C. Matz, May 9, 1911, Rt. Rev. Nicholas C. Matz manuscript collection, Archdiocese of Denver archives (hereafter cited as Matz papers).
8. Rt. Rev. N. C. Matz, Letter to J. K. Mullen, January 20, 1913, Matz papers.
9. J. K. Mullen, Letter to Rt. Rev. N. C. Matz, July 13, 1911, Matz papers. Mullen deeded his portion of the block to the Immaculate Conception Cathedral Association.
10. Rt. Rev. N. C. Matz, Letter to J. K. Mullen, January 20, 1913; J. K. Mullen, Letter to Rt. Rev. N. C. Matz, March 2, 1914, Matz papers.
11. J. K. Mullen, Letter to Rt. Rev. N. C. Matz, March 2, 1914, Matz papers.
12. J. K. Mullen, Letter to Rt. Rev. N. C. Matz, November 16, 1914, Matz papers.
13. J. K. Mullen, Letter to Rt. Rev. N. C. Matz, March 2, 1914, Matz papers.
14. Thomas J. Noel, *Colorado Catholicism and the Archdiocese of Denver, 1857–1989* (Niwot: University Press of Colorado, 1989), 107.
15. J. K. Mullen, Letter to Mother Germaine, August 30, 1916, Mullen papers, WHDDPL.

16. *Denver Post*, July 12, 1916: 7.

17. J. K. Mullen, Letter to Mother Germaine, August 30, 1916, Mullen papers, WHDDPL.

18. J. K. Mullen, "Draft of Conveyance" handwritten manuscript, Mullen papers, WHDDPL.

19. J. K. Mullen, Letter to Mother Germaine, August 30, 1916, Mullen papers, WHDDPL.

20. James F. Kennedy, esq., Letter to J. K. Mullen, June 17, 1916, Mullen papers, WHDDPL.

21. J. K. Mullen, "Draft of Conveyance"; J. H. Reddin, esq., Letter to J. K. Mullen, October 25, 1916, Mullen papers, WHDDPL.

22. "Warranty Deed Between J. K. Mullen and the Little Sisters of the Poor," September 16, 1916, Mullen papers, WHDDPL.

23. Mother Germaine, Telegraph to J. K. Mullen, September 11, 1916, Mullen papers, WHDDPL; Noel, *Colorado Catholicism*, 108.

24. "Deed of Gift Between J. K. Mullen and St. Mary's Academy of Leavenworth, Kansas," December 27, 1919, Mullen papers, WHDDPL.

25. Noel, *Colorado Catholicism*, 108.

26. *Denver Post,* August 22, 1917: 9.

27. "Home for the Aged Expense Sheet," Mullen papers, WHDDPL.

28. The first occupants were admitted in April 1918. *Rocky Mountain News (RMN)*, September 2, 1918: 4.

29. *Denver Catholic Register*, September 5, 1918. The Home for the Aged has experienced lows to match the highs. In August 1923, Mullen's daughter Katherine O'Connor was found guilty of possession of liquor in violation of the Volstead Act. Described in purple prose by the *Denver Post* as "a woman of fashion in search of unusual thrills," O'Connor assisted the pastor of Arvada's Shrine of St. Anne, Father Walter Grace, in funneling forty cases of Early Times whiskey through the Home for the Aged into private hands. Grace received two years in prison for his part in the scheme, as well as for forging permits for sacramental wine. Accompanied by her father, O'Connor pled guilty to her charges and was fined $400. Mullen, a dedicated teetotaler who wrote of Prohibition, "I don't think that in all this broad land you could find a dozen fair-minded men that wouldn't be willing to take a gun in their hands and fight rather than see the saloon back again," but believed the government-imposed Volstead Act to be "a complete failure," reportedly wept with shame. Sources: J. K. Mullen, Letter to L. L. Breckenridge, November 5, 1928, Mullen papers, Colorado Historical Society; *Denver Post*, April 9, 1922: 1; March 19, 1923: 1; August 2, 1923: 1.

30. *RMN*, July 31, 1932: 7.

31. *RMN*, January 24, 1948: 17; *Denver Post*, June 5, 1935: 15; March 16, 1973: 7HH.

32. *RMN*, December 10, 1974: 50.

33. *RMN*, May 17, 1989: 3C.

17

THE "TIDAL WAVE"

Postwar Prosperity and the Ku Klux Klan, 1920–1925

We have come in like a tidal wave . . .

—J. K. Mullen, May 15, 1920[1]

Controversy aside, the wartime economy propelled the fortunes of the Colorado Milling and Elevator Company forward, in J. K. Mullen's words, like a "tidal wave." The phrase aptly embodies both the possibilities and dangers of J. K.'s enterprises in the period of national insecurity following the First World War. Overlapping philanthropic and investment projects divided the capitalist's attentions. After a brief postwar flush, the CM&E suffered from the agricultural market collapse that lay hidden behind the national business boom. Nationalism fueled a new wave of bigotry against Catholics, Jews, African Americans, and immigrants. The aging financier also faced his own physical decline and the passing of his beloved wife. Combined, these factors motivated J. K. to initiate many of his finest social and religious projects. The "tidal wave" of the 1920s inspired the philanthropist to build a lasting legacy that included the building of a Catholic church for Denver's Hispanic community, a library for the Catholic University of America, endowments to Regis College, plans for a vocational school for orphaned boys, and the creation of a benevolent foundation to perpetuate his generosity.

In 1920, the seventy-two-year-old businessman realized the limits of his relentless work ethic. In March, he collapsed on a business trip to the remote town of El Centro, California. While his wife and daughters rushed from an abbreviated vacation at the seaside resort of

Coronado and Fathers McMenamin, Grace, O'Ryan, and O'Dwyer detrained from Denver, surgeons operated to remove an obstruction from the capitalist's bowels. Postoperative pneumonia set in as Father Mac prepared to guide his benefactor into eternity.[2]

For twenty-four hours, J. K.'s life hung by a thread. Even as he recovered, Oscar Malo worried about long-term prospects of "our big boss." He wrote to CM&E general manager Herbert Johnson, "When you take his age into consideration and the many after effects of an attack such as this, I am very much afraid it is going to be a long time before he can get on his feet again . . . and be the same man that he was prior to this." Malo underestimated the determination of his iron-willed father-in-law. Brushing off admonishments that the trip back across the Rockies was tantamount to "suicide," J. K. made alarming demands to return home.[3] His doctors convinced their patient to convalesce in California, emphasizing their point on a humiliating and painful train ride back to Los Angeles. Orderlies were unable to pass their stretcher-bound patient through the train's narrow passenger entry. Instead, they hoisted him through a window and slung him into a hammock for the journey.[4]

Restless and wheel-chair bound, he fidgeted in a sunny "little Garden of Eden" at the Beverly Hills Hotel while his strength returned. The idyll was far from tranquil. "Ever since I have been in bed," he wrote Johnson, "there has been no time that I could stop thinking about the business."[5] By May 2, although he could barely cross his room without assistance, Mullen renewed his demands to leave. "If he is just strong enough to . . . handle himself to and on the train so that we won't have to take him on a stretcher I believe we can make it," Malo worried philosophically. "At any rate . . . we have no alternative. He is very determined to go and so go we must."[6]

Mullen's impatience was propelled by visions of the burgeoning market for flour in California. "[California] is a wonderful state," he exclaimed from the hospital. "I am sure it is going to increase in population very fast . . . the land is too valuable for them to raise wheat." He proposed an ambitious string of CM&E stations between Pueblo and Dodge City to capture "all of the wheat raised in the Arkansas Valley . . . and easily worked off in California."[7] In order to serve the consumers of the Golden State, he directed Johnson to build a warehouse and elevator in Los Angeles and a mill in Salt Lake City. The CM&E

THE COLORADO MILLING & ELEVATOR COMPANY
Location of Operating Properties

LEGEND:
Flour Mills ▼
Grain Elevators •
Grain Warehouses ○
Bean Warehouses ▫

By 1924, the Colorado Milling and Elevator Company owned nearly three hundred mills, warehouses, and elevators reaching from Oregon to Missouri. The company's domination of flour production and distribution in the Rocky Mountain West allowed it to weather the farming recession of the 1920s and 1930s, but no further expansion took place until after the Second World War. Courtesy, William S. Jackson Business Records Collection, Colorado Historical Society.

purchased a broker, the Sunset Milling and Grain Company in Los Angeles, but never completed the elevator. J. K. also urged Johnson to continue expanding in order to protect the prosperity of the company and its staff:

> I think it is absolutely necessary to expand in order to make places for our men that have been with us so long . . . We have a splendid lot of employees and assistants and they must be encouraged in the belief that if they continue to remain in our employ their interests will be safely guarded.[8]

Expansion equaled job security, both for the trust's employees and its officers.

The capitalist put the finishing touches on his agricultural empire between 1920 and 1923. When wheat prices softened that year, the CM&E's expansion plans stalled for the next two decades.[9] He also borrowed heavily, taking $1 million from outside sources and $400,000 from CM&E reserves to add the last available shares of the milling corporation to his estate. Although by 1925 he owned 90 percent of all CM&E stock, J. K. worried about the state of his personal finances for perhaps the first time since the 1890s. The stagnation of agricultural prices, combined with his philanthropic obligations overextended his credit. Lamenting, "I haven't any loose money," he reluctantly asked his daughters for assistance. Stung by their hesitation, he used his powers as trustee of his daughters' CM&E shares to surreptitiously dip into their dividends.[10]

Increasingly, infirmity gnawed at Mullen's physical capabilities. Malo had correctly assessed the long-term prognosis for his boss. No amount of ambition allowed J. K. to keep up the physically demanding workload he had so long pursued. He remained an invalid for a year following his operation. As a result, J. K. was forced to delegate authority at an unprecedented level. He divided his responsibilities between his "splendid lot of employees," particularly to managers and directors such as Malo, Stephen Knight, Robert Kelly, and Maurice Dolan. Infirmity also dampened his ability to endure long sojourns to his outlying mills. When in February 1924 the officers of the CM&E traveled to Claflin, Kansas, to appoint a new manager, J. K. stayed home. He sent a note that began: "This is the first and only plant that I call to mind . . . for a great many years that [I have] not been present and assisted personally in the installation."[11]

"WHAT WOULD YOU HAVE ME DO?": J. K. MULLEN AND THE KLAN

In addition to health problems and the disagreeable task of ceding day-to-day authority at the CM&E, Mullen needed his vigor to withstand one last wave of anti-Catholic hysteria. Denver historian Tom Noel writes, "The hooded nightmare for Colorado Catholics [as well as Jewish and African Americans] began in 1921" when Ku Klux Klan imperial wizard William Joseph Simmons established the "Denver Doers

Club" at the Brown Palace Hotel.[12] Under the guidance of "Doctor" John Galen Locke, "Kolorado's Klan" grew in power until its per capita membership was second only to Indiana. The Klan's cry for reform against promiscuity, bootlegging, crime, and un-American behavior attracted perhaps 17,000 Denverites and 24,000 Coloradans at its peak. Catholics felt threatened by the Klan's "100% American" rhetoric, their physical and verbal harassment, their boycotts, their control of governmental offices, and their legislative attacks on Catholic schools and sacramental wine permits. Brandishing CYANA ("Catholics, you are not Americans") cigars, Colorado Klansmen were on the whole ineffective in achieving their agenda. Nevertheless, their brief prominence marked a dark period in Colorado ethnic history.[13]

The rise of the Klan chilled Colorado's leading Catholic layman. Even before the war, claimed American Federation of Labor organizer and Catholic convert David Goldstein, Denver's "anti-Catholic spirit was intense."[14] Mullen's success, coupled with his support of the Church, had long made him a prominent target for Catholic-baiters. The latest incarnation of anti-Catholic sentiment coincided with the 1921 ordination of the philanthropist, along with other leading lay Catholics William D. McPhee, John H. Reddin, and Frank Kirchhof, to the order of the Knights of St. Gregory.[15] The honor designated Mullen as one of the most prominent supporters of the Papacy in Colorado.

That his enterprises might be singled out for Klan harassment appalled the financier. Mullen considered his own acculturation to be one of his greatest defenses against intolerance. As he wrote in 1922, "In order to make a living, I have always dealt with non-Catholics."[16] He cultivated friendly social and business relationships with members and even ministers of the dominant religion. Over the years he even developed critical opinions about certain tenants of his own faith that were shared by many Protestants. He blamed Church corruption and abuse for the decline of Catholicism. He believed ostentation and the failure to apply common sense drove poor, everyday Catholics into other denominations. On various occasions, he had criticized contemporary Church dogma, fund-raising tactics, and authoritarian, incompetent, or corrupt clergymen.[17] As evidenced by his resignation from the cathedral building committee in 1909, he was even willing to defend Protestant denominations against the smears of his own bishop.

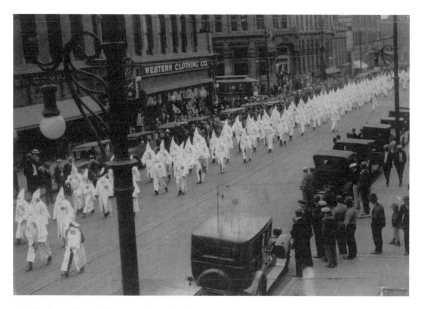

Masked members of the Ku Klux Klan formed an intrusive part of Colorado's scenery in the 1920s. Particularly influential on the High Plains, rural Klansmen blamed their economic woes on high-profile Catholics such as J. K. Mullen. To the despair of many in the Catholic community, Mullen accommodated the Klan and quietly rode out the storm. Courtesy, Western History Dept., Denver Public Library.

Indeed, J. K.'s behavior during the Klan crisis must have exasperated those who looked to the financier to join their defense of Catholic institutions. He criticized Father Matthew Smith, the crusading editor of the *Denver Catholic Register*, for excoriating the Klan in the pages of his journal. Smith's articles, Mullen complained, stirred up "much trouble and additional annoyance" among his Protestant customers.[18] When Bishop John Henry Tihen pressured Mullen to purge alleged Klansmen from his payroll, J. K. defended an employee:

> He is loyal to our interests as Old Dog Tray; he is on the job every day in the year. He may be a member of the [KKK] but, all the same, I believe he is honest and capable . . . How are you going to find out for certain whether he is or not? Suppose . . . I should displace him for someone else? Where are you going to get anyone else that will do any better?[19]

Besides, Mullen argued, he could ill afford *not* to employ Klansmen:

> A manager in Idaho [reported] that he had been approached continually to join—and that he declined to do so . . . He further said that the other

elevators were apparently controlled by that element. Well, what was the result? He stands in the doorway of the elevator and sees load after load of grain go by his door . . . and the plant isn't earning enough to pay his salary. We might just as well close the place up.

Left alone, J. K. hoped the Klan hysteria might fade away, as episodes of intolerance had on other occasions. He feared that friction between the Klan and its critics would intensify prejudice against Catholics in general and his "child," the CM&E, in particular. Although the CM&E board of directors contained seven Protestants to just four Catholics and retained many local Protestants as managers, the perception of the company as a "Catholic" institution was commonplace. J. K. felt he could point out the damage KKK chapters had done to other flour millers. Managers, particularly in rural Kansas and Idaho, received boycott threats from local Klansmen. The bakers of one southern Kansas town embargoed CM&E flour entirely. Another Catholic miller in Kansas had gone bankrupt as a result of the Klan boycotts, Mullen believed. Firing pro-Klan managers, he feared, threatened to create a nativist backlash that would shut down the CM&E's Kansas and Idaho mills before spreading into Colorado.[20]

J. K. responded by taking the offensive against the Klan's critics. When his family received a "deceitful and despicable" circular entitled "Catholic Business Men of Denver . . . Do Not Patronize Heretics. Deal with Roman Catholics Only," he demanded to know of Tihen:

> What are you going to do about it? Our salesmen go out and sell our goods . . . and are met at the door and the grocers say to them: "Well, why should we trade with you? You put out a circular in which you request Catholics to trade only with . . . Catholics."[21]

He also considered making a large grant to a Protestant institution, such as the Iliff School of Theology, as a gesture of interdenominational cooperation. Tihen privately chastised Mullen for his ingratiating scheme and advised against placing financial security ahead of the principles of Catholicism. Although he conceded that many admirable Protestants existed, Tihen reminded his patron that "there are good men who are wets . . . but you do not therefore approve bootlegging."[22] Ultimately, his arguments persuaded the philanthropist. Mullen pledged $15,000 to the Regis College drive but pointedly donated $300 to the Iliff School as well.[23]

The evils of the Klan posed a dilemma. As a Catholic, Mullen deplored the message and tactics of the "Ku Kluxers [who] are making us lots of trouble."[24] As a businessman, he was reluctant to antagonize Protestant customers who supported the popular organization. "We have to deal with them—buy from them—sell from them—trust them with our goods—and borrow money from them . . . I had to depend on these men for assistance continually—and have to do so yet."[25] Faced with the possibility of losing business by rocking the boat, he decided that a conservative, accommodating response was the most prudent.

His unwillingness to confront the Klan opens him to criticism, but his perspective is at least understandable. Financially exposed by large endowments, leveraged to the maximum in business, declining in health, and preoccupied with the failing health of his wife, Mullen drew upon his experiences as a member of a Catholic minority in a hostile Protestant society. His judgment warned him to protect his business interests first. Never in his life had the businessman lived in a place where Irish Catholics had enjoyed full security from intolerance. His protégé, the Tammany politician Frank Kernan, had achieved respectability by appealing to mainstream cultural ideals such as temperance—and defeat because of his Catholic affiliation. Mullen's own livelihood had been threatened by American Protective Association boycotts during the 1890s. Now, potential Klan boycotts threatened to damage his company and his hard-earned fortune. The safest choice, J. K. concluded, was not to speak out like Father Smith of the *Register* or clean his own house of Klansmen as Tihen suggested, but instead to work toward mending the divisions between the Catholic and Protestant communities. Even so, his conscience seemed to prick him slightly as he rationalized to Tihen, "If the services of an anti-Catholic are of very much more value to this Company than the services of a Catholic—and then if I use the profits of this Company . . . to help every Catholic institution—I think I am on the right track."[26]

NOTES

1. J. K. Mullen, Letter to H. E. Johnson, May 15, 1920, Herbert E. Johnson collection.
2. Oscar L. Malo, Telegram to Rt. Rev. J. H. Tihen, March 31, 1920, Rt. Rev. John Henry Tihen manuscript collection, Archdiocese of Denver archives (hereafter cited as Tihen papers); Rev. Hugh L. McMenamin, Telegram to Rt. Rev. J. H. Tihen, April 5, 1920, Tihen papers.

3. Oscar. L. Malo, Letter to H. E. Johnson, April 10, 1920, Johnson collection.
4. Oscar L. Malo, Letter to H. E. Johnson, May 1920, Johnson collection.
5. J. K. Mullen, Letter to H. E. Johnson, May 15, 1920, Johnson collection.
6. J. K. Mullen, Letter to H. E. Johnson, May 15, 1920; O. L. Malo, Letter to H. E. Johnson, May 2, 1920, both from Johnson collection.
7. J. K. Mullen, Letter to H. E. Johnson, May 15, 1920, Johnson collection.
8. Ibid.
9. Union Securities Corporation, "Prospectus of the Colorado Milling and Elevator Co.," August 1943, William S. Jackson business records collection, MSS 1074, Colorado Historical Society.
10. J. K. Mullen, Letter to Rt. Rev. J. H. Tihen, February 3, 1925, Tihen papers; J. K. Mullen, Letter to Ella M. Weckbaugh, July 6, 1925, and Letter to Ella M. Weckbaugh, May Dower, Catherine O'Connor, and Edith Malo, Denver, Colorado, 1928, both in Weckbaugh family collection.
11. J. K. Mullen, Letter to W. S. Bunt, February 12, 1924, Weckbaugh family collection.
12. Thomas J. Noel, *Colorado Catholicism and the Archdiocese of Denver, 1857–1989* (Niwot: University Press of Colorado, 1989), 97.
13. Ibid., 98–100.
14. Cited in Christopher Kauffman, *Faith and Fraternalism: The History of the Knights of Columbus, 1882–1982* (Cambridge, Mass.: Harper & Row, 1982), 178–179.
15. *Rocky Mountain News*, August 7, 1921: 1.
16. J. K. Mullen, Letter to Rt. Rev. J. H. Tihen, November 25, 1922, Tihen papers.
17. For examples, see J. K. Mullen, Letter to Rt. Rev. N. C. Matz, October 9, 1903, Letter to Rt. Rev. T. J. Shahan, September 18, 1923, and Letter to Rt. Rev. J. H. Tihen, November 22, 1925, all in Tihen papers; Letter to Ella M. Weckbaugh, August 21, 1925, Weckbaugh family collection.
18. J. K. Mullen, Letter to Rt. Rev. J. H. Tihen, January 13, 1925, Tihen papers.
19. This and Mullen's subsequent defense of his Klan-affiliated employees cited in J. K. Mullen, Letter to Rt. Rev. J. H. Tihen, March 13, 1925, Tihen papers.
20. J. K. Mullen, Letter to Rt. Rev. J. H. Tihen, January 13, 1925, Tihen papers.
21. J. K. Mullen, Letter to Rt. Rev. J. H. Tihen, June 24, 1924, Tihen papers.
22. Rt. Rev. J. H. Tihen, Letter to J. K. Mullen, March 1923, Tihen papers.
23. J. K. Mullen, Letter to Rt. Rev. J. H. Tihen, March 7, 1923, Tihen papers.
24. J. K. Mullen, Letter to Ella M. Weckbaugh, July 6, 1925, Weckbaugh family collection.
25. J. K. Mullen, Letter to Rt. Rev. J. H. Tihen, March 3, 1923, Tihen papers.
26. Ibid.

18

"FOR RELIGIOUS, CHARITABLE, BENEVOLENT, AND EDUCATIONAL PURPOSES"

The Mullen Library and Foundation

HELPING "EVERY CATHOLIC INSTITUTION," or at least as many as were within his means, remained a high priority. The physical demands of Mullen's advancing age required the miller to slow his hectic pace. After 1924, when he declared his semiretirement, he chose to spend more time worrying about the pleasant problems of grandfatherhood. His grand-children—Eleanore and Joseph Kernan Weckbaugh; Kenneth, Edith ("CiCi") and John F. Malo; Frank Louis "Teddy" Tettemer; and John and Katherine O'Connor—were sources of great pride and perplexity. A letter among his extended correspondence to John O'Connor, away at boarding school, reveals his typical mixture:

> I have been wondering whether or not you have made up your mind to be a traveling musician. I have been led to believe so because some time ago you paid a barrel of money for a saxophone and some of the boys told me you bought a silver mounted Jew's Harp and now you write me and tell me you would like to have $50.00 to buy a banjo. My Good Lord! When I grew up as a boy you could get a good banjo for $1.50 or $2.00. You must want a silver mounted banjo. I now hear that you are president of the baseball club and in charge of the school publications and that you are a good hand at cricket, tennis, and basketball. By Jove! I don't see how you can find time to attend to your studies.[1]

J. K. required more time to attend to his wife. Her ailment, which worsened steadily between 1922 and 1925, became an increasing source of preoccupation. On an October 1922 anniversary trip, the business-man, never one to easily separate business and pleasure, shuttled back and forth between complicated financial negotiations in New York

Mullen took a direct hand in raising his grandchildren, including, left to right, John Mullen O'Connor, Oscar Malo Jr., Katherine Mullen O'Connor, Joseph Kernan Weckbaugh, Eleanore Mullen Weckbaugh, Frank L. "Teddy" Tettemer Jr., Edith "Cici" Malo. In addition to educating them, and sheltering many of them, he prepared them to take on the responsibilities of philanthropy. Courtesy, Weckbaugh family collection.

City and Kate's sickbed in an Atlantic City resort. By October 1924, the worried husband spent long nights tending to her discomfort.[2] His own terse correspondence belies the anxiety that he felt during this trying period. In March 1923, he referred elliptically to Kate's continued poor health in a letter to his granddaughter Eleanore Weckbaugh: "Your Grandma isn't any worse but she isn't much, if any, better."[3] One year and one day later, he constructed a three-word report to his daughter Ella before moving quickly on to the next subject—"Mother the same."[4] Coping with the pain of slowly losing Kate overwhelmed the emotionally reserved businessman. Those who knew him understood that he lacked the capability to express his emotions outwardly. He had always found it easier to display his emotions in actions than in flowery prose.

Concerns about Kate's physical deterioration and recognition of his forthcoming generation of heirs created in the philanthropist the impetus to build on his legacy. The direction of those actions was clear—more than ever, Kate's illness underscored the importance of her role as the

John and Kate Mullen, c. 1921. J. K.'s warm relationship with his wife served as the foundation of family philanthropy. The evidence indicates that, unlike many of his social contemporaries, J. K. remained faithful to his wife throughout their marriage. The urge to please his "darling Kate" led to his greatest charitable endowments. Courtesy, Weckbaugh family collection.

guardian angel of family philanthropy. As if aware of their short remaining time together, Mullen responded to her sickness with a frenzy of large-scale philanthropic spending. Prior to her death, J. K. created some of his most enduring endowments for his "darling Kate's" approval.

J. K. enacted the most ambitious of all his projects—the 1923 establishment of a memorial library at the Catholic University of America—during this period. Lacking a formal education himself, Mullen pressured his children and grandchildren to excel in their studies, paid for their education in East Coast finishing schools, and underwrote local libraries generously.[5] The chancellor of Catholic University, Bishop Thomas J. Shahan, was an old friend and political supporter. Patronage of this high-profile Catholic institution, moreover, would reflect well on Catholicism nationally.

The financier initially pledged $500,000 worth of municipal bonds, which he ultimately increased to $750,000. The construction taxed his personal assets. When he received the first bill of $124,173.90, he wrote to Shahan, "I will continue to send in this money as fast as you call on me . . . but . . . when you call on me for such big amounts I have to raise some money myself."[6] For the money, his "J. K. Mullen of Denver Memorial Library" was a marvel. Designed by the Washington architectural firm of Murphy and Olmstead, the edifice boasted a "noble row" of Romanesque columns across the façade. Sheathed in white Kentucky limestone, standing three stories tall, lit by ample windows and an interior courtyard, the edifice shone like a "gem." Italian marble lined the interior concourse, providing a noble presentation for the 300,000 books in the university's collection. The books themselves included rare and antique sets, including the 40,000-volume Lima collection of South American literature, a 10,000-volume collection of Irish history, language, antiquities, art, and literature, the 10,000-volume Archbishop Curley American Catholic collection, the 20,000-volume Hyvernat Oriental collection of Egyptian and Middle Eastern texts, and 30,000 volumes of the Clementine Papal library. To his pleasure, Mullen received praise from Pope Pius XI. "May God bless the generous donor," the pontiff reportedly remarked.[7]

Asked for his opinion of the structure, Mullen was characteristically reserved. He responded that the library was "wonderfully nice . . . a handsome, dignified structure . . . the only criticism I can make is . . . that the front door is too small. I think it should have been very much larger."[8]

Spurred on by Kate's illness, J. K. made several other large contributions. In November 1923, he returned to Oriskany Falls, New York, to donate $31,000 for a brick replacement of the wooden St. Joseph's Catholic Church that his brother Patrick had helped finance.[9] He complemented his wife's 1924 donation of the family "homestead" on Ninth and Lawrence Streets with a pledge to finish the construction of St. Cajetan's Catholic Church after her death.[10] Finally, after long discussions with Kate, J. K. founded a long-term, nonprofit charitable organization to fund "religious, charitable, benevolent, and educational purposes" beyond the lifetime of himself, his wife, and his daughters.[11]

By the mid-1920s, J. K. spent considerable time managing the resources dedicated to the upkeep of his charitable endowments. His three largest trusts—the $54,000 operating fund for the Mullen Home for the Aged, the recently closed fund for the retirement of the

Immaculate Conception Cathedral debt, and a new $500,000 fund for the construction of the Catholic University Library—amounted to over $750,000. The charitable capital accrued large tax liabilities. In order to protect them, J. K. assigned his securities to the safekeeping of the Denver (Catholic Charities) Community Chest. Padded though these trusts were, the money was inadequately protected from long-term drainage through state and federal taxation.[12]

On the one hand, Mullen needed to release the tax pressure on his benevolent revenues. He also felt a pressing commitment to erect a philanthropic fund that would transcend the lifetimes of himself and Kate. "We were all very much in favor of . . . something in the nature of an obligation that would rest on our children and our children's children," he wrote.[13] J. K. encouraged his children and grandchildren to remain mindful of the needs of the poor. If the prospects for fulfilling their own charitable aspirations could be protected for the future, John and Kate need not worry about their philanthropic legacy. Under the Revenue Act of 1916, moreover, philanthropic corporations were allowed to declare deductions on their income taxes. Mullen and his family concluded that the creation of an "exclusive family trust" that embodied a nonprofit, private foundation fulfilled both ends nicely.[14]

On May 19, 1924, J. K., Kate, Ella, May, Katherine, Edith, and their families met with attorney John H. Reddin at John and Kate's home to organize the Denver Catholic Charitable and Benevolent Society (DCC&BS). Duly electing themselves as directors, the family resolved to file incorporation papers. On May 27, the directors met again to elect J. K. as president and treasurer, Kate as first vice president, and each daughter as a sequential vice president in order of age. The next day, the DCC&BS received its certificate of incorporation from the State of Colorado.[15]

J. K. offered a starting donation of $10,000 in "good municipal bonds" for the charitable and benevolent purposes of the organization. The foundation's initial fund quickly increased. Kate requested that J. K. donate 460 shares of CM&E stock to which she added 5,560 of her own shares, raising the fund to $656,000. At the end of June 1924, Mullen leased a safety-deposit box at the First National Bank of Denver for the safekeeping of Benevolent Society assets. He deposited an additional $250,000 worth of Canadian municipal and civic bonds, which he had purchased for the J. K. Mullen Investment Co. in 1923.

Now, Mullen rededicated their income for "such religious, charitable, benevolent, and educational purposes as your directors may deem worthy of assistance."[16]

Kate's serious condition drove the initial rush to incorporate. Mullen therefore reacted with frustration when the federal government delayed the approval of tax-exempt status. Final approval came in January 1925, although the foundation funds remained with the Denver Community Chest until March 31, 1925.[17] By then, Kate had passed away. Her daughters unanimously memorialized her and J. K. by changing the foundation's name to "The John K. and Catherine S. Mullen Benevolent Corporation" over J. K.'s objection.[18] He protested, "I didn't like to use my name since the death of my dear wife . . . I feel that in memory of her great help, her name should be used." For once, his family overruled him, pointing out that, "no one [else] has put a dollar into the fund."[19] Under any name, the foundation pleased its creator. To an Internal Revenue Service official, he reported, "The fund . . . is now a very substantial amount . . . the interest will enable the members of my family and their children . . . to help take care of the poor."[20] Contributions of additional CM&E stock and further municipal-bond donations, combined with the addition of Catherine Mullen's estate (4,700 shares of CM&E stock and other assets valued at over $770,000), created a $799,000 fund by 1926. By Mullen's death in August 1929, the principle had grown to $1.42 million, with $300,000 in disbursable capital.[21]

Second in establishment only to Colonel Albert E. Humphreys's 1922 benevolent foundation, the John K. and Catherine S. Mullen Foundation supported a variety of secular and religious charities, including many of Kate's pet projects.[22] A list of disbursements between May 28, 1924, and May 28, 1926, shows individual gifts to Catholic priests amounting to $3,300 and endowments to Regis College ($1,000), Catholic Daughters ($1,000), the Dominican Sisters of the Sick Poor ($520), the St. Vincent de Paul Society ($500), the Missionary Sisters of the Sacred Heart ($350), and St. Vincent's Orphanage ($300). The foundation also supported such non-Catholic charities as the University of Denver Buchtel Memorial Fund ($1,000), Children's Hospital ($200), National Jewish Hospital ($200), Reverend Jim Goodheart's Sunshine Rescue Mission ($125), and the Craig Colony for Orphaned Boys ($100).[23]

The foundation scored a triumph when the Catholic University of America granted permission to disburse ten scholarships to deserving Colorado lay scholars annually. The philanthropist took very seriously his responsibility for distributing the five full scholarships—including room, board, and tuition—and the five tuition stipends. In October 1926, he requested materials on entrance requirements so that he could "call [students'] attention to rules, regulations, and conditions regarding their entrance."[24]

Mullen personally chose the recipients of the Catholic University scholarships "during his lifetime."[25] Despite the family-centered board of directors, the foundation remained mostly his responsibility. Out of respect for Kate, the board left the office of first vice president vacant until after John's death in 1929. Only after the philanthropist passed away did the family move to fill the spots left vacant by the couple.[26] The succeeding officers remained true to many of their founders' interests, even as they pursued their own charitable goals. The foundation completed the Mullen Home for Boys in 1932 and continued to support the vocational school until 1952. Likewise, the foundation continued to allocate ten scholarships to the Catholic University for seventy years, finally transferring their commitment to Regis University of Denver in 1996.

THE DEATH OF CATHERINE SMITH MULLEN

The creation of the Benevolent Foundation as well as ongoing acts of private philanthropy seemed to buoy Kate's spirits. She rejuvenated enough to celebrate her fiftieth wedding anniversary in October 1924, before returning to her sickbed for the last time. During the last few months, teams of specialists passed through her bedroom, testing, examining, and consulting to no avail. Drifting from one complication to the next, Kate weakened until J. K. confessed to Tihen, "I doubt very much, my Dear Bishop, whether or not she will ever again be able to get up."[27] Her husband stayed by her side night after sleepless night and spent long days helping her arrange her final affairs.[28]

The long, painful battle ended for seventy-four-year-old Catherine Smith Mullen on the morning of March 23, 1925. She died in bed, at home, surrounded by loving children and grandchildren. Her death sent a ripple of sympathy through the city. Both the *Denver Post* and the *Rocky Mountain News* ran front-page memorials to "the friend of

Catherine Smith Mullen, c. 1920, was described as "a blue-eyed, pretty, bright-souled girl," and a "reflection of inspiration." Her inspiration moved beyond reflection when she actively raised funds for the Catholic parish in Central City, St. Vincent's Orphanage, the St. Vincent de Paul Society, St. Joseph Hospital, and the Immaculate Conception Cathedral. By donating her "homestead" at Ninth and Lawrence Streets, Kate kicked off the drive to build St. Cajetan's Catholic Church. Courtesy, Timothy O'Connor collection.

the friendless." The *Denver Catholic Register* noted that the wife of the prominent Catholic philanthropist "was not frequently mentioned in the newspapers, because she was of an exceedingly modest and retiring nature. Yet all Catholic Denver knows that for more than 50 years she was a part, and oftenest the chief part, of every Catholic activity."[29]

On the day of her funeral, the Denver Grain Exchange closed in Catherine's honor. The bells of the Immaculate Conception Cathedral pealed as the bereaved overflowed the pews inside. So many mourners packed the cavernous cathedral that ushers hurriedly opened the choir loft to accommodate the overflow.[30] Foremost among the bereaved were the beneficiaries of Kate's favorite charities: the boys of St. Vincent's Orphanage sat on one side of her lily-enshrouded casket, while elderly residents of the J. K. Mullen and Family Home for the Aged occupied the other. Longtime friend Monsignor William O'Ryan eulogized the departed:

> Peace on her soul; she loved the poor and the orphaned; she pitied the broken and aged poor . . . Her life made her unafraid to die, and her last words, "Into Thy hands I commit my spirit," were the expression of a faith that was built on a rock of absolute belief and goodness and mercy.[31]

Afterwards, mourners followed behind the black-draped carriage to a hillside location overlooking a field of grain at Mt. Olivet cemetery.

Although long anticipated, the new widower faltered following Kate's death. Writing five months later, J. K. confessed to his oldest daughter, "I visit your Mother's grave two or three times every week. I have never missed a Sunday when I was in Denver."[32] Brooding over her grave, he must have reflected over how much he depended on her activism and love of the poor and orphaned for direction. Everyone who knew the Mullen family was aware of Catherine's guidance, companionship, and spirit and how much "her home, her family, and her church filled her life."[33] Most of those who formed an opinion underestimated her role as a counselor and initiator of charity.

C. W. Hurd characterized Catherine as the passive partner: "She was not a driving force but her influence was inspirational." This depiction is understandable. Seventy-five years after her death, Kate is an unknowable figure. It would be nice to understand more about this woman who matured from a spirited pioneer girl but, true to the Victorian norms of her upbringing, she remains, in Hurd's words, "a reflection of inspiration."[34] Only in glimpses does Kate's personality shine through. Reverent and shy, lacking public social aspirations, Kate could cow even her formidable husband at home. She kept up with politics and religious issues and did not fear to express herself. Not long after women received the vote in Colorado, J. K. found himself mediating between his outraged spouse and his political ally, Thomas Patterson, "Now Kate please don't pitch into Tom about the parties or alliance or whatever you call them."[35] Despite her illness—or perhaps to relieve it—she remained active in Catholic fund-raising affairs until late in life. As late as 1923, J. K. reported her hosting ladies' aid meetings of up to 125 guests "sitting up on the stairway and out on the veranda."[36] Finally, she kept her husband's devotion through all the years of their marriage.

With her death, Denver lost one of its greatest organizers of Catholic charity. Alongside her husband's charities, Kate had cultivated her own favorite causes among Denver's homeless, orphans, and elderly.[37] Her own husband, remembered as one of Denver's greatest philanthropists, declared his debt to her guidance on virtually every major endowment. Today, few remember Kate's love of philanthropy when they praise Mullen for his grand acts of public largesse. She was truly a grand pioneer women whose charitable impulses, direction, and money made countless acts of kindness possible.

NOTES

1. J. K. Mullen, Letter to John O'Connor, June 16, 1924, Weckbaugh family collection.
2. J. K. Mullen, Letter to Rt. Rev. J. H. Tihen, November 25, 1922, Rt. Rev. John Henry Tihen manuscript collection, Archdiocese of Denver archives (hereafter cited as Tihen papers); John O'Connor, Letter to J. K. Mullen, October 10, 1924, Weckbaugh family collection.
3. J. K. Mullen, Letter to Eleanore Weckbaugh, March 6, 1923, Weckbaugh family collection.
4. J. K. Mullen, Letter to Ella M. Weckbaugh, March 7, 1924, Weckbaugh family collection.
5. Walter S. Weckbaugh, personal interview, July 21, 1997.
6. *Denver Post*, September 27, 1924: 5; J. K. Mullen, Letter to Rt. Rev. T. J. Shahan, June 5, 1925, Mullen papers, Western History Dept., Denver Public Library (WHDDPL).
7. Description and quote cited in *Denver Catholic Register* (*DCR*), August 22, 1929.
8. J. K. Mullen, Letter to Rt. Rev. T. J. Shahan, December 15, 1927, Mullen papers, WHDDPL.

9. *Denver Post*, February 17, 1928: 2; Mullen dedicated the church to "the glory of God and the memory of Dennis and Ellen Mulrey Mullen . . . and as a tribute to his boyhood home and his boyhood friends."

10. J. K. Mullen, Letter to Ella M. Weckbaugh, August 21, 1925, Weckbaugh family collection.

11. Denver Catholic Charitable and Benevolent Society (DCC&BS), "Minutes of Organization Meeting," May 19, 1924, J. K. Mullen Foundation, Inc., manuscript collection, WHDDPL (hereafter cited as Mullen Foundation papers).

12. Thomas J. Noel, with Kevin E. Rucker and Stephen J. Leonard, *Colorado Givers: A History of Philanthropic Heroes* (Niwot: University Press of Colorado, 1998), 101–102.

13. J. K. Mullen, Letter to Denver Community Chest, March, 1925, Mullen Foundation papers.

14. Walter S. Weckbaugh, personal interview, July 21, 1997; Noel, Rucker, and Leonard, 101; J. K. Mullen, Letter to Denver Community Chest, March 1925, Mullen Foundation papers.

15. DCC&BS, "Minutes of Organization Meeting," May 19, 1924; "Minutes," May 27, 1924; "Certificate of Incorporation," May 28, 1924, all in Mullen Foundation papers.

16. J. K. Mullen, Letter to the Board of Directors, DCC&BS, June 25, 1924, Mullen Foundation papers.

17. DCC&BS, "Minutes," April 1, 1925; George T. Evans, Internal Revenue Service, Letter to J. K. Mullen, January 5, 1925, both in Mullen Foundation papers.

18. DCC&BS, "Minutes," April 1, 1925, Mullen Foundation papers.

19. J. K. Mullen, Letter to Frank W. Howbert, Internal Revenue Service, April 4, 1925, Mullen Foundation papers.

20. Ibid.

21. C. S. Mullen's estate cited in *Denver Post*, May 29, 1925: 1. John K. and Catherine S. Mullen Benevolent Foundation Corp., "Minutes of a Special Meeting of the Board," August 20, 1929; "Comparative Balance Sheet," August 9, 1929, both in Mullen Foundation papers.

22. Noel, Rucker, and Leonard, 107.

23. John K. and Catherine S. Mullen Benevolent Corp., "Income and Disbursements, May 28, 1924, to May 28, 1926," Mullen Foundation papers.

24. J. K. Mullen, Letter to Rt. Rev. T. J. Shahan, October 19, 1926, Mullen Foundation papers.

25. Rt. Rev. Joseph Schrembs, "Certified Copy of Minutes of Meeting of the Board of Trustees of the Catholic University of America, September 14, 1926, Mullen Foundation Papers.

26. John K. and Catherine S. Mullen Benevolent Corp., "Income and Disbursements, May 28, 1924, to May 28, 1926," Mullen Foundation papers.

27. J. K. Mullen, Letter to Rt. Rev. J. H. Tihen, February 3, 1925, Tihen papers.

28. John O'Connor, Letter to J. K. Mullen, October 10, 1924, Weckbaugh family collection.

29. *Denver Post*, March 23, 1925: 1; *Rocky Mountain News*, March 23, 1925: 1; *DCR*, March 26, 1925: 1.

30. *Denver Post*, March 23, 1925: 1.

31. *DCR*, March 26, 1925: 1; *Denver Post*, March 26, 1925: 29.

32. J. K. Mullen, Letter to Ella M. Weckbaugh, July 6, 1925, Weckbaugh family collection.

33. Charles W. Hurd, "J. K. Mullen, Milling Magnate of Colorado," *The Colorado Magazine* XXIX:2 (April 1952): 110.

34. Ibid.

35. J. K. Mullen, Letter to Catherine S. Mullen, May 12, 1894, Mullen papers, Colorado Historical Society.

36. J. K. Mullen, Letter to Eleanore Weckbaugh, March 6, 1923, Weckbaugh family collection.

37. *DCR*, February 5, 1925: 8.

19

ST. CAJETAN'S CATHOLIC CHURCH

KATE'S CHARITABLE IMPULSES and their influence on her husband were never more apparent than in the endowment of St. Cajetan's Catholic Church in West Denver. By 1922, the demographics of the old neighborhood where John and Kate had gotten their start had changed dramatically. By the 1920s, employers in Colorado's multimillion-dollar sugar beet industry increasingly depended on the annual labor of thousands of Spanish-speaking workers from Mexico, New Mexico, and southern Colorado. Although their labor was welcomed, the Mexican and Spanish-American harvesters often discovered that their cultural presence was not. They subsisted on meager seasonal wages and both groups were subject to deportation without pay. Mexicans and Spanish Americans were excluded from stores, segregated into "Ragtowns" owned by the sugar companies, or forced to migrate to Denver for the winter.[1]

Even in Denver, Hispanos and Chicanos often experienced appalling conditions. Presbyterian minister Robert McLean described one Chicano section of Denver as "a district which looks as if both God and Denver had forgotten it."[2] West Denver, where many Hispanos and Chicanos relocated, was only marginally better. In large part because of the presence of three Colorado Milling and Elevator mills, the community had become a semi-industrial enclave. The Mullens were just one of many upwardly mobile Irish families who fled for more prosperous addresses. Hispanic and Chicano workers replaced the departing residents. For the remaining working-class Irish, the demographic change created a familiar pattern of ethnic tension that harkened back

217

to the problems between themselves and the established German community in the 1870s and 1880s.

Ironically, the Spanish-speaking migration revitalized the parish of St. Leo's, which had continued to struggle after its financial misadventure in the 1890s. The new flood of worshipers, estimated by the *Denver Catholic Register* at around 1,200, tested Monsignor William O'Ryan's meager resources.[3] His established flock—Irish, working-class, and conservative—pressed the priest with complaints about the new parishioners. Likewise, O'Ryan's Hispanic parishioners requested more Spanish-language services and expressed their need for a religious and cultural community center. Relegated to Father Humphrey Martorell, the Spanish-speaking parishioners packed the basement of St. Leo's to hear separate Spanish-language services. Plagued with complaints by both the segregated Hispanos and the uneasy Irish parishioners, Monsignor O'Ryan began casting about for help.[4]

Welcomed for their labor but segregated because of their culture, much of Denver's Spanish-speaking population was relegated to West Denver—a seedy, semi-industrial enclave dominated by CM&E flour mills such as the Eagle Mill, left of center. Mullen paid for St. Cajetan's, right of center, to ensure that God did not forget His most faithful parishioners. Louis C. McClure photo. Courtesy, Western History Dept., Denver Public Library.

Missionary Father Bartholomew Caldentey of the Theatine Fathers tended to Spanish-speakers in Colorado. The order's founder, St. Cajetan of Vicenza, became the patron of Hispanos and Chicanos in West Denver. Courtesy, Thomas J. Noel collection.

Much help arrived with Father Bartholomew Caldentey, a Majorcan-born missionary who tended the souls of the approximately ten thousand Spanish-speaking residents scattered throughout the San Luis Valley.[5] St. Cajetan of Vicenza, Italy, founded Caldentey's order of Theatine Fathers in 1524. His was one of the oldest missions in Colorado, having arrived in the San Luis Valley almost with the first Spanish settlers. During the Lenten season of 1922, the missionary responded to Monsignor O'Ryan's invitation and journeyed from Antonito to preach to the congregation at St. Leo's. To everyone's astonishment, over 900 worshippers assembled from around the city to hear him speak. Such unprecedented attendance, along with a petition supporting a new parish that circulated among Spanish-American women, further underscored the dedication of the Hispanic Catholics to O'Ryan and his superior, Bishop John Henry Tihen.[6] With Tihen's blessing, Caldentey, O'Ryan, and Martorell began planning a new church exclusively for the Spanish-speaking faithful.

Caldentey and O'Ryan started a campaign to acquire land for the church and money for construction. Like many before them, they turned to J. K. Mullen as an established source of assistance. O'Ryan arranged a series of meetings to discuss the purchase of John and Kate's old home at 1178 Ninth Street, an ideal location for the new church. As he later recalled, the ailing "Mrs. Mullen expressed a deep interest in the project." To his surprise he learned that she, not J. K. owned the property. Moreover, she refused to sell the lots. Instead, Kate offered them to the parish as a gift.[7] The couple also donated $5,000 to initiate construction, accompanied by a challenge to the parish to raise matching funds.

When discussions began, Catherine Smith Mullen was already fighting the illness that would take her life. The illness cast a shadow of urgency on the project and contributed to her deep commitment. Donating her "homestead"—as J. K. referred to the property—ensured that the home where Kate and John had gotten their start would become the symbolic center of an entire community.

Despite an enthusiastic response, the newly established parish struggled to match their patron's challenge. Parishioners raised over $4,000—only to lose it again in a bank failure. Father Caldentey moved ahead anyway, holding church services and classes in the old Mullen house on Ninth Street. The parish borrowed $20,000 from the German-

American Bank to continue construction. Kate lived long enough to see ground broken for the foundation on October 1, 1924. Unfortunately, momentum shifted away again on January 1, 1925. When Father Caldentey was called to Rome to assume the office of Superior General of the Theatine Order, he reluctantly left the parish coffers empty with only a covered basement to show for it. Nevertheless, half a church was better than none. Under Father Martorell, the basement of St. Cajetan's "resounded with masses, classes, and meetings."[8] Ever optimistic, the parish looked to St. Cajetan and their faith to see them through.

After Kate's death in March 1925, her husband saw to it that her wish and the parishioners' prayers were answered. The construction delays disappointed him. "When Mother and I gave up our homestead to those people, we did it with the expectation that there would be a church built thereon,"[9] J. K. observed. "They have been holding services in the basement for about a month, and although the basement is much larger than St. Leo's it isn't big enough to hold them. They are flocking into the basement from all over the City."[10] A lifelong advocate of piety, Mullen could not long bear to see such dedication go unrewarded. After consulting with Bishop Tihen, he paid off the parish's outstanding debt. J. K. insisted that the plan submitted by architect Robert Willison reflect a Hispanic design. To that end, Mullen specified "a good concrete Church . . . not a shabby structure" complemented by a "stuccoed—or cemented brick—white or cream surface." He also instructed contractor Frank Kirchhof to complete the church for "whatever it costs." (Kirchhof's bill: $47,708.)[11]

By late August 1925, the striking mission revival church was nearly finished. Mullen, now a widower of seventy-eight, described the final touches in a letter to his eldest daughter, Ella, who was then vacationing in Europe. Ella's full descriptions of European cafés and cathedrals delighted the patriarch and his grandchildren when read aloud at the dinner table. Mullen noted with pleasure that Superior General Caldentey had attended her in Rome. The evocation of his name inspired the philanthropist to explain,

> You probably understand that they began construction of [St. Cajetan's] Church, and that they were only going to finish the Basement . . . But I concluded that if they began holding Services in the basement, they would stay there for a great many years; and that was not in accordance with the

221

St. Cajetan's Catholic Church, located on the site of the Mullen family "homestead" at 1178 Ninth Street, closed the circle of J. K.'s rise to prosperity. Although critics accused Mullen of bankrolling the church to rid his Immaculate Conception Cathedral of Hispanic worshippers, J. K. believed that "the best Christians were to be found in the small, little Churches . . . instead of in the big Churches in the big cities." He hoped his structure would "give encouragement and hope to thousands of poor Mexicans and poor Spaniards." William J. Convery photo.

wishes of my dear Wife—your Mother . . . I am very pleased to think that we decided to finish the Church . . . I am sure that if your Mother had been permitted to live, she would have been very much interested in the construction.[12]

The St. Cajetan's endowment represented the closure of a wide circle. Just as West Denver once promised a new life for him and his wife, it now promised the same for the St. Cajetan's parish. A thriving church now occupied the site of his family "homestead." That term, used repeatedly by J. K. during the negotiations, signified the opportunity that he hoped to provide for Mexican and Spanish-American residents. At a time when Hispanos and Chicanos found it difficult to preserve their cultural integrity in a climate of intense discrimination, Mullen could proudly point to St. Cajetan's—where he and his wife began their lives of charitable giving—as the center of the Spanish-speaking community.[13] The church represented a memorial to the pioneer spirit that he assumed he and his wife exemplified. At the same time, he hoped to honor a community in which he recognized the folk values that he believed were necessary to improve the condition of society.

In later years, word spread that J. K. built St. Cajetan's to rid his own place of worship, the Immaculate Conception Cathedral, of Hispanos. His statement, "I concluded that if they began holding Services in the basement, they would stay there for a great many years," hints at the impatience that might have contributed to the rumor. Several factors indicate that this allegation was untrue. The veteran temple builder recognized the extraordinary difficulties of raising funds to meet the needs of a parish church. Other Denver Catholic churches started off with basement congregations. Some took decades to raise enough construction funds. He knew from working with St. Leo's and the cathedral that overextended parishes often ran into fiscal trouble. Mullen simply concluded that his intervention was required in order to clear the church of confining debt.

The gesture also reflected his admiration of the Hispanic faithful. Replying to Ella's description of Europe's grand cathedrals, he reacted with distaste to the religious ostentation: "You know in some way or

Participants of a 1930s confirmation pose proudly outside St. Cajetan's Catholic Church. For nearly forty-five years the parish served as the heart of the Spanish-speaking community of West Denver. In addition to spiritual comfort, the church uplifted the neighborhood with financial, medical, and social aid. Courtesy, Thomas J. Noel collection.

another, I have always felt that the best Christians were to be found in the small, little Churches and the little, lowly places out in the country instead of in the big Churches in the big cities." He hoped that his simple church would "give encouragement and hope to thousands of poor Mexicans and poor Spaniards," which, in turn, would "tend to make them satisfied and contented; and they will become much better citizens." It is notable that Mullen recognized a distinction between Mexicans and Spanish-Americans that many of his contemporaries were unable to see. By helping the Chicano community, Mullen believed he was diffusing discontent through the inculcation of the highest civic and religious standards.

Mullen offered "whatever it takes" to finish the church of St. Cajetan's. For his money, he demanded a "good concrete Church . . . not a shabby structure" with a "stuccoed—or cemented brick—white and cream surface" to complement its mission revival exterior. Later cost overruns, such as a $7,800 invoice for fixtures and furnishings, provided cause for regret. Nevertheless, he agreed with contractor Frank Kirchoff that the hand-carved altar and pews were "a good job too." By offering baptisms, confirmations, weddings, and funerals, St. Cajetan's Church anchored a community and fulfilled Kate Mullen's hope that her homestead would serve as a home for thousands of Denver families. Courtesy, Thomas J. Noel collection.

If Mullen sympathized, he did so because the parishioners' work ethic fit his standards for the deserving poor. Since he had built the little Spanish church on Lawrence Street, J. K. also felt that he had some right to instruct the parishioners what to pray for. To that end, he ordered a commemorative bronze plaque installed just inside the church doorway that read:

> Pray for the soul of Catherine Smith Mullen who donated her old home that on its site this church of St. Cajetan's might be built. Dedicated in her memory by her loving husband, John Kernan Mullen.

Although twenty-five years had elapsed since the family had relocated to Quality Hill, the gesture indicates that the West Denver site still possessed a powerful symbolic meaning. This was also indicated by J. K's repeated use of the word "homestead" to describe the house on Ninth Street. The building played an important symbolic role in the self-proclaimed pioneer's rationale of his success. As historian Richard Huber describes the pioneer ethic, "If the pioneer was to land feet first on the frontier and not go under, he had to keep at it, work hard, and save his money."[14] The Hispanic and Chicano parishioners were the new pioneers who revitalized the notions of hard work and frugality by actively raising funds, attending services, and even crafting their own furnishings and altar for the new church.

Characteristically, Mullen's admiration for the local artisans was quashed somewhat when he received the furnishing bill for $7,771.58. Likewise, his enthusiasm was dampened when furniture, fixture, heating, plumbing, and landscaping bills continued to arrive for months after the building was finished. He complained to Tihen, arguing at one point that "the side walks are really not part of the church."[15] Nevertheless, he paid the bills, preferring personal expense to the suggestion that the parish collected its own funds in an undignified manner. In March 1926, he received a report of children selling raffle tickets in front of St. Cajetan's. Having spent so much to build the church, he was "very much humiliated" to hear of children "begging" for money. Begging, he wrote, undermined self-sufficiency and invited anti-Catholic criticism. "Just think of it!" he wrote. "Here's a great big rich Catholic Church sending out little children to beg."[16]

Despite his concern, if J. K. completed St. Cajetan's because he believed in the parishioners, he would not have discovered long-term cause for disappointment. The church became the focal point of Denver's

As a church without a parish, the old St. Cajetan's structure survives as a conference facility on the Auraria Higher Education Center campus. Along with the adjacent Ninth Street Park, St. Cajetan's serves as a reminder of the passages of life in West Denver's once-vibrant neighborhood. Courtesy, Thomas J. Noel collection.

rapidly increasing Mexican and Spanish-American community. Following Mullen's death, his family continued to support the church through the Mullen Benevolent Foundation. In 1934, the foundation sponsored the St. Cajetan (Ave Maria) Clinic on the former site of the CM&E's West Denver Roller Mills on Eighth and Curtis Streets. The following year, the family established a parochial school and Benedictine convent behind the church across Eighth Street, on the former site of the Excelsior Mill. The foundation subsidized tuition so that no family, no matter how large, paid more than $20.

St. Cajetan's remained central to the community's social fabric. The parish's credit union offered loans to start businesses or buy homes or cars. Community outreach programs helped those on the bottom of the economic heap. Such was the church's communal importance that when the Denver Urban Renewal Authority announced plans to demolish the structure in the late 1960s to make way for the Auraria

Higher Education Center campus, residents objected nearly unanimously. Protest resulted in a reevaluation of the demolition plan and St. Cajetan's was saved from destruction. The beautiful *iglesia* that Mullen built still stands as a campus conference center, well-preserved and cherished as a Denver landmark, but oddly sterile, as if lacking the appreciation of a healthy and loving congregation. The parish relocated to a new facility at 4000 West Alameda in 1975, but many former residents still remember their West Denver church as "the heart and soul of the now vanished community."[17]

NOTES

1. Sarah Deutsch, *No Separate Refuge: Culture, Class and Gender on an Anglo Hispanic Frontier in the American Southwest, 1880–1940* (New York: Oxford University Press, 1987), 135. The conditions of Spanish-speaking laborers in the Colorado beet fields were documented by the Knights of Columbus, who battled against the exploitation and discrimination. As a former Grand Master and co-founder of the Knights of Columbus chapter in Colorado, Mullen likely followed their activities with interest. Christopher Kauffman, *Faith and Fraternalism: The History of the Knights of Columbus, 1882–1982* (Cambridge, Mass.: Harper & Row, 1982), 288; *Denver Catholic Register* (*DCR*), January 1, 1925: 1.

2. Deutsch, 154.

3. *DCR*, January 8, 1925: 4.

4. *Denver Post*, May 22, 1965: 3B; *La Luz*, August 1973: 13.

5. *La Luz*, August 1973: 13.

6. Ibid.; Thomas J. Noel, *Colorado Catholicism and the Archdiocese of Denver, 1857–1989* (Niwot: University Press of Colorado, 1989), 344.

7. J. K. Mullen, Letter to Ella M. Weckbaugh, August 21, 1925, Weckbaugh family collection.

8. Noel, *Colorado Catholicism*, 345.

9. J. K. Mullen, Letter to Rt. Rev. J. H. Tihen, February 3, 1925, Rt. Rev. John Henry Tihen manuscript collection, Archdiocese of Denver archives (hereafter cited as Tihen papers).

10. J. K. Mullen, Letter to Ella M. Weckbaugh, August 21, 1925, Weckbaugh family collection.

11. J. K. Mullen, Letters to Rt. Rev. J. H. Tihen, March 9, 1923; April 29, 1925, Tihen papers.

12. This and subsequent justifications for completing the church are cited in J. K. Mullen, Letter to Ella M. Weckbaugh, August 21, 1925, Weckbaugh family collection.

13. Deutsch, 174.

14. Richard M. Huber, *The American Idea of Success* (New York: McGraw-Hill, 1971), 11.

15. J. K. Mullen, Letter to Rt. Rev. J. H. Tihen, January 25, 1926, Tihen papers.
16. J. K. Mullen, Letter to Rt. Rev. J. H. Tihen and Rev. William O'Ryan, March 10, 1926, Tihen papers.
17. Noel, *Colorado Catholicism,* 346; Jason Krupar, "The Churches of Auraria," Rosemary Fetter, ed., pamphlet (Denver: Auraria Office of the EVOA, 1994).

20

SIR KNIGHT MULLEN, 1925–1929

STILL MENTALLY VIGOROUS, the aging industrialist faced the final challenges of his life as determinedly as he had the first. They were rarely simple ones. Having survived another wave of national bigotry, agricultural stagnation now threatened his corporate "child." A new generation of company officers challenged the wisdom of Mullen's business philosophies. Declining health forced the flour baron first to consider selling the Colorado Milling and Elevator Company, then to retire. Restless in retirement, Mullen continued to maintain influence within his company, while finding ways to extend his legacy of philanthropy.

"MELTING INTO GOLD"

Age and ill health forced Mullen to cut back further on his workload. In early 1926, he visited the Mayo Clinic in order to treat a "baffling" illness. Semiretired, he spent much of his free time writing to his grandchildren or wrapping up loose affairs. In October 1926, he donated $9,500 from his new foundation to the oldest of Denver's Catholic charities, the St. Vincent de Paul Society. He also celebrated his eighty-first birthday in Washington, D.C., attending dedication ceremonies for the recently completed J. K. Mullen of Denver Memorial Library, in 1928.[1]

Still nominally president of the CM&E, he also continued to worry about the future of his company. A postwar agricultural depression halted the rapid expansion of wheat farming nationwide. As wheat prices continued to decline, many Colorado sodbusters left their farms for more promising occupations. Those who remained expanded onto

J. K. Mullen, c. 1925. Despite a vigorous workload and ambitious expansion plans, age, ill-health, and increased religious tensions began to catch up with the capitalist in the 1920s. Courtesy, Western History Dept., Denver Public Library.

dry-land farms on the High Plains to make up the difference.[2] The CM&E began to feel the pinch of the agricultural stagnation as early as 1923. Gradually, profits from accumulated wheat supplies failed to cover the cost of aggressive purchasing in the fall. This "unsatisfactory" phenomenon, which had not occurred in thirty years, precipitated a bitter disagreement among the directors. For the first time, Mullen's policy of borrowing heavily in the fall on the assumption that wheat prices always advanced in the spring came into question.[3] Mullen approached the argument brusquely, overruling the dissenters for the moment. It remained to be seen whether he had the stamina to overcome an all-out revolt.

J. K. also realized that the time approached when he would no longer be able to actively supervise his "child." Evaluating his heirs, the industrialist saw no one who stood ready to take control under such straitened circumstances. His daughters, who were probably more capable than he imagined, were out of the question. Like many

Farmers gambled on dry-land wheat during the First World War. By 1918 they reaped $4 per bushel. Drought and the collapse of the wartime market left dry-land boomers with the dusty taste of failure in their mouths. The slump dealt the CM&E its first major setback in thirty years while farmers blamed Mullen's stingy pricing for their losses during the 1920s. Louis C. McClure photo. Courtesy, Western History Dept., Denver Public Library.

contemporary capitalists, he believed that "when property of that kind was left in the hands of a woman she became a prey for designing people to try to get the best of her."[4] His grandchildren, though precocious, were still too young to take up the burden of management. Of his sons-in-law, two stood out. Oscar Malo, his longtime lieutenant, had looked after Mullen's real estate and securities investments for many years. John L. Dower, coming from old money in New York and Hartford, Connecticut, was another competent financial advisor. Yet Mullen worried that Malo and Dower, like most of the new generation of young businessmen, failed to appreciate the risks that Mullen had endured. They also lacked seasoning as practical millers. Nobody, it seemed, had earned the physical and symbolic scars that Mullen proudly possessed. Nor, Mullen believed, did anyone understand the subtleties of management that allowed him to keep tabs on a five-state industry.[5]

Another concern was the possibility of sibling rivalry. Mullen split his fortune into equal shares by folding his assets into the J. K. Mullen Investment Company. By dividing the shares equally among his daughters, he hoped to avoid any charges of favoritism. Turning over control of the CM&E to one branch of the family threatened to kindle bitter flames of jealousy among his remaining heirs. The fairest solution, it seemed, was to sell off the company and divide the proceeds among each of his daughters.[6]

In the spring of 1926, Mullen approached an unnamed acquaintance at a Denver banking house with an offer to sell his shares of the CM&E. For the price of $20 million, he agreed to relinquish his nearly absolute control of CM&E stock to an interested investment company. The offer piqued the interest of the New York firm of Dillon, Read and Company, who sent two partners to negotiate with the president. Accompanying the partners was "a large force" of Dillon-Read accountants, who combed the books of each of the thirty-four mills and two hundred CM&E elevators in Colorado, Idaho, Kansas, and Utah.[7] The *Denver Post*, long opposed to the virtual lock that the CM&E held on local wheat prices, shuddered at rumors that Dillon-Read secretly represented the huge General Foods milling conglomeration. *Post* writer Robert G. Dill regretted the potential loss of a local company that had "financed thousands of farmers . . . and has aided in many other ways in the building up of the farming communities."[8]

CM&E mills such as the Eagle, located on Seventh and Lawrence Streets, let Denver claim the title "Minneapolis of the West." Built on the site of Mullen's old Excelsior Mill, the Eagle added to the overall value of Mullen's milling empire. Louis McClure photo. Courtesy, Western History Dept., Denver Public Library.

The Mullen family joined the *Post* in regretting J. K.'s decision. Son-in-law John L. Dower wrote an impassioned letter illustrating the family's point of view:

> You are about to part with your great pet child. This creation of yours [represents] one of the great achievements of this Western country. Before melting it into gold let us consider the possibility of letting it stand and adding to its glory . . . I have at different times tried to make suggestions to you but have never met with much success or attention, and your attitude has caused me to feel that you had neither confidence in nor regard for my opinions, my judgment or my motives.[9]

Acting despite his father-in-law's reservations about his character, Dower offered an alternative plan. He would buy the stock on the same terms as Dillon-Read offered, bringing in employees as shareholding employee-owners. Dower appealed to the self-made millionaire in terms that Mullen understood. "Don't sell your great business . . . to the men of

Wall Street. It should go to the men who have been loyal and faithful, who have worked with you and for you, whose toil helped you make it what it is."[10]

Apparently impressed with Dower's passion, as well as the resolve of his daughters, Mullen canceled further negotiations. The *Denver Post* reported that the failure of the sale occurred because of J. K.'s characteristic unwillingness to compromise. According to the *Post*, a Dillon-Read negotiator suggested that a single CM&E mill was valued too highly. "You think that?" Mullen asked. "I do," replied the negotiator. To the surprise of the Dillon-Read team, Mullen picked up his hat, concluded, "Then good morning, gentlemen," and walked out.[11]

J. K. also rejected Dower's offer on behalf of the employees. Instead, the financier resumed his efforts to find a successor within his family. He quashed further rumors regarding the proposed sale of the CM&E. The trade magazine *Southwestern Miller* printed a letter attributed to the industrialist:

> My attention has been called to your article of Oct. 20 in regard to the sale of . . . the Colorado Milling and Elevator Co., and incidentally to the fact that I was more than 80 years of age . . . Our company is not at all anxious to either give away our Colorado M. & E. Co. milling property, or to sell it. Why should we? We like the business and the country needs it, and we are in love with our associates and our employees. They are our pals, and have been such for a generation or more . . . We do not care to sell out because we love the West. We love the cool breezes that come from the snow-clad hills in the summer time, and we love its rivers and its mountains, and its fields of golden grain, and we love the wonderful people, the pioneers that have made the country blossom like a rose. But we do not like to be called old. I have lived in Colorado over 50 years and have grown younger every year, and if I continue to live in Colorado long enough, I expect to die of infantile paralysis.[12]

"But we do not like to be called old . . ." The syrupy letter smacked of the CM&E's recently organized public-relations department (which included the father of playwright Mary Coyle Chase). Yet the undercurrent remained pure Mullen. Unable to stand the rigors of managing his corporate empire on a daily basis, the capitalist relied on vigorous executives such as Malo, Dower, Maurice C. Dolan, and Stephen Knight, who in turn continued to assert themselves in the formation of company policy.

During the winter of 1926–1927, weary from the rigors of negotiations, depressed by the stagnated price of wheat, bothered by
"lumbargo [*sic*]," and "not feeling very well of late," Mullen withdrew
to Long Beach, California, for a well-earned rest. Although the "boys"
at the CM&E-affiliated Sunset Milling and Grain Company attempted
to cure his doldrums with nightly card games, Mullen spent much of
his time in heavy contemplation. In early February, Mullen telegraphed
the board of directors of the CM&E that he intended to resign as
director and president. On February 9, he confirmed his decision.
Writing to "my very dear associates for the last forty years," he apolo-
gized for any hurt feelings he may have caused. "It is only natural for
an official that has held office such a great length of time to become at
times somewhat arbitrary." Feeling responsible for the declining profits of the company in the last few years, he attempted to explain his
actions. "Nineteen years out of twenty the price has advanced
sufficient[ly] between the time the wheat is received and the following
harvest to justify us and to give us a very substantial profit. But that
has not been so the last three or four years." Nevertheless, he hoped
that his retirement would not prevent the CM&E from continuing its
aggressive purchasing policy. The company was, after all, "in good
financial condition" with 6 million bushels of wheat on hand and
200,000 bushels stored in the countryside. He implored the company
to continue his practices.[13]

The directors replied with regret, refusing to accept his resignation until he returned to Colorado to help pick a successor. Although
they praised his "forty two years of hard and constant work in building
the Company," there were nevertheless a few private sighs of relief.[14]
Not the least of these came from Maurice C. Dolan, the manager of
the Excelsior Mill, who in April criticized his superior for taking extensive loans and purchasing too aggressively each fall. Perhaps it was
better, Dolan suggested, to let each local manager buy wheat at his
own price and according to his own needs. In an admittedly "big long
letter," Mullen dressed the young manager down. He reviewed the
litany of risks, obligations, and deferred gratification he had under-
taken since the formation of Mullen and Seth in 1875. Compared to
Dolan's generation, he observed, "You have been away from home but
very little. You have been able to sleep at home almost every night; and
occasionally you go off and have a little vacation; and you don't get

down to work very early."[15] Although he recognized that his health no longer permitted him to oversee his commercial empire, Mullen saw little in the next generation that allowed him to relax his vigil easily.

On February 5, 1927, J. K. Mullen began easing his fifty-year-old grip on the reigns of the CM&E. Agreeing to "make haste slowly," Mullen remained on partial duty while he and the board of directors determined the questions of transition.[16] He retained his position as chairman of the board of directors and temporarily extended his tenure as president when his designated successor, Oscar Malo, suffered a sprained ankle and broken ribs in a train accident.[17] At times, it was difficult to tell that the industrialist had retired at all. He accompanied the annual invoicing trips to Kansas and Missouri in the summers of 1927 and 1928. He also continued to keep abreast of CM&E affairs. As if starting fresh, the retiree filed papers of incorporation for the subsidiary Oregon Milling Company and drew up plans for elevators in Ontario and Nyssa, Oregon, in April 1928.[18]

The Mullen monument at Mt. Olivet Cemetery. Designed by Tiffany's of New York, the classical granite colonnade flanking the bronze statue of the Sacred Heart suggests cool grace and reflection. Visitors can enjoy the vistas of the Rocky Mountains and contemplate cemetery grounds that once grew wheat for the Colorado Milling and Elevator Co. Michael J. Convery photo. Courtesy, author's collection.

Family patronage and support was important to J. K. Mullen's sense of philanthropy. This plot at Mt. Olivet Cemetery contains the remains of J. K.'s mother, father, and sister. Michael J. Convery photo. Courtesy, author's collection.

Personal affairs kept J. K. busy as well. In June 1927 he commissioned Tiffany's of New York to design a monument for his family plot at Mt. Olivet Cemetery. Mullen's monument suggests cool grace and reflection. Built of granite, the elegant classical colonnade surrounds a larger-than-life bronze statue of the Sacred Heart designed by sculptor Harriet W. Rishmuth. Stone meditation benches flank the statue, allowing visitors to view the mesas to the south and west. The monument anchors the extended Mullen family plot, drawing visitors into a park within a park.[19] J. K. commissioned the design to counterpoint the nearby John F. Campion mausoleum, which he considered "nice, but somewhat squatty."[20]

Sensing, in his conservative way, a forthcoming financial crisis, he also inaugurated a personal campaign against the maintenance of large debts by poor parishes. In 1920, the Shrine of St. Anne in Arvada had purchased brick on credit from the Mullen-owned Denver Brick and Shale Company. Although the Denver Brick and Shale Co. assumed part of the costs, the church still owed $2,200 as late as 1927. As much as Mullen regretted placing a lien on a church, business was business. When Bishop John Tihen promptly paid the bill, the financier returned $1,000, feeling "a regular, definite obligation" to abrogate the interest.[21] He cleared St. Joseph's Church of Oriskany Falls from its debt of $1,500 and deposited another $1,500 at the Idaho Falls Catholic Church upon hearing that it owed $60,000 on its $95,000 construction bill. Concerned, he asked Bishop Tihen if he too had noticed the tendency of parishes to emulate the larger business community by carrying excessive obligations. Easy credit, he feared, disaffected poor Catholics who carried the burden of debt: "I am afraid it will be carried too far."[22] In December 1928, he noticed other symptoms of impending financial trouble, observing to Tihen, "I think there are more poor at this time than during any previous Christmas time. What is your opinion?"[23]

"THERE IS NOTHING WRONG WITH ME!"

Early the following year, the friend of Denver's poor was recognized as a member of the truly elite Catholic-American business class. On January 22, 1929, he was invested as a Knight of the Order of Malta, one of the highest honors bestowed on Catholic laymen by the papacy. The prestigious order traced its origin to the crusading medieval knights of St. John, who pledged themselves to the defense of Catholicism and to the care of the sick and poor. In the twentieth century, the honor went to "practical Catholics" (in the words of a representative) who had performed notable services to the Church. Previously restricted to notable European Catholics, knighthood had been opened to Americans only in recent months. J. K. joined James A. Farrell of United States Steel, Cornelius Kelly and John D. Ryan of Anaconda Copper, and Frederick J. Fisher of General Motors in the rarified air of America's elite Catholic businessmen.[24]

The summer of 1929 opened with the industrialist on a vigorous travel schedule. On his birthday, June 11, Mullen left on an inspection tour of CM&E properties in Kansas. He took an unannounced, and perhaps reflective, solo side trip through backcountry fields and farms, worrying his family with an uncharacteristic lack of communication.[25] He returned home briefly by June 17 to invite the Christian Brothers of New Mexico to take over his planned vocational home for orphaned boys.[26] Mid-July found the veteran miller on the road to Idaho Falls for the funeral of a longtime friend. On the way back, Mullen stopped in Salt Lake City to look after some business matters. There, he came down with a heavy cold that forced him to return home. The cold worsened. By July 25, pneumonia had settled in Mullen's lungs.[27]

Not for the first time, family members worried about Mullen's advanced age and physical condition. At the train station in Denver, he forecast to his welcoming daughters, "This is the end."[28] As always, he proved to be a vigorous, if difficult, patient. "There is nothing wrong with me!" he declared to examining doctors.[29] Indeed, J. K. improved enough to give doctors and family members false hopes before relapsing on August 2. The battle to draw each breath, as well as a high fever, taxed the strength of his already weakened heart.[30]

From bed in his home on Pennsylvania Street, Mullen exerted the last of his formidable will power in this final fight. Although Fathers O'Ryan and McMenamin administered last rites on the evening of August 2 and recited prayers for the dying all the following day, the patient rallied. He struggled in and out of consciousness for another week before finally succumbing at 7:25 A.M., Friday, August 9, 1929.[31]

Word of J. K. Mullen's death inspired an instant outpouring of sympathy that matched the philanthropist's stature. The directors of

After Mullen became the first Catholic layperson to lie in state at the Immaculate Conception Cathedral, pallbearers, including CM&E officers Stephen Knight, Maurice Dolan, Herbert E. Johnson, and Loyal Breckenridge, escort his remains to Mt. Olivet, August 12, 1929. Courtesy, Western History Dept., Denver Public Library.

the Colorado Milling and Elevator Company issued a quickly penned, lavishly printed memorial poem:

> He sleeps in the west, that he loved the best,
> In the land of the setting sun.
> The hum of the mill for him is still,
> And his long day's work is done.
> His kindly smile in the "after-while,"
> Will greet us again some day,
> When we earn our rest in the golden west
> Where our chieftain is "just away."[32]

Managers from both CM&E and competing mills sent letters of condolence to Oscar Malo. The chairman of the Minneapolis Grain Commission, Henry L. Hankinson, wrote Malo, "I have always . . . looked upon Mr. Mullen as the best friend I had in the world." On

August 15, the Denver Chamber of Commerce memorialized Mullen as "a Denver and civic leader." The *Denver Post* overdid itself in praise— as it had in criticism—calling the miller "Colorado's first citizen . . . tolerant, merciful, brave, and just in every way."[33]

Escorted by a Knights of Columbus honor guard, "Colorado's first citizen" made the final journey to his cathedral on Sunday, August 11. In accordance with his stature as Colorado's premiere Catholic bene- factor, the diocese honored Mullen as the first layman to lie in state at the Immaculate Conception Cathedral. His casket rested under a canopy of black and white streamers while mourners passed by.[34] The next morning, an overflow crowd attended his funeral, where, in the words of the *Post*, "the Catholic church . . . utilized all of its rich store of ceremony in tribute to the man who . . . had been its large benefac- tor."[35] The cathedral bells tolled eighty-two times—once for each year of the philanthropist's life. Following the requiem mass, Father William O'Ryan mounted the pulpit before the assembled rich and poor, busi- ness tycoons and politicians, elderly and orphaned, old friends, nuns, clergymen, and employees to eulogize Colorado's great Catholic patron:

> He was an Irishman. He was an American. He was a member of the Holy Catholic Church . . . He loved his country and all it means . . . As he was loyal to his city, so he was loyal to the church of his devotion . . . So he lived all through his life, a simple man, devoted to duty, his city, state, and church. He had a strong shoulder to lean on the faith of his fathers . . . It will be remembered in the hearts of his people for many and many a changing generation.[36]

NOTES

1. *Denver Post*, January 29, 1926: 18; July 12, 1928: 23.
2. Carl Abbott, Stephen J. Leonard, and David McComb, *Colorado: A History of the Centennial State*, 3d ed. (Niwot: University Press of Colorado, 1994), 176– 177.
3. J. K. Mullen, Letter to Directors, CM&E, February 9, 1927, Weckbaugh family collection.
4. J. K. Mullen, Letter to Ella M. Weckbaugh, May Dower, Catherine O'Connor, and Edith Malo, Denver, Colorado, 1928, Weckbaugh family collection (here- after cited as Letter to his daughters).
5. *Denver Post*, May 6, 1926: 10.
6. J. K. Mullen, Letter to his daughters, 1928; Walter S. Weckbaugh, personal interview, July 21, 1997.

7. *Denver Post*, May 6, 1926: 10.

8. Ibid.

9. John L. Dower, Letter to J. K. Mullen, June 5, 1926, John Kernan Mullen manuscript collection, MSS 705 (Mullen papers), Colorado Historical Society (CHS).

10. Ibid.

11. *Denver Post*, August 14, 1929: 1.

12. *Southwestern Miller*, August 13, 1929: 33.

13. J. K. Mullen, Letter to Directors, CM&E, February 9, 1927, Weckbaugh family collection.

14. Board of Directors, CM&E, Letter to J. K. Mullen, February 5, 1927, Weckbaugh family collection.

15. J. K. Mullen, Letter to Maurice C. Dolan, April 19, 1927, Mullen papers, CHS.

16. J. K. Mullen, Letter to Directors, CM&E, February 9, 1927, Weckbaugh family collection.

17. G. B. Irwin, mgr., Hungarian Mills, Letter to Oscar L. Malo, June 19, 1929, John Kernan Mullen manuscript collection, Western History Dept., Denver Public Library (WHDDPL); *Denver Post*, September 16, 1927: 26.

18. J. K. Mullen, Letter to Rt. Rev. J. H. Tihen, June 14, 1927, Rt. Rev. John Henry Tihen manuscript collection, Archdiocese of Denver archives (hereafter cited as Tihen papers); *Denver Post*, April 27, 1928: 28.

19. *Denver Post*, June 6, 1927: 4.

20. J. K. Mullen, Letter to Rt. Rev. J. H. Tihen, April 12, 1925, Tihen papers.

21. J. K. Mullen, Letters to Rt. Rev. J. H. Tihen, June 4, 1927; June 14, 1927, Tihen papers.

22. *Denver Post*, February 17, 1928: 2; J. K. Mullen, Letter to Rt. Rev. J. H. Tihen, June 14, 1927, Tihen papers.

23. J. K. Mullen, Letter to Rt. Rev. J. H. Tihen, December 14, 1928, Tihen papers.

24. *Denver Catholic Register* (*DCR*), January 24, 1929: 1.

25. *Denver Post*, June 11, 1929: 3.

26. J. K. Mullen, Letter to Rt. Rev. J. H. Tihen and Rev. Brother Arsenius, July 15, 1929, J. K. Mullen Home for Boys papers, Archdiocese of Denver archives.

27. *Denver Post*, July 26, 1929: 10.

28. *DCR*, August 18, 1929: 2.

29. Ruth Vincent Novack, "Give While You Live," *St. Anthony Messenger* (November 1947): 55.

30. *Denver Post*, August 3, 1929: 1.

31. *Denver Post*, August 9, 1929: 1.

32. C. E. Williams, Colorado Milling and Elevator Co., Letter to employees and friends of the CM&E, August 16, 1929, Mullen papers, CHS.

33. H. L. Hankinson, Letter to Oscar Malo, August 6, 1929, Mullen papers, WHDDPL; *Denver Magazine* 21:17 (August 15, 1929); *Denver Post*, August 12, 1929: 1.

34. *DCR*, August 18, 1929: 2.

35. *Denver Post*, August 12, 1929: 4.

36. Ibid.

21

THE J. K. MULLEN HOME FOR BOYS

It must not be forgotten that good wheat may be spoiled in grinding to such an extent that no after treatment will save it.

—R. JAMES ABERNATHEY[1]

A PROJECT OF GREAT IMPORTANCE—one intended to "round out" his and Kate's lives—lay unfinished on the deceased philanthropist's desk. On April 27, 1929, Catholic Charities founder Father John R. Mulroy and five committee members of the Diocesan Holy Name Society had issued a report describing the need for a vocational school for homeless adolescent boys. Under Colorado law, local orphanages were required to release boys from their care upon completion of the eighth grade. With few opportunities for higher education and without the basic skills of a trade, young males between the ages of twelve and eighteen tended to drift into trouble. In many cases, the report concluded, these directionless adolescents became, like Pinocchio's Lost Boys, "questionable characters" who would soon belong in "Golden, Buena Vista, and, with some exceptions, to the devil." Having found "fifty Catholic boys in Denver . . . who were in urgent need of a home with active Catholic influence," the committee recommended the construction of an instructional boarding home as soon as possible.[2]

In order to plug what it called a "leakage at the bunghole," the Holy Name Committee called on Colorado's prominent Catholic citizens to step forward with financial help. With these funds, the Holy Name Society intended to buy and maintain one of three potential vocational schools: a rural ranch "where boys may farm on a large scale," a suburban farm "where boys can engage in gardening, rabbit breeding, and chicken raising," or an urban home convenient to city jobs.[3] Although the report addressed no particular individual, in all likelihood Mulroy aimed this sermon-in-disguise at J. K. Mullen. As chairman of Catholic Charities, Mulroy and his predecessors had depended on Mullen family charity for similar social projects in the past. They had rarely been disappointed.[4]

If Mulroy chose to appeal to Mullen's sympathies for homeless boys and girls, he read his audience well. Both John and Kate were well aware of the social conditions of homeless children. Their concern for the children who fell between the cracks of society may be traced to an exchange of letters with the director of the Sunshine Rescue Mission, Reverend James Goodheart, in 1918 and 1919. In January 1919, Mullen read that Rev. Goodheart had recently taken in two preadolescent boys expelled from the State Home for Dependents, one of whom was accused of shooting the home's superintendent. While praising "my dear Rev. Goodheart" for taking in the boys, he blamed their lack of morals on the absence of daily religious indoctrination. Without the parents to act as proper role models, and provide religious instruction or education, J. K. feared that the boys would become "a menace to society." He focused on the absence of religious influences, writing, "I am one of those, Jim Goodheart, who believes that this [lack of responsibility] is primarily due to a lack of religious teaching in their early youth." In the hope that Rev. Goodheart would take his opinion to heart, the philanthropist enclosed a $50 check.[5]

More support for orphaned children came from Catherine. Although the *Denver Catholic Register* correctly called J. K. Mullen a "chief benefactor" of St. Vincent's Orphan Asylum, he quickly credited his wife for direction.[6] Growing up without a father perhaps made her sensitive to the plight of orphans and insufficiently supported children, because in one form or another, Catherine made helping orphans a central part of her life. During the panic of 1893, she entreated her husband to take in the son of a hard-luck friend. Kate donated her own funds to establish the St. Joseph Hospital Baby Annex, which nurtured orphaned and homeless infants.[7] She also contributed much of her time to the Sacred Heart Aid Society and to the St. Vincent's Ladies' Aid Society, which supported Denver's Mount St. Vincent Orphan Asylum. Evolving out of Denver's Dorcas Society, the upper-

Kate Mullen spent a lifetime caring for "motherless and fatherless waifs" such as these at St. Vincent's Orphanage. Kate and her husband both feared that, without proper guidance, these lost boys were in danger of going to prisons in "Golden, Buena Vista, and, with some exceptions, to the devil." Courtesy, Colorado Historical Society.

middle-class Catholic Ladies' Aid Society rededicated itself to the care of over two hundred orphan children between the ages of six months and fifteen years in 1884 and assumed the task of raising funds for the new community orphanage.[8]

The Ladies' Aid Society earned most of the orphanage's modest operating revenue by sponsoring annual New Year's Eve balls and through summer outings for the parentless children at Denver's parks and gardens. Catherine was a key promoter of these summer outings. In 1902, she was elected president of the society and, with Mary Elitch, opened Elitch's Gardens for annual summer picnics to benefit "these motherless and fatherless waifs."[9] As an organizer of the Elitch's picnic, Catherine was thrust into a reluctant public role. She normally preferred working behind the scenes as a yeoman organizer of the Ladies' Aid Society, advancing the ideals of the club as secretary, treasurer, and vice president. Her conviction infected her husband's motivations for philanthropy. When Mullen exchanged fifteen acres of land north of St. Vincent's Orphanage to the Sisters of Charity for $1 on Christmas, 1919, he cited his wife's influence.[10]

J. K. underscored Kate's involvement when he described their idea for a school for orphaned adolescent boys:

> During her lifetime and just previous to her death, we agreed together that we should round out our lives if possible by the construction of this build-ing and by creating a foundation . . . amounting to $150,000 or $200,000 to pay the estimated cost of the grounds and improvements . . . to maintain permanently and continuously eighty to one hundred boys—to feed them, house them, clothe them properly and give them the benefit of a good Christian Education.[11]

In early 1929, Mullen remained convinced that the greatest need for homeless and orphaned boys and girls was for "a good Christian Education." Within a few months, he included the need for secular training as well. Almost a year before the Holy Name Society issued its report, Mullen personally wrote to the most successful organizer of vocational homes for boys, Father Edward J. Flanagan, for advice. From his Boys' Home in Omaha, Father Flanagan happily responded to a man whose "reputation has traveled North, South, East, and West . . . because of your outstanding qualities as a Catholic gentleman."[12] Flanagan described the dimensions, furnishings, and construction of his living quarters, as well as the method by which he established his own home. Most importantly, he stressed the need to train the boys in some sort of vocation, speaking in crisp terms that Mullen understood:

> I consider a trade for every young fellow a most necessary asset . . . because these children do not have the advantages of boys from well established homes . . . If our boys slip, they fall, and they remain fallen if they haven't the strength of character to get up and go ahead.

Flanagan encouraged Mullen's efforts, sent instructional literature, and offered to "come out at my own expense to give whatever information or help that I could."

More help arrived from the Christian Brothers mission in Santa Fe, New Mexico. Distinguished by their distinctive, double-breasted collars, the Christian Brothers had dedicated themselves to Christian instruction. On June 17, 1928, Mullen invited the Brothers to Colo-rado to take over his proposed school. In a July 15 letter to Bishop Tihen and Christian Brother Arsenius, J. K. mentioned his efforts to find a suitable property and outlined his intended organizational plan. While the day-to-day operations would fall under the Christian Brothers' care, the problems of fund-raising, as well as of long-term policy, would fall to a board of directors comprised of "good, loyal, faithful, honest Christian gentlemen of this city." As far as Mullen was concerned, the duty of the directors was to watch out for "extraordinary or unnecessary expenditures." However, he planned to set up funding so that the directors could "afford to and doubtless be very liberal."[13]

His heirs resumed Mullen's plans, interrupted by his death the following month. After reviewing over fifty sites, daughters May, Ella, and Edith and grandchildren Katherine O'Connor Grant and John M. O'Connor purchased the Shirley Farms Dairy through the Mullen Benevolent Foundation in 1931. The 900-acre farm, located at 3601 South Lowell Boulevard, was converted into a working school while the newly admitted boys began classes at Regis College. Barns and dairy buildings were remodeled while dormitories and a chapel were

J. K. Mullen consulted Sunshine Rescue Mission minister James Goodheart and Boys' Town founder Father Edward J. Flanagan before recruiting the Christian Brothers, pictured above, to administrate his home for orphan boys. Dedicated to Christian education, the order continues to guide students at the private J. K. Mullen High School in southwest Denver. Courtesy, Western History Dept., Denver Public Library.

The Mullen Benevolent Foundation selected the 900-acre Shirley Farms Dairy, at 3601 South Lowell Boulevard, after reviewing over fifty potential sites. New dormitories and a chapel complemented the existing barns and dairy buildings. Resident boys learned the skills of husbandry and agriculture while raising livestock, wheat, hay, and alfalfa on a profitable dairy farm. During the Second World War, the home's patriotic Holsteins, Mullen Jewel Mercury and Mullen Valentine Mercury, held state production records for dairy products. Bill Smythe photo. Courtesy, Western History Dept., Denver Public Library.

constructed.[14] The first fifty boys, along with their goats, sheep, rabbits, dogs, and parakeets, moved into the new quarters on April 8, 1932. Within five years, the vocational school had added a gymnasium, cattle and poultry sheds, a tool house, a dairy house, and a greenhouse. The boys, products of orphanages and foster homes, annually harvested in the neighborhood of fifteen tons of alfalfa, wheat, barley, oats, and corn. The students also operated a working dairy to pay for operating expenses. Nevertheless, the Home continued to receive the bulk of its support from the Mullen Benevolent Foundation. In 1950, the Benevolent Foundation constructed new classroom buildings and paid for a $70,000 auditorium in 1952. In 1956, in response to changing priorities by the Christian Brothers, the boarding school closed.[15] Renamed the J. K. Mullen High School, the institution

Boys from the Mullen Home proudly display their husbandry skills. Mullen Home graduates became officers in the Public Service Company, Goodyear, Standard Oil, and the United States Army. Two died in combat during the Second World War. Several became members of the Christian Brothers. At least one alumnus distinguished himself in a fashion that Mullen would not have approved. "Beat Angel" Neal Cassady briefly attended the Home for Boys. The one-time car thief pioneered the Beat Generation's signature Bohemian lifestyle and legendary drug use. Influential Beat writers such as Jack Kerouac, Allen Ginsberg, and Tom Wolfe celebrated Cassady's hip decadence even as he burned himself out through marijuana, LSD, and alcohol abuse. Courtesy, Western History Dept., Denver Public Library.

began accepting day students in a new $650,000 facility financed by the Mullen Foundation. In 1980, the Mullen Foundation transferred the grounds to the Christian Brothers for the sum of $500,000.[16] Today, J. K. Mullen High School continues to operate as one of Colorado's elite independent prep schools.

NOTES

1. R. James Abernathey, *Practical Hints for Mill Building* (Moline, Ill.: R. James Abernathey, 1880), 58, microfilm copy, Auraria Library, Denver, Colorado.
2. Rev. John R. Mulroy et al., "Report of Investigation and Planning Committee to the Diocesan Holy Name Society," April 27, 1929, John K. Mullen collection, Western History Dept., Denver Public Library (WHDDPL).
3. Mulroy et al.

4. Thomas J. Noel, *Colorado Catholicism and the Archdiocese of Denver, 1857–1989* (Niwot: University Press of Colorado, 1989),105–106.

5. J. K. Mullen, Letter to Rev. James Goodheart, January 13, 1919, Weckbaugh family collection. While no record exists of the boys' eventual fate, Mullen's accusation seemed to aptly fit their guardian. Plagued by a nervous breakdown and accusations of financial improprieties and alcoholic "drunken orgies," Rev. Goodheart retired from public life by 1927. See Marcia T. Goldstein, "Homelessness in Denver," *University of Colorado Historical Studies Journal* VI (1989): 11.

6. *Denver Catholic Register*, September 25, 1958: 2.

7. J. K. Mullen, Letter to Catherine S. Mullen, September 2, 1893, John Kernan Mullen manuscript collection, MSS 705 (Mullen papers), Colorado Historical Society (CHS); Noel, *Colorado Catholicism*, 106.

8. Taking their name from the New Testament seamstress who sewed garments for the poor (Acts 9:36–41), these indefatigable women organized to collect toys, clothing, and food for Denver's poor and indigent in 1882. By 1884, the society, now one hundred strong, was overwhelmed by requests for assistance. A society spokeswoman commented that "calls on our purses are so numerous that we are often tempted to tighten the strings against all appeals for assistance" (*Denver Times*, December 6, 1901: 12). When Bishop Machebeuf and the Sisters of Charity established the Mount St. Vincent Orphan Asylum in 1884, the ladies redirected their efforts to the support of the new institution.

9. *Denver Times*, August 8, 1902: 3.

10. J. K. Mullen, "Deed of Gift between J. K. Mullen and St. Mary's Academy of Leavenworth, Kansas," December 27, 1919, Mullen papers, WHDDPL.

11. J. K. Mullen, Letter to Rt. Rev. J. H. Tihen and Vy. Rev. Brother Arsenius, F.S.C., July 15, 1929, J. K. Mullen Home for Boys manuscript collection, Archdiocese of Denver archives (hereafter cited as Home for Boys papers).

12. This and subsequent quotes from Father Flanagan cited in Rev. Edward J. Flanagan, Letter to J. K. Mullen, May 14, 1928, Mullen papers, CHS.

13. J. K. Mullen, Letter to Rt. Rev. J. H. Tihen and Rev. Brother Arsenius, July 15, 1929, Home for Boys papers.

14. *Denver Post*, January 1, 1932: 12; January 31, 1932: 12; Noel, *Colorado Catholicism*, 134.

15. *Rocky Mountain News*, April 8, 1932: 12; Noel, *Colorado Catholicism*, 134–135; Rev. Elmer J. Kolka, Letter to Most Rev. Urban J. Vehr, July 24, 1956, Rt. Rev. John Henry Tihen manuscript collection, Archdiocese of Denver archives.

16. "Quit Claim Deed Between Mullen Benevolent Corp. and the Christian Brothers," September, 10, 1980, Mullen Benevolent Corp. papers, J. K. Mullen Foundation, Inc., manuscript collection, Western History Dept., Denver Public Library.

22

THE LEGACY OF JOHN KERNAN MULLEN

ON A STORMY WINTER NIGHT IN DECEMBER 1926, J. K. Mullen answered a knock at the door to find a ragged, bright-eyed, and nearly toothless woman standing on the sill, fingering a large ebony crucifix that hung against her breast. J. K. recognized the shivering apparition as Elizabeth McCourt "Baby Doe" Tabor, the widow of millionaire Horace Tabor. Forty years before, Baby Doe had presided with her husband over Denver's gilded age. Now destitute, she waited in the snow until Mullen invited her into the warmth of his home. "It's a bad night to be walking the streets," he observed. "It's nothing to the Leadville blizzards," she replied. "I'm used to a hard life."[1] She asked to be excused for the lateness of the hour, as well as for her lack of an invitation, but she wished to discuss "a matter of life and death." Escorted to J. K.'s study, Baby Doe unfolded what Mullen later described as "a real out West story."[2]

The rags-to-riches-to-rags saga of Horace Tabor and his paramour cum soulmate was well known to the businessman. When he died penniless in 1899, Tabor left Baby Doe with little except mounting debts, a murky claim to his properties, and the single-minded desire to restore the Tabor fortune to its former glory.[3] From her cabin above Leadville, Baby Doe tenaciously defended the last piece of the Tabor empire, the Matchless Mine. "I'll never let the Matchless go while there's breath in my body," she told a banker who questioned her determination.[4] Alternately pursuing and evading lawsuits, the widow appealed to Jesus and "protective spirits" to defend her nearly worthless mine from claimants, litigants, and hallucinatory "devils" and "monsters" who tormented her as she prayed.

By early 1926, her need for miracles increased. She owed over $14,000 in damages, legal fees, and interest against her claim. A strong believer in Christian mysticism, Baby Doe meticulously recorded her vivid dreams and visions. In April, she beheld the apparition of a "large big common man's hands" signing a document that would help set her free.[5] Soon after, Tabor's widow descended into Denver to seek out the

Horace Austin Warner Tabor and his second wife, Elizabeth Bouliel McCourt "Baby Doe," were two members, along with Horace's first wife, Augusta Pierce, of Colorado's most celebrated love triangle. Unlike Mullen, Tabor made and lost his fortune through sometimes reckless mining speculation.

owner of those hands. Her appeals to Denver's Catholic clergy led to a unanimous referral to the city's premier philanthropist—J. K. Mullen.

Finishing her story, Baby Doe reminded the philanthropist how her late husband, a deathbed convert to Catholicism, had died in the embrace of the Church. Repeatedly fondling and kissing her oversized crucifix—a gesture that unnerved the patron—she invoked Mullen's

Mullen supposedly loaned the Tabors money in exchange for a mortgage on the Matchless Mine. Although this is unlikely, J. K. still refused to stand by as Baby Doe struggled in the 1920s. Courtesy, Western History Dept., Denver Public Library.

reputation for philanthropy and appealed to him as a member of Denver's Catholic elite. Could he step forward once again and help the beleaguered widow?

Mullen could. The next morning, he recalled, "I went down to the Bank and borrowed $14,000." He requested that his attorney, John Reddin, clear up Baby Doe's legal difficulties. J. K. instructed the widow to keep his assistance anonymous. In return, J. K. had Baby Doe sign over a mortgage on the Matchless, which she would repay with profits from the mine. As security, he requested the abstract of title from Tabor's widow. It was not forthcoming, nor did receipts appear. Pressing the issue, Mullen received troubling excuses from Baby Doe. "I am indeed sad and grieved to have caused the gentleman [Mullen] anxiety," she wrote Reddin. Nevertheless, she couldn't trust the mails. The abstract had been misplaced. The snows were too deep. The "Evil people who have . . . persecuted us" sabotaged mine machinery. Her subcontractor was an "evil man . . . who hates all Catholics."[6]

J. K. sent agents to Leadville to resolve the matter. They found Baby Doe unaccountably diverted from appointments or unexpectedly absent from home. Her continued evasion forced the philanthropist to conclude that Senator Tabor had never transferred clear title to his wife. In time, he considered her a squatter. Mullen's investment in the Matchless proved to be equally disappointing. An "occasional" check for $180 or $190 appeared irregularly from the mine's smelting company. By now suspicious that Baby Doe was working the mine at less than full capacity, Mullen sent a mining engineer to inspect his investment. Mrs. Tabor successfully avoided the engineer for several days, forcing him to return empty-handed.

By December 27, 1927, Baby Doe owed $1,120 in interest payments, with no prospect of recovery. "The property is not being worked at all," Mullen complained. "It is just laying there and the timbers are rotting." On December 29, Mullen foreclosed on the Matchless, despite an eleventh-hour appeal for leniency from *Denver Catholic Register* editor Father Matthew Smith. "In all my fifty years of experience in Denver," Mullen explained, "nearly all the difficulties and losses that I had encountered arose by reason of dealings that I had with my close friends . . . the party referred to is just another case."[7]

Nevertheless, the businessman-philanthropist preserved the dignity of the eccentric widow. On the snowy night when she first sought

"I am night watch and I watch all the while when I am not sleeping," Baby Doe wrote. She maintained her solitary vigil at the Matchless Mine, protecting it from "evil men," "persecutors," and hallucinatory "monsters" who tormented her in the night. Mullen believed that Mrs. Tabor sincerely wished to develop the mine property, but he soon realized her instability made the goal impossible. "In all my fifty years of experience in Denver," Mullen complained, "nearly all the difficulties and losses that I had encountered arose by reason of dealings that I had with my close friends." Courtesy, Western History Dept., Denver Public Library.

his help, Baby Doe had stressed her belief that "the Crucifix would bring her through all right." Mullen refused to let her faith go unrewarded. He established the Shorego Mining Company to oversee the Matchless and protect Baby Doe from liability. (Upon his death in 1929, Mullen's forty-three shares in the Shorego Mining Co. were worth $7,150.) Additionally, the philanthropist and his family permitted Baby Doe to maintain the illusion of ownership, letting her live in her cabin rent-free and providing assistance when her pride permitted it, until her solitary death from exposure in March 1935.

J. K.'s private assistance of Denver's former Silver Queen says much about the nature of the philanthropist's legacy. His aid combined personal charity, piety, sensitivity, friendship, and fiscal pragmatism— in all, a neat sum of the financier's priorities. The capitalist's legacy transcended his social values. Upon his death, the former mill hand's personal estate was estimated to be worth $6,622,049.51 (see Appendix B). Likewise, Mullen left behind the seventh largest milling company in the United States. The Colorado Milling and Elevator Company controlled approximately $27 million worth of wheat, supported approximately 850 employees, and delivered flour to forty-one states. The combined worth of the CM&E mills, elevators, and warehouses was estimated at approximately $20 million.

J. K.'s heirs continued to operate Mullen's "child." "The company was built up by our father. It was his pride," May Dower told a *Denver Post* reporter on August 22, 1929. Selling out would be "ungracious . . . We will [continue to] operate the mills as they have always been operated." Just as quickly, the family quarreled over the future management of the firm. Since Mullen's resignation in 1927, Edith's husband, Oscar Malo, had served as company president and chairman of the board of directors. One month after Mullen's death, the remaining three daughters removed Malo from the presidency in favor of May's husband, John L. Dower. Although the move represented an attempt to share the responsibilities of management, the ouster, executed in secret, damaged the relationship between the Malos and the rest of the family. Oscar resigned as chairman and terminated his association with the milling firm. A reconstituted board of directors appointed Stephen Knight as chairman and revised the voting system to exclude minority stockholders such as the Malos.[8]

The familial rift marked an inauspicious decade for the CM&E. Led by John Dower, the CM&E entered the disastrous years of the Great Depression. Overextended and under-irrigated, Colorado farms literally blew away in the arid years from 1933 to 1938.[9] The CM&E survived the Dust Bowl era despite a 15 percent decrease in farmsteads, the failure of four company mills, and occasional disastrous years. Despite years such as 1938, when the firm lost $858,000, and although on average the company operated at less than half its rated capacity during the 1930s, it accumulated an annual net average of $439,568 between 1935 and 1941.[10] Nevertheless, the strain of management taxed Dower and his advisors, some of whom, such as Edmond Ryan and Herb Johnson, had come out of retirement to assist the firm.

Even these veteran managers struggled to adjust to significant changes that overtook the flour-making business. New economic forces began to transform the milling industry in the 1920s. Just as small family farms gave way to corporate agribusiness, so proprietary milling companies yielded to corporate firms. White-collar management specialists who lacked specific milling training replaced workaday milling capitalists such as Mullen. The new breed of corporate miller ran their mills as isolated units of a larger economic bureaucracy.[11] Recognizing the trend of corporate investment, Mullen's heirs concluded that the operation of the family-oriented milling company would become increasingly difficult.

Rumors of a pending sale circulated as early as 1938, but the continuing depression discouraged potential buyers. Finally, on May 22, 1943, Dower negotiated the sale of 79,464 shares (98.38 percent) of CM&E stock to a New York–based holding company, Union Securities Investment Co., for $13,776,850.40. On June 12, the holding company sold off $3,410,000 worth of stock to the Chicago-based Paul H. Davis & Co., the Wall Street firm of Hornblower & Weeks, and minority interests to (Charles) Boettcher & Co. and Bosworth, Chanute, Loughridge & Co. of Denver.[12] Upon completion of the sale, Dower retired from active service. Reelected to the board of directors in June, he died shortly thereafter.[13]

In the postwar age of increasing competition, efficient highway transportation, and corporate consolidation, the Colorado Milling and Elevator Co. dissolved into the larger world of agribusiness. In 1968, the CM&E merged with the Great Western Sugar Company to form the Great Western United conglomerate. Two years later, Great Western United sold its milling concerns to Peavy Incorporated, which in turn sold the dwindling CM&E to the Omaha-based Consolidated Agriculture Company (ConAgra).[14] One by one, Colorado's aging mills closed, burned down, or consolidated. Nevertheless, the Hungarian brand name survives. ConAgra relocated the Hungarian Mills to Commerce City, Colorado, northeast of downtown Denver, during the urban renewal movement of the late 1960s. Each package of Hungarian High-Altitude Flour commemorates the introduction of the Hungarian milling process by J. K. Mullen in a small printed history on the label.

The economic revival of Denver's lower downtown district promises to resuscitate a former CM&E mill. In 1997, developers led by

By 1970, the Hungarian Flour Mill and Elevators had survived the breakup of the CM&E, two depressions, and a massive fire. But, like the not-yet-expanded Mile High Stadium in the background, the brick-and-concrete structure could not withstand the forces of urban renewal. Courtesy, Denver Urban Renewal Authority, Thomas J. Noel collection.

Historic Denver founder Dana Crawford began restoring the abandoned Longmont Farmer's Mill into luxury apartments. Taking advantage of memories of the familiar CM&E "Pride of Denver" brand logo that formerly adorned the concrete grain silos, developers rechristened the last surviving Denver mill as the "Flour Mill Lofts." The new lofts offer proximity to Coors Field, access to LoDo's nightlife, and a chance to live in a historic National Register structure.[15]

By contrast, survival proved elusive for the Oriskany Falls mill where Mullen received his first employment, although the village itself has changed little from when Mullen boarded the westward-bound stagecoach. After converting to rollers in 1887, the mill continued to attract local farmers until 1962. Converted to a feed store, the mill provided seed, fertilizer, farm supplies, and custom grinding to local husbandmen until competition from larger corporate mills forced its closure in 1983.[16] The building remained abandoned for thirteen years. Village authorities tried to claim the structure for unpaid taxes, but were pre-

vented by an unclear title, and an absconding developer. In the meantime, vandals attempted to destroy the old mill on several occasions.
Following a number of failed efforts, Halloween pranksters succeeded
in burning down the old mill in 1996.[17]

In addition to managing the challenged milling company, the family continued to support Mullen's legacy of philanthropy. After completing Mullen's home for orphaned boys in 1932, the family continued to provide for Denver's poor, elderly, orphaned, and ill, mixing
personal philanthropic ambitions with the traditional goals of the
founder. Contributions of the 1930s included a clubhouse and addition to the Home for the Aged (1932) and the foundation of two
mountain camps for Denver's poor boys and girls—Camp Santa Maria
(Mr. and Mrs. John Dower, 1931) and Camp St. Malo, with its St.
Catherine's Chapel (Mr. and Mrs. Oscar Malo, 1934).[18] Ella Mullen
Weckbaugh contributed a $117,000 Temple Buell–designed nurses'
home to St. Joseph Hospital in 1933. Remembering her mother's special relationship with the Sisters of Charity, she christened the building the Catherine Smith Mullen Home.[19]

*The ruins of the Oriskany Falls, New York, mill. On October 31, 1996, vandals made
another Mullen landmark a piece of history. William J. Convery photo.*

Mullen's charitable principles endure in the family-oriented charitable foundations. Noting the "very strong underlying current" of family philanthropy, board member Walter S. Weckbaugh commented, "I think it is just fascinating how his really worthwhile philosophies have been passed through the generations . . . That tradition will be carried forward."[20] The J. K. Mullen Foundation adheres closely to Mullen's ideal of an "exclusive family trust" for the "benefit of religious, charitable, educational, and benevolent purposes." With a board of family

Mullen gets it done

Mustangs are second to no one

By Neil H. Devlin
Denver Post High School Sports Editor

For the first time in so many postseasons, they didn't crumble like a stale cookie.

They didn't wilt under the spotlight and they certainly didn't buckle under the pressure of perhaps Colorado's most vocal and demanding following, a group whose expectations are as lofty as any.

There were some anxious moments Saturday afternoon, yes, but the ghosts of previous playoff poisonings were tamed by the antidote of finally winning it all after an entire generation of past performers had come and gone through school doors.

Riding yet another dominating performance by its front walls, Mullen won its first championship in 18 years at Brother Bernard De La Salle Stadium by physically handling archrival Cherry Creek 23-14.

The Class 5A title, the Mustangs' first in Colorado's largest classification, capped a 13-1 campaign. And they did it in rousing fashion, outhitting and outexecuting a somewhat surprising Bruins bunch that ended 11-3 and kept it very much a game until about five min-

SATURDAY'S TITLE GAMES

CLASS 5A
Mullen 23, Cherry Creek 14

CLASS 4A
Rampart 35, Sierra 20

CLASS 3A
Faith Christ. 21, Brush 19

COVERAGE, 15-18C

Please see MULLEN on 15C

The Denver Post John Leyba

Mullen's Vernard Bond, who rushed for 212 yards, scores in the third quarter against Cherry Creek.

Although his name is still celebrated as a prep-school football powerhouse, J. K. Mullen's contributions to Colorado's philanthropy and economic development are largely forgotten.

members, the Mullen Foundation endows traditional institutions such as Regis College and St. Joseph's Hospital as well as newer causes such as the Winter Park Blind Skiers Program and the Dumb Friends League. A recent endowment to the newly remodeled Denver Public Library created the J. K. Mullen Manuscript Room in the Western History Department. This gesture, echoing Mullen's interest in literacy, libraries, and education, promises to link the philanthropist with western history for thousands of researchers who will work underneath the gaze of his portrait. Likewise, family philanthropies such as the Mary M. Dower Benevolent Foundation, the Weckbaugh Foundation, and the Eleanore Mullen Weckbaugh Foundation continue to support civic, cultural, youth-oriented, medical, educational, and religious institutions.[21] Supported by assets worth more than $12.75 million in 1994, as well as by trustees who share their founder's concern with charity, these three foundations provide a solid philanthropic legacy.

Denver is a far different place than the village that J. K. Mullen first saw in 1871. J. K.'s adopted city prepares to enter the twenty-first century as a metropolis of more than 2 million. There is little that the Irish immigrant would recognize at first glance. His far-flung agricultural empire is subsumed by corporate agribusinesses. His house on Pennsylvania Street is a bygone memory. The religious intolerance that he opposed has subsided, if only to be replaced by other forms of bigotry. Still, the philanthropist would probably be pleased to know that many of the monuments he erected are still enjoyed by the people who need them the most. The Denver Catholic diocese, the Immaculate Conception Cathedral, Catholic Charities, and the United Way—struggling institutions that he supported in the hope of making a better future—have become flourishing, stable institutions that serve millions. For this pioneer Colorado businessman-philanthropist, the greatest honor would have been to know his contributions continue to help.

NOTES

1. John Burke, *The Legend of Baby Doe* (New York: G. P. Putnam's Sons, 1974), 237.
2. This and subsequent references to the interview with Baby Doe, as well as to the events cited below, are related in J. K. Mullen, Letter to Rev. Matthew Smith, December 8, 1927, Timothy O'Connor collection, Denver, Colorado. See also Rev. Matthew Smith, Letter to J. K. Mullen, December 6, 1927, Timothy

O'Connor collection, Denver, Colorado; Charles W. Hurd, "J. K. Mullen, Milling Magnate of Colorado," *The Colorado Magazine* XXIX:2 (April 1952): 116.

3. Duane A. Smith, *Horace Tabor: His Life and Legend*, 2d ed. (Niwot: University Press of Colorado, 1989), 302, 314.

4. Burke, 232–233.

5. Elizabeth B. Tabor, journal entry, April 26, 1926, Tabor collection, MSS 614, Colorado Historical Society (CHS).

6. Elizabeth B. Tabor, Letter to John Reddin, c. 1927, Tabor collection, MSS 614, CHS.

7. J. K. Mullen, Letter to Rev. Matthew Smith, December 8, 1927, Timothy O'Connor collection, Denver, Colorado.

8. *Rocky Mountain News* (*RMN*), August 15, 1927: 14; *Denver Post*, September 13, 1929: 1; August 18, 1931: 1; Charles B. Kuhlman, *The Development of the Flour Milling Industry in the United States, With Special Reference to Minneapolis* (Boston: Houghton Mifflin Co., 1929), 201.

9. Carl Abbott, Stephen J. Leonard, and David McComb, *Colorado: A History of the Centennial State*, 3d ed. (Niwot: University Press of Colorado, 1994), 177.

10. Union Securities Corporation, "Prospectus of the Colorado Milling and Elevator Co.," August 1943, William S. Jackson business records collection, MSS 1074, CHS.

11. Robert Murray Frame, "The Progressive Millers: A Cultural and Intellectual Portrait of the Flour Milling Industry, 1870–1930" (Ph.D. diss., University of Minnesota, 1980), 210.

12. H. E. Johnson, "Report to Stockholders of the Colorado Milling and Elevator Co.," July 1939, Herbert E. Johnson manuscript collection (hereafter cited as Johnson collection); Securities and Exchange Commission, "Securities Act of 1933, Release No. 2964, In the Matter of the Colorado Milling and Elevator Co.," December 20, 1943, Johnson collection.

13. Union Securities Corp., "CM&E Prospectus," August 1943, William S. Jackson business records collection, MSS 1074, CHS.

14. *Denver Post*, July 1, 1969: 73; Peter Grant and John F. Malo, personal interview, March 2, 1998.

15. "Flour Power," *RMN*, October 22, 1997: 1B.

16. A. Stella Cieslak, ed., *The Colonel's Hat: A History of the Township of Augusta* (Oriskany Falls, N.Y.: Limestone Ridge Historical Society, 1976), 82.

17. Stella Cieslak, Letter to author, August 20, 1997.

18. *Denver Post*, December 30, 1932: 2.

19. *Denver Post*, October 12, 1933: 3.

20. Walter S. Weckbaugh, personal interview, July 21, 1997.

21. *Colorado Foundation Directory* (Denver: Junior League of Denver, 1994–1995), 79, 96.

APPENDIX A

Freehold Properties Owned by the
Colorado Milling and Elevator Company, 1889

Name	*Location*	*Structure*	*Power Source*	*Grind/Storage Cap.*
Hungarian Mills *Elevator* *Meal and Feed Mill* *Warehouse*	Denver	Stone/Brick Wood/Metal Brick Brick	Steam	1,600 sacks/day 300,000 bu. wheat 230,000 lbs. bran
Crescent Mills *Elevator* *Warehouse*	Denver	Stone/Brick Stone/Brick Stone/Brick	Steam	1,000 sacks/day 20,000 bu. wheat 50,000 lbs. bran
Excelsior Mills *Elevator* *Warehouse*	Denver	Stone/Brick Stone/Brick Stone/Brick	Steam	600 sacks/day 50,000 bu. wheat 30,000 lbs. bran
Roller Mills *Warehouse*	Denver	Stone/Brick Stone/Brick	Water	500 sacks/day 40,000 bu. wheat 25,000 lbs. bran 20,000 sacks flour
Rock Mills *Warehouse*	Golden	Stone/Brick Stone/Brick	Water	400 sacks/day 20,000 bu. wheat 20,000 sacks flour
Longmont Mills *Elevator*	Longmont	Frame	Steam	500 sacks/day 130,000 bu. wheat
Lindell Mills *Elevator* *Warehouse*	Fort Collins	Stone/Brick Brick/Wood	Water	800 sacks/day 130,000 bu. wheat 40,000 lbs. bran 10,000 sacks flour

continued on next page

Name	Location	Structure	Power Source	Grind/Storage Cap.
Model Mills	Greeley	Brick	Steam	400 sacks/day
Elevator		Wood/Brick		80,000 bu. wheat
Warehouse				20,000 sacks flour
Berthoud Elevator				60,000 bu. wheat
Erie Elevator				10,000 bu. wheat
Total grinding capacity:				5,800 sacks/day
Total wheat storage capacity:				840,000 bu.
Total bran storage capacity:				375,000 lbs.
Total flour storage capacity:				70,000+ sacks

Source: "Statement of Earnings and Disposition, Colorado Milling and Elevator Co., for the years ending July 31, 1889," Mullen papers, MSS 705, CHS.

APPENDIX B

J. K. Mullen Estate Tax Assessment

STOCKS

Company	Shares	Value
J. K. Mullen Investment Co.	11,095	$1,775,200.00
Colorado M&E Co.	9,804	1,617,660.00
Mountain States Telephone Co.	1,080	166,300.00
First National Bank	120	36,000.00
McPhee and McGinnity Co.	330	23,250.00
International Trust Co.	20	9,000.00
Denrado Land and Invst. Co.	125	8,750.00
Shorego Mining Co.	43	7,150.00
Oak Hills Coal Co.	58	2,900.00
American National Bank	20	2,500.00
West Side Construction Co.	50	2,500.00
Others	—	101,584.00
Unpaid dividends		183,970.98
Total Stocks		$3,904,364.98

BONDS

United States Treasury, state, and municipal bonds	$1,740,411.50
Moffat Tunnel Improvement District	700,000.00
City and County of Denver Water Works	131,000.00
Accrued interest	30,756.33
Total Bonds	$2,602,167.83

TRUST FUNDS
Moffat Tunnel Improvement Dist. bonds $39,000.00
(Set aside for Father William O'Ryan and James
W. and Hattie Denio. Beneficiaries to receive
$100/month for lifetime.)

REAL ESTATE
Colorado $ 20,000.00
Idaho   890.00

NOTES AND MORTGAGES   190,983.70

ACCOUNTS RECEIVABLE, CASH, AUTOMOBILES, MISC. PROPERTY   8,941.34

Total Value: $6,746,347.85

Source: Denver Post, Dec. 20, 30, 1929.

WORKS CITED

Abbott, Carl, Stephen J. Leonard, and David McComb. *Colorado: A History of the Centennial State*. 3d ed. Niwot: University Press of Colorado, 1994.

Abernathey, R. James. *Practical Hints for Mill Building*. Moline, Ill.: R. James Abernathey, 1880. Microfilm copy. Auraria Library. Denver, Colorado.

Archdiocese of Denver. Archives. Denver, Colorado.

Immaculate Conception Cathedral. Manuscript collection.

"Cathedral Building Fund Fair, Nov. 27–Dec. 13, 1902, at Coliseum Hall." Souvenir Program.

"Financial Statement of the Immaculate Conception Cathedral Association." Sept. 24, 1910.

"General Financial Statement, Immaculate Conception Cathedral." 1901, 1903.

Matz, Rt. Rev. Nicholas C. "Circular Letter." March 28, 1895.

McMenamin, Rev. H. L. "The Shadow of Debt." Circular. Dec. 19, 1915.

Mullen, J. K. Letters to Rev. H. L. McMenamin. July 8, 1921; Oct. 21, 1921.

Little Sisters of the Poor/Home for the Aged. Manuscript collection.

"The Little Sisters of the Poor." Booklet. London: Burns, Oates, & Washbourne, Ltd.

Matz, Rt. Rev. Nicholas C. Manuscript collection.

Matz, Rt. Rev. Nicholas C. Letters to J. K. Mullen. Apr. 21, 1909; Jan. 20, 1913.

Letter to Ella M. Weckbaugh. Jan. 27, 1913.

Mullen, John K. Letters to Rt. Rev. N. C. Matz. Oct. 9, 1903; Apr. 12, 1909; May 2, 1909; May 9, 1911; July 13, 1911; July 14, 1911; Sept. 18, 1913; March 2, 1914; Nov. 16, 1914.

Naughten, Rev. Bernard E. Letter to Rev. Brady, St. Mary's of the Assumption Catholic Church, Central City, Colorado. Feb. 28, 1913.

Mullen, J. K. Letter to Northwestern Life Insurance Co. 1902.

Mullen, J. K., Home for Boys. Manuscript collection.

    Mullen, John K. Letter to Rt. Rev. J. Henry Tihen and Vy. Rev. Brother Arsenius, F.S.C. July 15, 1929.

St. Leo the Great Catholic Church. Manuscript collection.

Tihen, Rt. Rev. John Henry. Manuscript collection.

    "Constitution and By-Laws of the St. Patrick's Catholic Mutual Benevolent Society of Denver." Denver: Labor Enquirer Printing House, 1881.

    Kolka, Rev. Elmer J. Letter to Most Rev. Urban J. Vehr, July 24, 1956.

    Malo, Oscar L. Telegram to Rt. Rev. J. Henry Tihen. March 31, 1920.

    McMenamin, Rev. Hugh L. Telegram to Rt. Rev. J. Henry Tihen. Apr. 5, 1920.

    Mullen, John K. Letter to Rev. H. L. McMenamin. June 30, 1909.

    ———. Letter to Rt. Rev. N. C. Matz. Apr. 2, 1915.

    ———. Letters to Rt. Rev. J. Henry Tihen. 1921; Oct. 17, 1922; Nov. 1922; Nov. 25, 1922; March 3, 1923; March 6, 1923; March 7, 1923; March 9, 1923; March 13, 1923; June 24, 1924; Jan. 13, 1925; Jan. 19, 1925; Feb. 3, 1925; March 13, 1925; Apr. 12, 1925; Apr. 29, 1925; Nov. 22, 1925; March 10, 1926; June 4, 1927; June 14, 1927; Feb. 4, 1928; Aug. 22, 1928; Dec. 14, 1928; Apr. 24, 1929.

    ———. Letter to Rt. Rev. Thomas J. Shahan, chancellor, Catholic University of America. Sept. 18, 1923.

    ———. Letter to Rev. Mayer, Crook, Colorado. Aug. 21, 1925.

    Shahan, Rt. Rev. Thomas J. Letter to Sec. Joseph P. Tumulty. Dec. 23, 1917.

    Smith, Rev. Matthew. Letter to J. K. Mullen. May 1926.

    Tihen, Rt. Rev. J. Henry. Letters to J. K. Mullen. Nov. 1922; March 1923.

    ———. Letter to John Forbes. Jan. 1923.

Arps, Louisa Ward. *Denver in Slices*. Denver: Sage Books, 1959.

Athearn, Robert G. *The Mythic West in Twentieth-Century America*. Lawrence: University Press of Kansas, 1986.

Beetle, C. David H. *Along the Oriskany*. Utica, N.Y.: Utica Observer-Dispatch, 1947.

Bellinger, R. Edward, ed. *Roots in the Hollow, Life in the Falls: A History of the Village of Oriskany Falls, New York*. 2d ed. Oriskany Falls, N.Y.: Limestone Ridge Historical Society, 1989.

Bernstein, Paul. *American Work Values: Their Origin and Development*. Albany: State University of New York Press, 1997.

Bird, Isabella L. *A Lady's Life in the Rocky Mountains*. 1878. Reprint. Norman: University of Oklahoma Press, 1988.

"Bird's Eye View of Denver, Colorado, 1908." Map. Denver: Bird's Eye View Publishing Co., 1907.

Birmingham, Steven. *Real Lace: America's Irish Rich*. New York: Harper & Row, 1973.

Brown, Thomas N. *Irish-American Nationalism, 1870–1890*. Philadelphia: J. B. Lippincott Co., 1966.

Brundage, David. *The Making of Western Labor Radicalism: Denver's Organized*

Workers, 1878–1905. Urbana: University of Illinois Press, 1994.

——. *The Producing Classes and the Saloon: Denver in the 1880s.* New York: Tamiment Institute, 1985.

Burke, John. *The Legend of Baby Doe: The Life and Times of the Silver Queen of the West.* New York: G. P. Putnam's Sons, 1974.

Byers, William Newton. *Encyclopedia of Biography of Colorado: History of Colorado.* Chicago: The Century Publishing and Engraving Co., 1901.

Cashman, Sean Dennis. *America in the Gilded Age.* 3d ed. New York: New York University Press, 1993.

Cieslak, A. Stella, ed. *The Colonel's Hat: A History of the Township of Augusta.* Oriskany Falls, N.Y.: Limestone Ridge Historical Society, 1976.

Cieslak, Stella. Letter to author. August 20, 1997.

Colorado Business Directories, 1877–1882. Microfilm.

Colorado Catholic. Mar. 15, 1894: 1.

Colorado Farmer and Livestock Journal. Sept. 3, 1874: 569; Aug. 11, 1879: 4; Aug. 14, 1879: 4; Aug. 21, 1879: 4; Sept. 4, 1879: 4; March 10, 1881: 4; Jan. 7, 1886: 1; Jan. 14, 1886: 4; Jan. 28, 1886: 1.

Colorado Foundation Directory. Denver: Junior League of Denver, 1994–1995.

Colorado Historical Society. Denver, Colorado.

    Jackson, William S. Business records collection. MSS 1074.

        Union Securities Corporation. "Prospectus of the Colorado Milling and Elevator Co." August 1943.

    Mullen, John Kernan. Manuscript collection. MSS 705.

        Colorado Milling and Elevator Company. "Statement of Earnings and Disposition for the Years Ending July 31, 1889."

        Dower, John L. Letter to J. K. Mullen. June 5, 1926.

        Flanagan, Rev. Edward J. Letter to J. K. Mullen. May 14, 1928.

        McLoon, Frank. Letter to J. K. Mullen. Oct. 2, 1921

        Mullen, Catherine S. Letters to J. K. Mullen. July 17, 1889; July 21, 1889; July 26, 1889.

        Mullen, John K. "Article of Agreement Made and Entered Into This Twenty-Fourth Day of July, A.D. 1886, Between John K. Mullen and Dennis W. Mullen."

        ——. Letters to Catherine S. Mullen. May 19, 1876; Feb. 22, 1877; June 21,1880; July 1, 1880; July 4, 1880; July 17, 1880; May 18, 1881; Sept. 4, 1886; Aug. 10, 1890; Nov. 9, 1890; Dec. 24, 1890; March 16, 1892; March 18, 1892; March 16, 1893; May 13, 1893; May 16, 1893; Aug. 11, 1893; Aug. 14, 1893; Aug. 15, 1893; Aug. 30, 1893; Sept. 2, 1893; Sept. 3, 1893; Aug. 14, 1894; July 30, 1900.

        ——. Letters to Rev. Raymond J. Mullen, S. J. May 5, 1916; Dec. 1921.

        ——. Letter to John J. Mullen. June 1, 1926.

        ——. Letter to A. J. Simonson. July 30, 1926.

        ——. Letter to Maurice C. Dolan. CM&E. Apr. 19, 1927.

——. Letters to Loyal L. Breckenridge, Idaho Falls Milling and Elevator Co. Nov. 2, 1928; Nov. 5, 1928.

——. "Our Duties as Catholic Citizens." Handwritten manuscript. 1912.

——. "Promissory Notes on Excelsior Mills." Nov. 20, 1878.

——. "Statement Concerning the Individual Business of J. K. Mullen." May 25, 1902.

Mullin, Patrick H. Letters to J. K. Mullen. July 7, 1872; Oct. 6, 1874.

O'Donnell, esq., T. J. Letters to J. K. Mullen. Oct. 15, 1897; Nov. 12, 1902; Nov. 13, 1902.

Smith, esq., Milton. Letters to J. K. Mullen. Aug. 24, 1989; Aug. 29, 1898; Aug. 30, 1897; Sept. 4, 1898.

Williams, C. E. Colorado Milling and Elevator Co. Letter to employees and friends of the CM&E. Aug. 16, 1929.

Corbett, Hoye, and Ballenger. *Denver City Directory*, 1874–1885. Microfilm. Western History Dept., Denver Public Library. Denver, Colorado.

Denver Catholic Register. May 16, 1907: 1; Sept. 5, 1918; Jan. 8, 1925: 4; Jan. 1, 1925: 1; Feb. 5, 1925: 8; March 26, 1925: 1; Aug. 18, 1929: 2; Aug. 22, 1929; Sept. 25, 1958: 2.

Denver Magazine. 21:17, Aug. 15, 1929.

Denver Post. July 30, 1906: 1; June 9, 1907; June 4, 1909: 15; March 7, 1913: 1; Aug. 24, 1914: 6; Apr. 13, 1917: 18: July 4, 1917: 3; Aug. 10, 1917: 1; Aug. 22, 1918: 9; Dec. 10, 1917: 5; Dec. 21, 1917: 5; Jan. 17, 1918: 1; Jan. 22, 1918: 1; June 30, 1918: 15; Aug. 10, 1918: 7; Aug 18, 1918: 5; Sept. 13, 1918: 7; Apr. 23, 1919: 13, 18; Apr. 9, 1922: 1; March 19, 1923: 1; Aug. 2, 1923: 1; Sept. 27, 1924: 5; March 23, 1925: 1; March 26, 1925: 29; May 29, 1925: 1; Jan. 29, 1926: 18; May 6, 1926: 10; June 6, 1927: 4; Sept. 16, 1927: 26; Feb. 17, 1928: 2; Apr. 27, 1928: 28; July 12, 1928: 23; March 28, 1929: 1; June 11, 1929: 3; July 26, 1929; Aug. 3, 1929: 1; Aug. 9, 1929: 1; Aug. 12, 1929: 1, 4; Aug. 14, 1929: 1; Aug. 22, 1929; Sept. 13, 1929: 1; Dec. 20, 1929: 36; Dec. 30, 1929: 1; Feb. 1, 1931; Aug. 18, 1931: 1; Jan. 1, 1932: 12; Jan. 31, 1932: 12; Dec. 30, 1932: 2; Oct. 12, 1933: 3; June 5, 1935: 15; Oct. 27, 1952: 1; Apr. 17, 1965: 6B; May 22, 1965: 3B; July 1, 1969: 73; March 16, 1973: 7HH; July 19, 1997: B3; July 20, 1997: E5.

Denver Republican. June 14, 1903: 26; Oct. 7, 1906.

Denver Times. Sept. 5, 1892: 5; July 1, 1898: 2; July 2, 1892: 6; March 8, 1899: 1; March 9, 1899: 8; March 15, 1899: 6; Apr. 3, 1899: 6; June 12, 1901: 1; June 26, 1901: 11; Dec. 6, 1901: 12; Aug. 8, 1902: 3; May 1, 1913: 1.

Desmond, Humphrey J. *The A.P.A. Movement*. New York: Arno Press and New York Times, 1969.

Deutsch, Sarah. *No Separate Refuge: Culture, Class, and Gender on an Anglo-Hispanic Frontier in the American Southwest, 1880–1940*. New York: Oxford University Press, 1987.

Diner, Hasia R. *Erin's Daughters in America: Irish Immigrant Women in the Nineteenth*

Century. Baltimore: Johns Hopkins University Press, 1983.

Dorsett, Lyle W. *The Queen City: A History of Denver*. Boulder: Pruett Publishing Co., 1977.

East Galway Family Historical Society Company Ltd. Letter to John F. Malo. Nov. 30, 1999.

Edwards, Ruth Dudley. *An Atlas of Irish History*. London: Meuthen & Co., 1973.

Ellis, David M., James A. Frost, Harold C. Syrett, and Harry J. Carman. *A Short History of New York State*. Ithaca: New York University Press, 1957.

Ellis, McDonough & Co. *Perspective Map of the City of Denver, Colorado, 1889*. William S. Jackson map collection. Western History Dept., Denver Public Library.

Emmons, David M. *The Butte Irish: Class and Ethnicity in an American Mining Town, 1875–1925*. Urbana: University of Illinois Press, 1989.

Everitt, John. "The Early Development of the Flour Milling Industry on the Prairies." *Journal of Historical Geography* 19:3 (1993): 278–298.

Feeley, Thomas Francis. "Leadership in the Early Colorado Catholic Church." Ph.D. diss., University of Denver, 1973.

Fetter, Rosemary. "A Walking Tour of Ninth Street Historic Park." Pamphlet. Denver: Auraria Higher Education Center, 1976.

Fisher, Franklin M., and Peter Temin. "Regional Specialization and the Supply of Wheat in the United States, 1867–1914." *Review of Economics and Statistics* 52:2 (1970): 134–149.

Foner, Eric. *Politics and Ideology in the Age of the Civil War*. New York: Oxford University Press, 1980.

Frame, Robert Murray. "The Progressive Millers: A Cultural and Intellectual Portrait of the Flour Milling Industry, 1870–1930." Ph.D. diss., University of Minnesota, 1980.

Gallagher, Dennis. Personal interview. Denver, Colorado, Nov. 24, 1997.

Goldstein, Marcia T. "Homelessness in Denver." *University of Colorado Historical Studies Journal* VI (1989): 1–25.

Goodstein, Phil. *The Ghosts of Denver: Capitol Hill*. Denver: New Social Publications, 1996.

Grant, Peter. Personal interview. Denver, Colorado, March 2, 1998.

Greeley, Andrew M. *That Most Distressful Nation: The Taming of the American Irish*. Chicago: Quadrangle Books, 1972.

Hafen, LeRoy, ed. *Colorado and Its People: A Narrative and Topical History of the Centennial State*. New York: Lewis Historical Publishing Co., 1948.

Harley, C. Knick. "Western Settlement and the Price of Wheat, 1872–1913." *Journal of Economic History* 38:4 (Dec. 1978): 865–878.

Hawley, Ellis W. *The Great War and the Search for a Modern Order: A History of the American People and their Institutions, 1917–1933*. New York: St. Martin's

Press, 1979.

Higham, John. *Strangers in the Land: Patterns of American Nativism, 1860–1925.* 2d ed. New Brunswick, N.J.: Rutgers University Press, 1988.

Huber, Richard M. *The American Idea of Success.* New York: McGraw-Hill, 1971.

Hurd, Charles W. "J. K. Mullen, Milling Magnate of Colorado." *The Colorado Magazine* XXIX:2 (April 1952): 104–118.

Johnson, Herbert E. Manuscript collection. Midland, Michigan.

    Johnson, Herbert E. Letter to J. K. Mullen. Dec. 27, 1920.

    ——. "Report to the Stockholders of the Colorado Milling and Elevator Co." July 1939.

    ——. Letter to Guy Thomas, president, Colorado Milling and Elevator Co., Denver, Colorado. June 10, 1943.

    Malo, Oscar L. Letters to Herbert E. Johnson, general manager, Colorado Milling and Elevator Co. Apr. 10, 1920; May 1920; May 2, 1920.

    Mullen, John K. "The Policy of Our Company and the Dignity and Responsibility of a Merchant." Typed speech transcript. Sept. 10, 1912.

    ——. Letter to Herbert E. Johnson. May 15, 1920.

    ——. Letters to Rev. Matthew Smith. Dec. 7, 1927; Dec. 8, 1927.

Kauffman, Christopher. *Faith and Fraternalism: The History of the Knights of Columbus, 1882–1982.* Cambridge, Mass.: Harper & Row, 1982.

Kennedy, David M. *Over Here: The First World War and American Society.* New York: Oxford University Press, 1980.

"Kernan, Francis." Biographical file. Oneida County Historical Society, Utica, New York.

Krupar, Jason. "The Churches of Auraria." Rosemary Fetter, ed. Pamphlet. Denver: Auraria Office of the EVOA, 1994.

Kuhlmann, Charles Byron. *The Development of the Flour Milling Industry in the United States, With Special Reference to the Industry in Minneapolis.* Boston: Houghton-Mifflin Co., 1929.

La Luz. Aug. 1973: 13.

Leonard, Stephen J. "Denver's Foreign-Born Immigrants, 1859–1900." Ph.D. diss., Claremont Graduate School, 1971.

——, and Thomas J. Noel. *Denver: Mining Camp to Metropolis.* Niwot: University Press of Colorado, 1990.

Levy, Edwin Lewis. "Elitch's Gardens, Denver, Colorado: A History of the Oldest Summer Theatre in the United States." Ph.D. diss., Columbia University, 1960.

Lewis, Samuel. *A Topographical Dictionary of Ireland.* Vol. 1. 1837. Reprint. London: Kennikat Press, 1970.

Luebbers, David J. "Directory of Ninth Street Historic Park, 1871–1900." Unpublished manuscript. Dec. 1977. Dept. of Planning and Development, Auraria Higher Education Center, Denver, Colorado.

Malo, John F. Personal interview. Denver, Colorado, March 2, 1998.

Marshall, Elaine Tettemer. Letter to the author. March 14, 1999.

McMenamin, Rev. Hugh L. *Diamond Jubilee of the Cathedral Parish, Denver, Colorado.* Denver: Frank J. Wolf Printers, 1935.

——. *The Pinnacled Glory of the West: Cathedral of the Immaculate Conception.* Denver: Smith-Brooks Printing, 1912.

Morris, Edmund. *The Rise of Theodore Roosevelt.* New York: Ballantine Books, 1979.

Mullendore, William C. *History of the United States Food Administration, 1917–1919.* Stanford: Stanford University Press, 1941.

Municipal Facts. Denver: City and County of Denver. Feb. 12, 1910; Jan. 14, 1911; Oct. 1918; Apr. 1919.

Myers, Sandra L. *Westering Women and the Frontier Experience, 1800–1915.* Albuquerque: University of New Mexico Press, 1982.

New York Times. Oct. 27, 1872: 3; Oct. 28, 1872: 5.

Noel, Thomas J. *The City and the Saloon, Denver, 1858–1916.* Lincoln: University of Nebraska Press, 1982.

——. *Colorado Catholicism and the Archdiocese of Denver, 1857–1989.* Niwot: University Press of Colorado, 1989.

——, Paul F. Mahoney, and Richard E. Stevens. *Historical Atlas of Colorado.* Norman: University of Oklahoma Press, 1994.

——, and Barbara S. Norgren. *Denver: The City Beautiful and Its Architects, 1893–1941.* Denver: Historic Denver Inc., 1987.

——, with Kevin E. Rucker and Stephen J. Leonard. *Colorado Givers: A History of Philanthropic Heroes.* Niwot: University Press of Colorado, 1998.

Novack, Ruth Vincent. "Give While You Live." *St. Anthony Messenger,* Nov. 1947.

"Obituary of Dennis W. Mullen," *The Trail* IX:1 (June 1916): 29.

O'Connor, Timothy. Personal interview. Denver, Colorado, Dec. 4, 11, 1997.

O'Connor, Timothy. Manuscript collection. Denver, Colorado.
　　O'Connor, Katherine Mullen. Scrapbook.
　　Smith, Rev. Matthew. Letter to J. K. Mullen, Dec. 6, 1927.

Proctor, A. Phimister. *Sculptor in Buckskin.* Hester E. Proctor, ed. Norman: University of Oklahoma Press, 1971.

Pula, Cheryl A., and Philip A. Bean. "Utica's Irish Heritage." In *Ethnic Utica,* James S. Pula, ed. Utica, N.Y.: Utica College of Syracuse University, 1994.

Rocky Mountain News. Oct. 27, 1859: 2; Sept. 3, 1874; Oct. 22,1874; May 22, 1879; June 12, 1879; July 10, 1879; Jan. 1, 1880: 16; July 15, 1880: 5; Aug. 9, 1880; Aug. 29, 1880: 1; Oct. 20, 1880: 3; Dec. 23, 1880: 3; Jan. 1, 1881: 24; Jan. 13, 1881: 1; Jan. 21, 1881: 5; July 19, 1881: 2; July 21, 1881: 5; Aug. 18, 1881: 4; Oct. 17, 1881: 6; Nov. 11, 1881: 4; Jan. 1, 1882: 13; Jan. 13, 1882: 8; Jan. 24, 1882: 1; March 25, 1882: 7; May 6, 1882: 8; July 27, 1882; Sept. 13, 1882: 4; Jan. 10, 1883: 3; Jan. 14, 1883: 2; March 6, 1883: 4; March 14, 1883: 8; July 3, 1883; Dec. 25, 1883: 9; March 1, 1884: 1; Aug.

12, 1884: 7; Feb. 15, 1885: 8; Aug. 29, 1885: 8; March 14, 1886: 2; Jan. 22, 1888: 4; Feb. 7, 1889: 6; July 19, 1893: 2; Sept. 2, 1918: 4; Aug. 7, 1921: 1; March 23, 1925: 1; Aug. 15, 1927: 11; Apr. 8, 1932: 12; July 31, 1932: 7; Jan. 24, 1948: 17; March 1, 1965; Dec. 10, 1974: 50; May 17, 1989: 3C; June 26, 1997: 5A.

Securities and Exchange Commission. "Securities Act of 1933, Release No. 2964, In the Matter of the Colorado Milling and Elevator Co." Dec. 30, 1943.

Sevier, Sheila. Private manuscript collection. Denver, Colorado.
    Snow, Robert M. Promissory notes to J. K. Mullen. July 17, 25, 1871.
    Morris, W. Letter to J. K. Mullen. March 24, 1876.
    ——. Letter to J. K. Mullen. May 23, 1876.
    O'Connor, Katherine Mullen. Letter to James E. O'Connor. Apr. 23, 1908.
    "Why Don't You Get a Father-in-Law Worth While? He's in Denver." Undated, unidentified newspaper clipping.

Silver Standard (Silver Plume, Colorado). Aug. 19, 1893: 1.

Smith, Duane A. *Horace Tabor: His Life and Legend.* Boulder: Colorado Associated University Press, 1973.

——. *Rocky Mountain Mining Camps: The Urban Frontier.* 2d ed. Niwot: University Press of Colorado, 1992.

Southwestern Miller. Aug. 12, 1929: 33.

Steinal, Alvin T. *History of Agriculture in Colorado.* Ft. Collins: Colorado State Agricultural College, 1926.

U.S. Department of Commerce. Bureau of the Census. "Immigrants by Country: 1820–1970." *Historical Statistics of the United States: Colonial Times to 1970.* Vol. 1. Washington, D.C.: GPO, 1976.

——. *Manuscript Census, Population Schedules: 1865.* Town of Augusta, Oneida County, New York. Microfilm copy. Utica Public Library, Utica, New York.

——. "Prices and Price Indexes." *Historical Statistics of the United States, Colonial Times to the Present.* Vol. 1. Washington, D.C.: GPO, 1976.

Weckbaugh, Anne. Personal interview. Englewood, Colorado, Feb. 6, 1998.

Weckbaugh family private manuscript collection. Denver, Colorado.
    Board of Directors, CM&E. Letter to J. K. Mullen. Feb. 5, 1927.
    Buchtel, Henry A. Letter to President Woodrow Wilson. Dec. 24, 1917.
    Dines, Tyson S. Letter to J. K. Mullen. Dec. 21, 1906.
    "J. K. Mullen Mill Cleared of Charge." Unattributed, undated newspaper clipping.
    Mullen, John K. "The Family Register of John K. Mullen and Kate Theressa Smith, his wife."
    ——. Letter to Catherine S. Mullen. May 19, 1876.
    ——. Letter to David H. Moffat. Dec. 29, 1906.
    ——. "The Duties and Obligations of Merchants and Manufacturers." Speech transcript. 1912.

——. Letter to the stockholders of the Colorado Milling and Elevator Co. March 9, 1917.

——. Letter to Frederick G. Bonfils and Harry H. Tammen, owners, the *Denver Post*. Dec. 14, 1917.

——. Letters to Henry A. Buchtel, chancellor, University of Denver. Dec. 13, 1917; Dec. 14, 1917; July 9, 1918.

——. Letter to Frederick G. Bonfils. Dec. 24, 1918.

——. Letter to Rev. James Goodheart, Jan. 13, 1919.

——. Letter to Eleanore Weckbaugh. March 6, 1923.

——. Letter to W. S. Bunt, mgr., Claflin Flour Mills, Claflin, Kansas. Feb. 12, 1924.

——. Letters to Ella M. Weckbaugh. March 7, 1924; July 6, 1925; Aug. 21, 1925; Aug. 25, 1925.

——. Letter to the Directors, CM&E. Feb. 9, 1927.

——. Letter to Ella M. Weckbaugh, May Dower, Katherine O'Connor, and Edith Malo. Denver, Colorado. 1928.

——. Letter to George F. Cottrell. Denver, Colorado. Jan. 25, 1929.

Mullin, Patrick H., Oriskany Falls, New York. Letters to J. K. Mullen. Aug. 3, 1872; Sept. 23, 1872; March 16, 1873; Aug. 3, 1873.

O'Connor, John. Letter to J. K. Mullen. Oct. 10, 1924.

Shahan, Rt. Rev. Thomas J. Letter to Henry A. Buchtel. Dec. 23, 1917.

United States Council of National Defense. "Certificate of Acknowledgement to J. K. Mullen." June 28, 1919.

Weckbaugh, Walter S. Personal interview. Denver, Colorado, July 21, 1997.

Western History Department, Denver Public Library, Denver, Colorado.

Malo, Oscar Louis. Manuscript collection.

Oscar L. Malo. Circular No. 160 to District Managers, Managers, and Employees of the CM&E. Dec. 18, 1928.

Mullen, John Kernan. Manuscript collection.

Colorado Milling and Elevator Co. "Memorandum to the Board of Directors." Sept. 19, 1919.

Germaine, Mother Provincial, Little Sisters of the Poor (Mary Sicot). Telegraph to J. K. Mullen. Sept. 11, 1916.

Hankinson, H. L. Letter to Oscar L. Malo. Aug. 6, 1929.

Irwin, G. B., mgr. of Hungarian Mills. Letter to Oscar L. Malo, June 19, 1929.

Kennedy, James F., esq. Letter to J. K. Mullen. June 17, 1916.

Malo, Oscar L. Letter to Richard McCloud. March 28, 1927.

McCloud, Richard. Letter to Oscar L. Malo. March 24, 1927.

Mullen, John K. "Personal Ledger Book, 1900–1905."

——. "Deed of Gift Between J. K. Mullen and St. Mary's Academy of Leavenworth, Kansas." Dec. 27, 1919.

——. "Draft of Conveyance." Handwritten manuscript.

——. "Home for the Aged Expense Sheet."

——. Letters to Sister Germaine, Mother Provincial, Little Sisters of the Poor.

June 12, 1916; Aug. 30, 1916.

——. "Warranty Deed Between J. K. Mullen and the Little Sisters of the Poor." Sept. 16, 1916.

——. Letters to Rt. Rev. Thomas J. Shahan. June 5, 1925; Dec. 15, 1927.

Mulroy, Rev. John R., et al. "Report of Investigation and Planning Committee to the Diocesan Holy Name Society." Apr. 27, 1929.

Reddin, John H., esq. Letter to J. K. Mullen. Oct. 25, 1916.

Mullen, J. K., Foundation, Inc. Manuscript collection.

Denver Catholic Charitable and Benevolent Society. "Minutes of Organization Meeting." May 19, 1924.

——. "Certificate of Incorporation." May 28, 1924.

——. "Minutes." May 27, 1924; Apr. 1, 1925.

Evans, George T., Internal Revenue Service. Letter to J. K. Mullen. Jan. 5, 1925.

J. K. and C. S. Benevolent Foundation Corp. "Income and Disbursements, May 28, 1924, to May 28, 1926."

——. "Comparative Balance Sheet." Aug. 9, 1929.

——. "Minutes of a Special Meeting of the Board of Directors." Aug. 20, 1929.

Mullen, J. K. Letter to the Board of Directors, Denver Catholic Charitable and Benevolent Society. June 25, 1924.

——. Letter to the Denver Community Chest. March 1925.

——. Letter to Frank W. Howbert, Internal Revenue Service. Apr. 4, 1925.

——. Letter to Rt. Rev. Thomas J. Shahan. Oct. 19, 1926.

Schrembs, Rt. Rev. Joseph. "Certified Copy of Minutes of Meeting of the Board of Trustees of the Catholic University of America." Sept. 14, 1926.

Wiebe, Robert H. *The Search for Order, 1877–1920*. New York: Hill and Wang, 1967.

Wyllie, Irvin G. *The Self-Made Man in America*. New York: The Free Press, 1954.

Yelland, Starr. "The Life of J. K. Mullen as Narrated by Starr Yelland on *Inside Story*. Sponsored by the Colorado National Bank." Unpublished manuscript. John Kernan Mullen papers. Western History Dept., Denver Public Library, Denver, Colorado.

INDEX

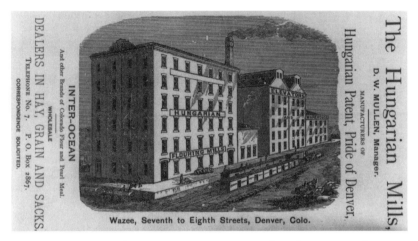

Hungarian Mills advertisement. Courtesy, Colorado Historical Society.